COMMON CORE MATHEMATICS

NEW YORK EDITION

Grade 1, Module 4: Place Value, Comparison, Addition and Subtraction to 40

JB JOSSEY-BASS

A Wiley Brand

Cover design by Chris Clary

Published by Jossey-Bass
A Wiley Brand
One Montgomery Street, Suite 1200, San Francisco, CA 94104-4594—www.josseybass.com

ISBN: 978-1-118-81124-5

Printed in the United States of America
FIRST EDITION
PB Printing   10 9 8 7 6 5 4 3 2 1

WELCOME

Dear Teacher,

Thank you for your interest in Common Core's curriculum in mathematics. Common Core is a non-profit organization based in Washington, DC dedicated to helping K-12 public schoolteachers use the power of high-quality content to improve instruction.[1] We are led by a board of master teachers, scholars, and current and former school, district, and state education leaders. Common Core has responded to the Common Core State Standards' (CCSS) call for "content-rich curriculum"[2] by creating new, CCSS-based curriculum materials in mathematics, English Language Arts, history, and (soon) the arts. All of our materials are written by teachers who are among the nation's foremost experts on the new standards.

In 2012 Common Core won three contracts from the New York State Education Department to create a PreKindergarten–12th grade mathematics curriculum for the teachers of that state, and to conduct associated professional development. The book you hold contains a portion of that work. In order to respond to demand in New York and elsewhere, modules of the curriculum will continue to be published, on a rolling basis, as they are completed. This curriculum is based on New York's version of the CCSS (the CCLS, or Common Core Learning Standards). Common Core will be releasing an enhanced version of the curriculum this summer on our website, commoncore.org. That version also will be published by Jossey-Bass, a Wiley brand.

Common Core's curriculum materials are not merely aligned to the new standards, they take the CCSS as their very foundation. Our work in math takes its shape from the expectations embedded in the new standards—including the instructional shifts and mathematical progressions, and the new expectations for student fluency, deep conceptual understanding, and application to real-life context. Similarly, our ELA and history curricula are deeply informed by the CCSS's new emphasis on close reading, increased use of informational text, and evidence-based writing.

Our curriculum is distinguished not only by its adherence to the CCSS. The math curriculum is based on a theory of teaching math that is proven to work. That theory posits that mathematical knowledge is most coherently and

---

1. Despite the coincidence of name, Common Core and the Common Core State Standards are not affiliated. Common Core was established in 2007, prior to the start of the Common Core State Standards Initiative, which was led by the National Governors Association and the Council for Chief State School Officers.
2. *Common Core State Standards for English Language Arts & Literacy in History/Social Studies, Science, and Technical Subjects* (Washington, DC: Common Core State Standards Initiative), 6.

effectively conveyed when it is taught in a sequence that follows the "story" of mathematics itself. This is why we call the elementary portion of this curriculum "The Story of Units," to be followed by "The Story of Ratios" in middle school, and "The Story of Functions" in high school. Mathematical concepts flow logically, from one to the next, in this curriculum. The sequencing has been joined with methods of instruction that have been proven to work, in this nation and abroad. These methods drive student understanding beyond process, to deep mastery of mathematical concepts. The goal of the curriculum is to produce students who are not merely literate, but fluent, in mathematics.

It is important to note that, as extensive as these curriculum materials are, they are not meant to be prescriptive. Rather, they are intended to provide a basis for teachers to hone their own craft through study, collaboration, training, and the application of their own expertise as professionals. At Common Core we believe deeply in the ability of teachers and in their central and irreplaceable role in shaping the classroom experience. We strive only to support and facilitate their important work.

The teachers and scholars who wrote these materials are listed beginning on the next page. Their deep knowledge of mathematics, of the CCSS, and of what works in classrooms defined this work in every respect. I would like to thank Louisiana State University professor of mathematics Scott Baldridge for the intellectual leadership he provides to this project. Teacher, trainer, and writer Robin Ramos is the most inspired math educator I've ever encountered. It is Robin and Scott's aspirations for what mathematics education in America *should* look like that is spelled out in these pages.

Finally, this work owes a debt to project director Nell McAnelly that is so deep I'm confident it never can be repaid. Nell, who leads LSU's Gordon A. Cain Center for STEM Literacy, oversees all aspects of our work for NYSED. She has spent days, nights, weekends, and many cancelled vacations toiling in her efforts to make it possible for this talented group of teacher-writers to produce their best work against impossible deadlines. I'm confident that in the years to come Scott, Robin, and Nell will be among those who will deserve to be credited with putting math instruction in our nation back on track.

Thank you for taking an interest in our work. Please join us at www.commoncore.org.

Lynne Munson
President and Executive Director
Common Core
Washington, DC
June 20, 2013

Common Core's K-5 Math Staff

Scott Baldridge, Lead Mathematician and Writer
Robin Ramos, Lead Writer, PreKindergarten-5
Jill Diniz, Lead Writer, 6-12
Ben McCarty, Mathematician

Nell McAnelly, Project Director
Tiah Alphonso, Associate Director
Jennifer Loftin, Associate Director
Catriona Anderson, Curriculum Manager,
    PreKindergarten-5

Sherri Adler, PreKindergarten
Debbie Andorka-Aceves, PreKindergarten

Kate McGill Austin, Kindergarten
Nancy Diorio, Kindergarten
Lacy Endo-Peery, Kindergarten
Melanie Gutierrez, Kindergarten
Nuhad Jamal, Kindergarten
Cecilia Rudzitis, Kindergarten
Shelly Snow, Kindergarten

Beth Barnes, First Grade
Lily Cavanaugh, First Grade
Ana Estela, First Grade
Kelley Isinger, First Grade
Kelly Spinks, First Grade
Marianne Strayton, First Grade
Hae Jung Yang, First Grade

Wendy Keehfus-Jones, Second Grade
Susan Midlarsky, Second Grade
Jenny Petrosino, Second Grade
Colleen Sheeron, Second Grade
Nancy Sommer, Second Grade
Lisa Watts-Lawton, Second Grade
MaryJo Wieland, Second Grade
Jessa Woods, Second Grade

Eric Angel, Third Grade
Greg Gorman, Third Grade
Susan Lee, Third Grade
Cristina Metcalf, Third Grade
Ann Rose Santoro, Third Grade
Kevin Tougher, Third Grade
Victoria Peacock, Third Grade
Saffron VanGalder, Third Grade

Katrina Abdussalaam, Fourth Grade
Kelly Alsup, Fourth Grade
Patti Dieck, Fourth Grade
Mary Jones, Fourth Grade
Soojin Lu, Fourth Grade
Tricia Salerno, Fourth Grade
Gail Smith, Fourth Grade
Eric Welch, Fourth Grade
Sam Wertheim, Fourth Grade
Erin Wheeler, Fourth Grade

Leslie Arceneaux, Fifth Grade
Adam Baker, Fifth Grade
Janice Fan, Fifth Grade
Peggy Golden, Fifth Grade
Halle Kananak, Fifth Grade
Shauntina Kerrison, Fifth Grade
Pat Mohr, Fifth Grade
Chris Sarlo, Fifth Grade

Additional Writers

Bill Davidson, Fluency Specialist
Robin Hecht, UDL Specialist
Simon Pfeil, Mathematician

Document Management Team

Tam Le, Document Manager
Jennifer Merchan, Copy Editor

Common Core

1
GRADE

Mathematics Curriculum

Table of Contents

GRADE 1 • MODULE 4

Place Value, Comparison, Addition and Subtraction to 40

Grade 1 • Module 4

Place Value, Comparison, Addition and Subtraction to 40

OVERVIEW

Module 4 builds upon Module 2's work with place value within 20, now focusing on the role of place value in the addition and subtraction of numbers to 40.

The module opens with Topic A, where students study, organize, and manipulate numbers within 40. Having worked with creating a ten and some ones in Module 2, students now recognize multiple tens and ones. Students use fingers, linking cubes, dimes, and pennies to represent numbers to 40 in various ways: from all ones to tens and ones (**1.NBT.2**). They use a place value chart to organize units. The topic closes with the identification of 1 more, 1 less, 10 more, and 10 less, as students learn to add or subtract *like* units (**1.NBT.5**).

In Topic B, students compare quantities and begin using the symbols for *greater than* (>) and *less than* (<) (**1.NBT.3**). Students demonstrate their understanding of place value when they recognize that 18 is less than 21 since 2 tens already have a greater value than 1 ten 8 ones. To support understanding, the first lesson in the topic focuses on identifying the greater or lesser amount. With this understanding, students label each of the quantities being compared and compare from left to right. Finally, students are introduced to the mathematical symbols, using the story of the alligator whose hungry mouth always opens toward the greater number. The abstract symbols are introduced after the conceptual foundation has been laid.

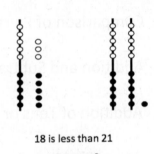

18 is less than 21

Topic C focuses on addition and subtraction of tens (**1.NBT.4, 1.NBT.6**). Having used concrete models in Topic A to represent 10 more and 10 less, students now recognize that just as 3 + 1 = 4, 3 tens + 1 ten = 4 tens. With this understanding, students add and subtract a multiple of 10 from another multiple of 10. The topic closes with the addition of multiples of 10 to numbers less than 40, e.g., 12 + 30.

In Topic D, students use familiar strategies to add two-digit and single-digit numbers within 40. Students apply the Level 2 strategy of counting on and use the Level 3 strategy of making ten, this time making *the next ten* (**1.NBT.4**). For instance, when adding 28 + 5, students break 5 into 2 and 3 so that they can make *the next ten*, which is 30, or 3 tens, and then add 3 to make 33. The topic closes with students sharing and critiquing peer strategies.

In Topic E, students consider new ways to represent larger quantities when approaching *put together/take apart with total or addend unknown* and *add to with result or change unknown* word problems. Students begin labeling drawings with numerals, and eventually move to tape diagrams to represent the problem pictorially (**1.OA.1**). Throughout this topic, students will continue developing their skills with adding single- and double-digit numbers, introduced in Topic D, during fluency activities.

The module closes with Topic F, focusing on adding like place value units as students add two-digit numbers. The topic begins with interpreting two-digit numbers in varied combinations of tens and ones (e.g., 34 = 34 ones = 3 tens 4 ones = 2 tens 14 ones = 1 ten 24 ones). This flexibility in representing a given number prepares students for addition with regrouping (e.g., 12 + 8 = 1 ten 10 ones = 2 tens or 18 + 16 = 2 tens 14 ones = 3 tens 4 ones). To close the module, students add pairs of numbers with varied sums in the ones to support flexibility in thinking.

Distribution of Instructional Minutes

This diagram represents a suggested distribution of instructional minutes based on the emphasis of particular lesson components in different lessons throughout the module.

- ■ Fluency Practice
- ▨ Concept Development
- ▨ Application Problems
- ■ Student Debrief

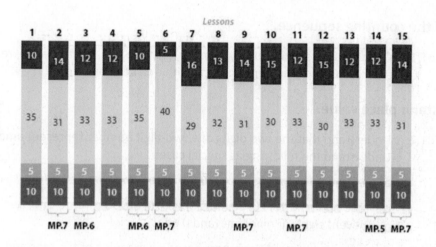

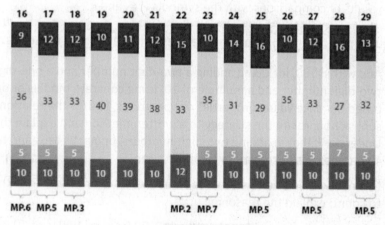

MP = Mathematical Practice

Focus Grade Level Standards[1]

Represent and solve problems involving addition and subtraction.[2]

1.OA.1   Use addition and subtraction within 20 to solve word problems involving situations of adding to, taking from, putting together, taking apart, and comparing, with unknowns in all positions, e.g., by using objects, drawings, and equations with a symbol for the unknown number to represent the problem. (See CCLS Glossary, Table 1.)

Extend the counting sequence.[3]

1.NBT.1   Count to 120, starting at any number less than 120. In this range, read and write numerals and represent a number of objects with a written numeral.

Understand place value.[4]

1.NBT.2   Understand that the two digits of a two-digit number represent amounts of tens and ones. Understand the following as special cases:

    a.   10 can be thought of as a bundle of ten ones – called a "ten."

    c.   The numbers 10, 20, 30, 40, 50, 60, 70, 80, 90 refer to one, two, three, four, five, six, seven, eight, or nine tens (and 0 ones).

1.NBT.3   Compare two two-digit numbers based on meaning of the tens and ones digits, recording the results of comparisons with the symbols >, =, and <.

Use place value understanding and properties of operations to add and subtract.[5]

1.NBT.4   Add within 100, including adding a two-digit number and a one-digit number, and adding a two-digit number and a multiple of 10, using concrete models or drawings and strategies based on place value, properties of operations, and/or the relationship between addition and subtraction; relate the strategy to a written method and explain the reasoning used. Understand that in adding two-digit numbers, one adds tens and tens, ones and ones, and sometimes it is necessary to compose a ten.

1.NBT.5   Given a two-digit number, mentally find 10 more or 10 less than the number, without having to count; explain the reasoning used.

1.NBT.6   Subtract multiples of 10 in the range 10–90 from multiples of 10 in the range 10–90 (positive or zero differences), using concrete models or drawings and strategies based on place value, properties of operations, and/or relationship between addition and subtraction; relate the strategy to a written method and explain the reasoning used.

---

[1] While the use of pennies and dimes will be used throughout the module, 1.MD.3 is not a focus grade level standard in Module 4. Instead, this standard will become a focal standard in Module 6, when all coins are introduced and used.

[2] The balance of this cluster is addressed in Module 2.

[3] Focus on numbers to 40.

[4] Focus on numbers to 40.

[5] Focus on numbers to 40.

	Module 4:	Place Value, Comparison, Addition and Subtraction to 40
	Date:	9/20/13

Foundational Standards

K.OA.3   Decompose numbers less than or equal to 10 into pairs in more than one way, e.g., by using objects or drawings, and record each decomposition by a drawing or equation (e.g., 5 = 2 + 3 and 5 = 4 + 1).

K.OA.4   For any number from 1 to 9, find the number that makes 10 when added to the given number, e.g., by using objects or drawings, and record the answer with a drawing or equation.

K.NBT.1   Compose and decompose numbers from 11 to 19 into ten ones and some further ones, e.g., by using objects or drawings, and record each composition or decomposition by a drawing or equation (e.g., 18 = 10 + 8); understand that these numbers are composed of ten ones and one, two, three, four, five, six, seven, eight, or nine ones.

Focus Standards for Mathematical Practice

MP.3   **Construct viable arguments and critique the reasoning of others.** Students describe and explain their strategies for adding within 40, and critique and adjust student samples to more efficiently solve addition problems.

MP.5   **Use appropriate tools strategically.** After learning varied representations and strategies for adding and subtracting pairs of two-digit numbers, students choose their preferred methods for representing and solving problems efficiently. Students may represent their computations using arrow notation, number bonds, quick ten drawings, and linking cubes. As they share their strategies, students explain their choice of counting on, making ten, adding tens and then ones, or adding ones and then tens.

MP.6   **Attend to precision.** Students recognize and distinguish between units, demonstrating an understanding of the difference between 3 tens and 3 ones. They use this understanding to compare numbers and to add like place value units.

MP.7   **Look for and make use of structure.** Students are introduced to the place value chart, deepening their understanding of the structure within our number system. Throughout the module, students use this structure as they add and subtract within 40. They recognize the similarities between 2 tens + 2 tens = 4 tens and 2 + 2 = 4, and use their understanding of tens and ones to explain the connection.

Overview of Module Topics and Lesson Objectives

Standards		Topics and Objectives		Days
1.NBT.1 **1.NBT.2** **1.NBT.5**	A	**Tens and Ones**		6
		Lesson 1:	Compare the efficiency of counting by ones and counting by tens.	
		Lesson 2:	Use the place value chart to record and name tens and ones within a two-digit number.	
		Lesson 3:	Interpret two-digit numbers as either tens and some ones or as all ones.	
		Lesson 4:	Write and interpret two-digit numbers as addition sentences that combine tens and ones.	
		Lesson 5:	Identify 10 more, 10 less, 1 more, and 1 less than a two-digit number.	
		Lesson 6:	Use dimes and pennies as representations of tens and ones.	
1.NBT.3 1.NBT.1 1.NBT.2	B	**Comparison of Pairs of Two-Digit Numbers**		4
		Lesson 7:	Compare two quantities, and identify the greater or lesser of the two given numerals.	
		Lesson 8:	Compare quantities and numerals from left to right.	
		Lessons 9–10:	Use the symbols >, =, and < to compare quantities and numerals.	
1.NBT.2 **1.NBT.4** **1.NBT.6**	C	**Addition and Subtraction of Tens**		2
		Lesson 11:	Add and subtract tens from a multiple of 10.	
		Lesson 12:	Add tens to a two-digit number.	
		Mid-Module Assessment: Topics A–C (assessment 1 day, return 1 day, remediation or further applications 1 day)		3
1.NBT.4	D	**Addition of Tens or Ones to a Two-Digit Number**		6
		Lessons 13–14:	Use counting on and the make ten strategy when adding across a ten.	
		Lesson 15:	Use single-digit sums to support solutions for analogous sums to 40.	
		Lessons 16–17:	Add ones and ones or tens and tens.	
		Lesson 18:	Share and critique peer strategies for adding two-digit numbers.	

COMMON CORE   Module 4:   Place Value, Comparison, Addition and Subtraction to 40
Date: 9/20/13

vi

Standards		Topics and Objectives	Days
1.OA.1	E	**Varied Problem Types Within 20**	4
		Lesson 19: Use tape diagrams as representations to solve *put together/take apart with total unknown* and *add to with result unknown* word problems.	
		Lessons 20–21: Recognize and make use of part–whole relationships within tape diagrams when solving a variety of problem types.	
		Lesson 22: Write word problems of varied types.	
1.NBT.4	F	**Addition of Tens and Ones to a Two-Digit Number**	7
		Lesson 23: Interpret two-digit numbers as tens and ones including cases with more than 9 ones.	
		Lessons 24–25: Add a pair of two-digit numbers when the ones digits have a sum less than or equal to 10.	
		Lessons 26–27: Add a pair of two-digit numbers when the ones digits have a sum greater than 10.	
		Lessons 28–29: Add a pair of two-digit numbers with varied sums in the ones.	
		End-of-Module Assessment: Topics D–F (assessment 1 day, return 1 day, remediation or further applications 1 day)	3
Total Number of Instructional Days			**35**

Terminology

New or Recently Introduced Terms

- \> (greater than)
- < (less than)
- Place value (quantity represented by a digit in a particular place within a number)

Familiar Terms and Symbols[6]

- Equal (=)
- Numerals
- Ones
- Tens

---

[6] These are terms and symbols students have seen previously.

Module 4: Place Value, Comparison, Addition and Subtraction to 40
Date: 9/20/13

Suggested Tools and Representations

- Arrow notation
- Comparison symbols: >, <, =
- Dime
- Hide Zero cards
- Hundred chart
- Number bond
- Penny
- Place Value Chart
- Quick Ten
- Rekenrek
- Tape Diagram

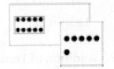

Arrow Notation

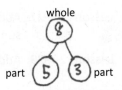

Hide Zero Cards

1	2	3	4	5	6	7	8	9	10
11	12	13	14	15	16	17	18	19	20
21	22	23	24	25	26	27	28	29	30
31	32	33	34	35	36	37	38	39	40

Hundred Chart to 40

Number Bond

tens	ones
3	4

Place Value Chart

Quick Ten

Rekenrek

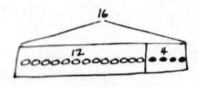

Tape Diagram

Scaffolds[7]

The scaffolds integrated into *A Story of Units* give alternatives for how students access information as well as express and demonstrate their learning. Strategically placed margin notes are provided within each lesson elaborating on the use of specific scaffolds at applicable times. They address many needs presented by English language learners, students with disabilities, students performing above grade level, and students performing below grade level. Many of the suggestions are applicable to more than one population. The charts included in Module 1 provide a general overview of the lesson-aligned scaffolds, organized by Universal Design for Learning (UDL) principles. To read more about the approach to differentiated instruction in *A Story of Units*, please refer to "How to Implement *A Story of Units*."

Assessment Summary

Type	Administered	Format	Standards Addressed
Mid-Module Assessment Task	After Topic C	Constructed response with rubric	1.NBT.1 1.NBT.2 1.NBT.3 1.NBT.4 1.NBT.5 1.NBT.6
End-of-Module Assessment Task	After Topic F	Constructed response with rubric	1.OA.1 1.NBT.1 1.NBT.2 1.NBT.3 1.NBT.4 1.NBT.5 1.NBT.6

---

[7] Students with disabilities may require Braille, large print, audio, or special digital files. Please visit the website, www.p12.nysed.gov/specialed/aim, for specific information on how to obtain student materials that satisfy the National Instructional Materials Accessibility Standard (NIMAS) format.

Topic A

Tens and Ones

1.NBT.1, 1.NBT.2, 1.NBT.5

Focus Standard:	1.NBT.1	Count to 120, starting at any number less than 120. In this range, read and write numerals and represent a number of objects with a written numeral.
	1.NBT.2	Understand that the two digits of a two-digit number represent amounts of tens and ones. Understand the following as special cases:
		a. 10 can be thought of as a bundle of ten ones – called a "ten."
		c. The numbers 10, 20, 30, 40, 50, 60, 70, 80, 90 refer to one, two, three, four, five, six, seven, eight, or nine tens (and 0 ones).
	1.NBT.5	Given a two-digit number, mentally find 10 more or 10 less than the number, without having to count; explain the reasoning used.
Instructional Days:	6	
Coherence -Links from:	G1–M2	Introduction to Place Value Through Addition and Subtraction Within 20
-Links to:	G2– M3	Place Value, Counting, and Comparison of Numbers to 1,000

Module 4 builds on students' work with teen numbers to now work within 40. Working within 40 helps students focus on the units, tens and ones, which can be easily modeled pictorially and concretely with these smaller numbers. The smaller numbers also allow students to count all while having an important experience of its inefficiency. Students' innate ability to subitize to 4 keeps the numbers friendly when both adding and subtracting tens for the first time and managing the new, complex task of considering both tens and ones when adding. Through their work within 40, students develop essential skills and concepts that generalize easily to numbers to 100 in Module 6.

In Lesson 1, students are presented with a collection of 20 to 40 items. They discuss and decide how to count the items, and then compare the efficiency of counting individual ones with counting tens and ones. Through this exploration, students come to understand the utility of ten as a unit: both as a method for counting, and for efficiently recording a given number (**1.NBT.1**, **1.NBT.2**). Students keep their own set of 40 linking cubes, organized as a kit of 4 ten-sticks, to use as they progress through the module.

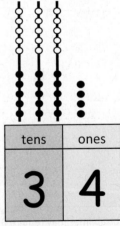

Place Value Chart

In Lesson 2, students represent and decompose two-digit numbers as tens and ones, and record their findings on a place value chart, supported by the familiar Hide Zero cards. Students share thoughts such as, "The 3 in 34 stands for 3 tens. And the 4 in 34 is just 4 ones!" Up to this point, students have worked with representations of ten where 10 ones are clearly visible (e.g., as two 5-groups).

While the digit 3 in 34 may appear smaller than the digit 4, its value is determined by its position. Use of the place value chart represents the students' first experience with this additional layer of abstraction.

Lesson 3 allows students to explore two-digit numbers as tens and ones, and as just ones. Students use their fingers to represent "bundled" tens and "unbundled" ones by clasping and unclasping their fingers. For example, students model 34 with 3 students showing their hands clasped to make a ten, and a fourth student showing 4 fingers to represent 4 ones. Taking student understanding of place value a step further, Lesson 4 asks students to decompose and compose two-digit numbers as addition equations. Students develop an understanding that "34 is the same as 30 + 4," as they move between writing the number when given the equations and writing the *equations* when given a number. Throughout these lessons, students use concrete objects and/or drawings in order to support their understanding and explain their thinking.

Topic A concludes with Lessons 5 and 6, where students use materials and drawings to find 10 more, 10 less, 1 more, and 1 less than a given number (**1.NBT.5**). In Lesson 5, students use the familiar linking cubes (organized into tens) and 5-group columns. They engage in conversation about patterns they observe, "I see that 10 less than 34 is just 1 less ten, so it must be 24!" Students represent how the number changed using arrow notation, or *the arrow way,* as shown to the right. Lesson 6 then introduces the dime and penny as representations of ten and one respectively.[1] Students make the connection between the familiar representations of tens and ones to the dime and the penny, and work to find 10 more, 10 less, 1 more, and 1 less.

$$34 \xrightarrow{+1} 35 \qquad 34 \xrightarrow{-1} 33$$

$$34 \xrightarrow{+10} 44 \qquad 34 \xrightarrow{-10} 24$$

arrow notation

A Teaching Sequence Towards Mastery of Tens and Ones

Objective 1: Compare the efficiency of counting by ones and counting by tens.
(Lesson 1)

Objective 2: Use the place value chart to record and name tens and ones within a two-digit number.
(Lesson 2)

Objective 3: Interpret two-digit numbers as either tens and some ones or as all ones.
(Lesson 3)

Objective 4: Write and interpret two-digit numbers as addition sentences that combine tens and ones.
(Lesson 4)

Objective 5: Identify 10 more, 10 less, 1 more, and 1 less than a two-digit number.
(Lesson 5)

Objective 6: Use dimes and pennies as representations of tens and ones.
(Lessons 6)

---

[1] Integrates the 1.MD.3 standard for dime and penny. This standard will become a focal standard in Module 6, when all 4 coins have been introduced.

Topic A:	Tens and Ones
Date:	9/20/13

Lesson 1

Objective: Compare the efficiency of counting by ones and counting by tens.

Suggested Lesson Structure

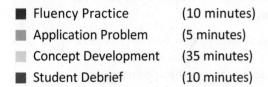 

■ Fluency Practice   (10 minutes)
■ Application Problem   (5 minutes)
■ Concept Development   (35 minutes)
■ Student Debrief   (10 minutes)
   Total Time   **(60 minutes)**

Fluency Practice (10 minutes)

- Break Apart Numbers **1.OA.6**   (4 minutes)
- Change 10 Pennies for 1 Dime **1.NBT.2**   (4 minutes)
- Happy Counting by Tens **1.NBT.5**   (2 minutes)

Break Apart Numbers (4 minutes)

Materials: (S) Personal white boards with break apart numbers template

Note: Reviewing decomposing numbers 5–9 supports Grade 1's required fluency of adding and subtracting within 10 and is an essential skill in order to apply the Level 3 addition strategy of making ten. If students struggle with this activity, consider repeating it in lieu of some of the fluency activities that provide practice with numbers to 20 and beyond.

Students complete as many *different* number bonds as they can in one minute. Take a poll of how many students completed all decompositions for 5, 6, etc., and celebrate accomplishments.

Change 10 Pennies for 1 Dime (4 minutes)

Materials: (T) 10 pennies, 1 dime (S) 10 pennies and 1 dime per pair

Note: This activity helps students to see that 10 cents is equal to 1 dime just as 10 ones are equal to 1 ten. This fluency activity is necessary to prepare students to utilize coins as abstract units that represent tens and ones in G1–M1–Lesson 6.

Lay out 10 pennies into 5-groups as students count (1 cent, 2 cents, etc.). Make sure students include the unit as they count.

Lesson 1:   Compare the efficiency of counting by ones and counting by tens.
Date: 9/20/13

4.A.

Change the 10 pennies for 1 dime and say, "10 pennies is equal to 10 cents." Repeat the exact same process but this time say, "10 pennies is equal to 1 dime." Students repeat the activity with a partner.

Happy Counting by Tens (2 minutes)

Note: Reviewing Happy Counting by Tens prepares students to recognize the efficiency of counting groups of 10 in today's lesson.

Happy Count by tens the regular way and Say Ten way from 0–120. To really reinforce place value, try alternating between counting the regular way and the Say Ten way.

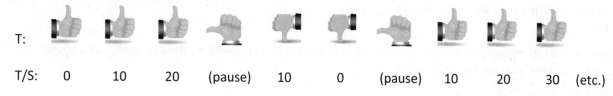

| T: | | | | | | | | | | |

| T/S: | 0 | 10 | 20 | (pause) | 10 | 0 | (pause) | 10 | 20 | 30 | (etc.) |

Application Problem (5 minutes)

Joy is holding 10 marbles in one hand and 10 marbles in the other hand. How many marbles does she have in all?

Note: This problem applies a doubles fact that is familiar to most students. Circulate and notice students that may need to count on to add the 2 tens. During the Debrief, students will relate the Application Problem to the efficiency of counting by tens instead of counting by ones.

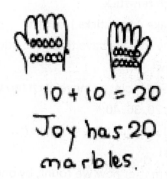

10 + 10 = 20
Joy has 20 marbles.

Concept Development (35 minutes)

Materials: (T) 40 linking cubes (2 colors, 20 of each), projector
(S) Resealable plastic bag with 40 separated linking cubes (2 colors, 20 of each)

Note: When preparing these bags, be sure to use the same two colors for every partner pair. In the later lessons, partners will be combining their cubes to represent numbers more than 20 with a single color. In this lesson, students may choose to count by twos and fives, although this is not a first grade standard.

Students sit at their tables with their bags of linking cubes.

T: You will be making your own math tool kit today! Look in your bag. How many cubes do you think are in your bag?

NOTES ON MULITPLE MEANS OF REPRESENTATION:

As students are counting, circulate and observe their counting levels. Not all students may be able to switch between counting ones and tens. Take some extra time with the students who need to practice counting these patterns. Play some counting games with the linking cubes. You may also want to send home some counting activities for these students to play at home.

S: (Look in bag and make prediction.)

T: Open your bag and count how many linking cubes there are.

T: Wow, there are a lot of cubes in our bags. What do you think is the best way to count them?

S: Count by ones. → Don't count by ones. There are too many cubes. → Count them by twos. → We can put them in 5-groups and count by fives. → Put them in 5-groups and count them by tens!

T: Arranging these cubes in 5-groups is a great idea! Arrange your cubes, and then count to see how many cubes there are.

As students arrange their linking cubes and count, circulate, taking note of students' methods.

T: How many linking cubes did you count?

S: 40 linking cubes.

T: Many of you did a great job putting your cubes in 5-groups and counting by fives or tens. Let's count by ones to make sure we have 40 cubes.

T/S: (Count by ones.)

T: Now let's count them by tens by making them into sticks of 10 cubes. Use the same color cubes for each ten-stick.

S: (Make 4 ten-sticks.)

T: Now that we have these ten-sticks, we can count by…

S: Tens!

T: Great! Point or move each ten to the side as you count.

S: 10, 20, 30, 40.

T: Did we still count 40 cubes?

S: Yes!

T: No matter how we count, by ones or by tens, we get to the same number. But which way was more efficient to count?

S: Organizing our cubes so we could count by tens was more efficient.

T: Also, sometimes when I count by ones and get distracted, I lose count. Then it takes even longer to count by ones because I have to start from the beginning again. But if I make tens, I wouldn't have to start all over again.

T: (Show 12 scattered individual cubes on the projector. Have another scattered set of 12 individual cubes set aside for later.) How can I make these quicker to count?

S: Organize them into 5-groups. → Organize them into ten-sticks.

T: Let's use ten-sticks. (Invite a student volunteer to demonstrate.)

T: Show me this same number of cubes using your own set. Organize them efficiently, like the ones on the board.

S: (Show one stick of 10 and 2 individual cubes.)

T: (Take out second set of scattered cubes.) Look at the 12 scattered cubes that I have and the 12 cubes you have in front of you. Which makes it easier for you to see 12 quickly?

S: The ones on my desk. → The ten-stick and 2 cubes are easier to see 12 quickly. I don't even need to count it. I can just *see* that it's 12.

Lesson 1: Compare the efficiency of counting by ones and counting by tens.
Date: 9/20/13

4.A.

T: Let's make a number bond to show the cubes we grouped and the extra cubes that we added to the grouped cubes. 12 is made of 10 and 2 extra ones.

Repeat the process with 22 scattered cubes. Next, simply call out numbers from 11 to 40 and invite students to show the number using their ten-sticks and extra ones in the suggested sequence: 3 tens 2 ones, 15, 25, 35, 3 tens 7 ones, 1 ten 7 ones, 1 ten 8 ones, 29, and 36.

Each time, have students create a number bond, representing the cubes that were grouped together as tens and the extra ones. Ask student volunteers to show how they counted their cubes to check their work. For example, for 35, one student may count, "10, 20, 30, 31, 32, 33, 34, 35." Another student may count, "10, 20, 30, and 5 is 35." Accept different ways of counting the ones, but always guide the students to count the tens first.

At the end of any lesson using the 40 linking cubes, students should regroup the cubes into 4 ten-sticks and store in the resealable bag for use during future lessons. These will become a part of their math toolkit for G1–Module 4.

Problem Set (10 minutes)

Students should do their personal best to complete the Problem Set within the allotted 10 minutes.

For some classes, it may be appropriate to modify the assignment by specifying which problems students should work on first. With this option, let the careful sequencing of the problem set guide your selections so that problems continue to be scaffolded. Balance word problems with other problem types to ensure a range of practice. Assign incomplete problems for homework or at another time during the day.

Student Debrief (8 minutes)

Lesson Objective: Compare the efficiency of counting by ones and counting by tens.

The Student Debrief is intended to invite reflection and active processing of the total lesson experience.

Invite students to review their solutions for the Problem Set. They should check work by comparing answers with a partner before going over answers as a class. Look for misconceptions or misunderstandings that can be addressed in the Debrief. Guide students in a conversation to debrief the Problem Set and process the lesson.

> NOTES ON
> MULTIPLE MEANS OF
> REPRESENATION:
>
> As you are calling out numbers from 11 to 40 for students to show the number using their ten-sticks, be sure to write the numbers so students can also see them. This will help any students in the class who are hearing impaired, visual learners or those students who may get behind while putting one of their ten-sticks together.

COMMON CORE™

Lesson 1:   Compare the efficiency of counting by ones and counting by tens.
Date: 9/20/13

4.A.6

You may choose to use any combination of the questions below to lead the discussion.

- Compare your answer to Problem 15 with your partner's. Did you get the same answer? What are the parts of your number bond? Explain your thinking. (Accept any variation that aligns with the picture. For example, students may correctly bond as 20 and 10, or 30 and 0.)

- What did you do to solve Problem 16? (Similar to Problem 15, there may be multiple correct answers.)

- What are the different ways we can group objects to make counting easier?

- How does organizing objects in groups of 10 help us?

- How did the Application Problem connect to today's lesson?

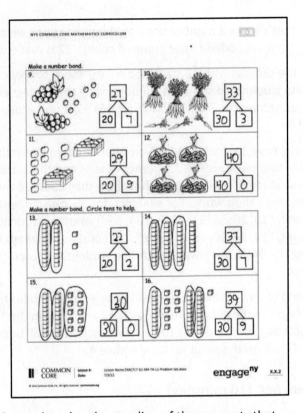

Exit Ticket (3 minutes)

After the Student Debrief, instruct students to complete the Exit Ticket. A review of their work will help you assess the students' understanding of the concepts that were presented in the lesson today and plan more effectively for future lessons. You may read the questions aloud to the students.

COMMON CORE™

Lesson 1:
Date:

Compare the efficiency of counting by ones and counting by tens.
9/20/13

4.A.

Break Apart Numbers

COMMON CORE™

Lesson 1: Compare the efficiency of counting by ones and counting by tens.
Date: 9/20/13

4.A.8

Name _____   Date _____

Circle groups of 10. Write the number.

1. There are _____ grapes.	2. There are _____ carrots.
3. There are _____ apples.	4. There are _____ peanuts.
5. There are _____ grapes.	6. There are _____ carrots.
7. There are _____ apples.	8. There are _____ peanuts.

Lesson 1:	Compare the efficiency of counting by ones and counting by tens.
Date:	9/20/13

4.A.

Make a number bond to show tens and ones.

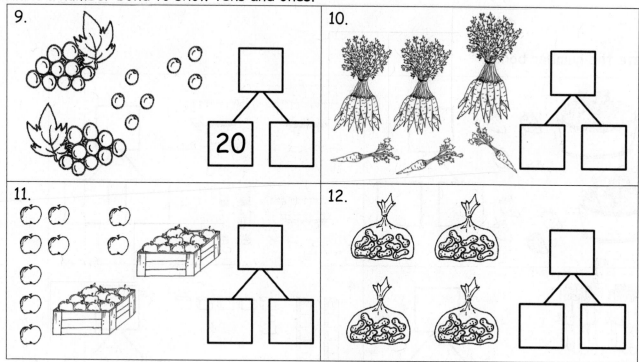

Make a number bond to show tens and ones. Circle tens to help.

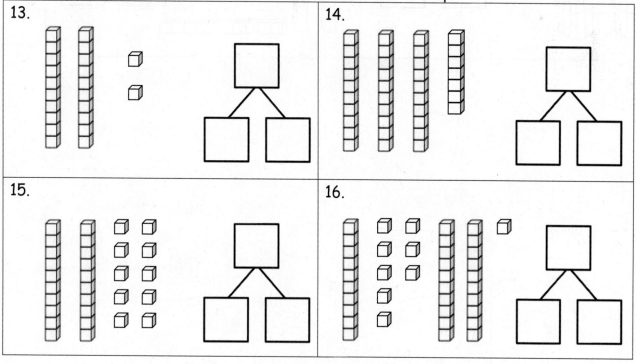

COMMON CORE

Lesson 1:   Compare the efficiency of counting by ones and counting by tens.
Date: 9/20/13

4.A.10

Name _____   Date _____

Complete the number bonds.

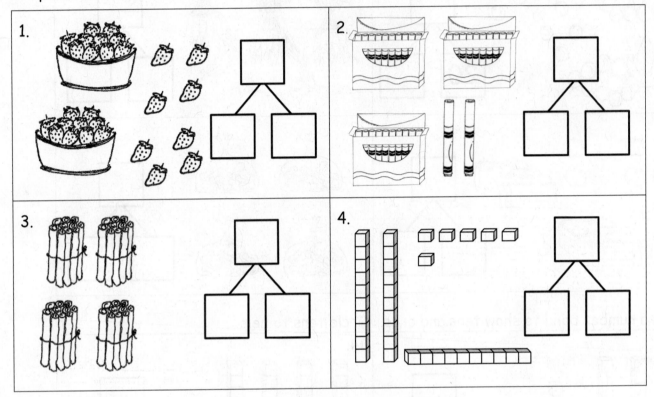

COMMON CORE™   Lesson 1:   Compare the efficiency of counting by ones and counting by tens.
Date: 9/20/13

4.A.1

Name _____ Date _____

Circle groups of 10 and write the number. Say the number the Say Ten way as you count.

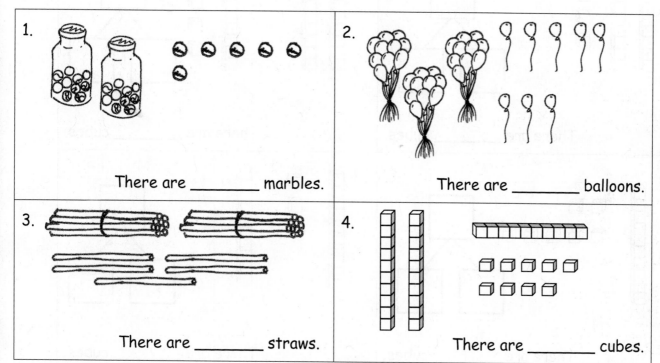

1. There are _____ marbles.

2. There are _____ balloons.

3. There are _____ straws.

4. There are _____ cubes.

Make a number bond to show tens and ones. Circle tens to help.

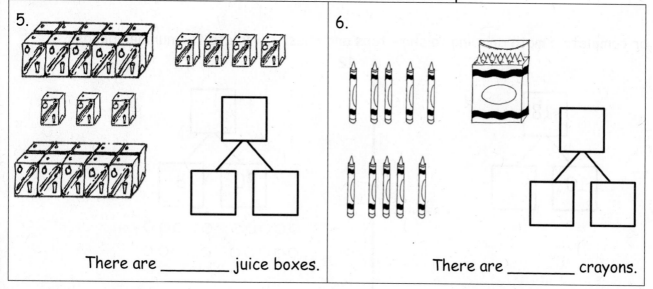

5. There are _____ juice boxes.

6. There are _____ crayons.

COMMON CORE

Lesson 1:   Compare the efficiency of counting by ones and counting by tens.
Date: 9/20/13

4.A.12

Make a number bond to show tens and ones. Circle tens to help.

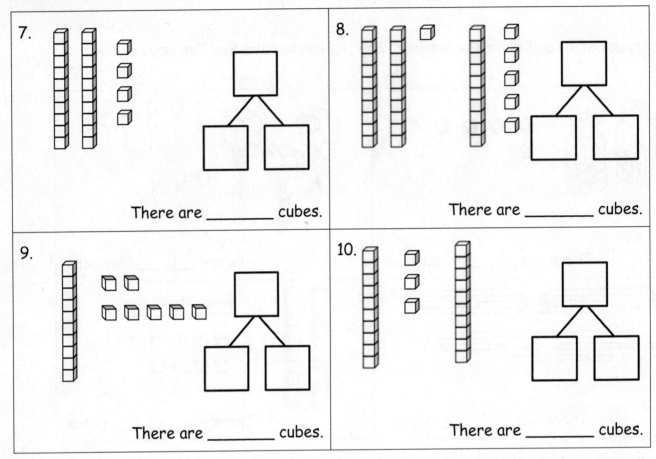

7.

There are _____ cubes.

8.

There are _____ cubes.

9.

There are _____ cubes.

10.

There are _____ cubes.

Make or complete a math drawing to show tens and ones. Complete the number bonds.

11.

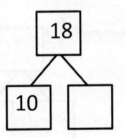

18

10

12.

30   3

○○○○○ ○○○○○
○○○○○ ○○○○○

Lesson 1:   Compare the efficiency of counting by ones and counting by tens.
Date: 9/20/13

4.A.1

Lesson 2

Objective: Use the place value chart to record and name tens and ones within a two-digit number.

Suggested Lesson Structure

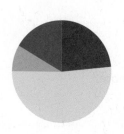

■ Fluency Practice   (14 minutes)
■ Application Problem   (5 minutes)
■ Concept Development   (31 minutes)
■ Student Debrief   (10 minutes)
   Total Time   **(60 minutes)**

Fluency Practice (14 minutes)

- Core Addition Fluency Review **1.OA.6**   (5 minutes)
- 3, 4, and 5 More **1.OA.6**   (4 minutes)
- Change 10 Pennies for 1 Dime **1.NBT.2**   (5 minutes)

Core Addition Fluency Review (5 minutes)

Materials: (S) Core Addition Fluency Review

Note: This addition review sheet contains the majority of addition facts within 10 (excluding some +0 and +1 facts), which are part of the required core fluency for Grade 1. Students will likely do well with this activity at this point in the year. If not, repeat some addition fluency activities from Module 1 and use this activity as an assessment tool to monitor progress.

Students complete as many problems as they can in three minutes. Choose a counting sequence for early finishers to practice on the back of their papers, such as counting by ones from 46 or counting by tens from 3. When time runs out, read the answers aloud so students can correct their work. Encourage students to remember how many they completed so they can try to improve their scores on future Core Addition Fluency Reviews.

NOTES ON MULTIPLE MEANS OF ACTION AND EXPRESSION:

Adjust written fluency games for students with motor delays. Give written fluency activities orally to students who may be slowed due to challenges with motor skills, allowing them to experience success with the math skills being addressed.

| Lesson 2: | Use the place value chart to record and name tens and ones within a two-digit number. | 4.A.14 |
| Date: | 9/20/13 | |

3, 4, and 5 More (4 minutes)

Note: This fluency activity provides practice with the grade level standard of addition within 20, while reinforcing the relationship between single-digit sums and their analogous teen sums.

T: On my signal, say the number that is 3 more.

T: 3 (snap).

S: 6.

T: 13 (snap).

S: 16.

Continue reviewing 3 more. Then review 4 and 5 more.

Change 10 Pennies for 1 Dime (5 minutes)

Materials: (S) 10 pennies and 2 dimes for each pair of students

Note: This fluency activity is necessary in order to prepare students to utilize coins as abstract representations of tens and ones in G1–M1–Lesson 6.

Students work in pairs. Partner A begins with 10 pennies. Partner B begins with 2 dimes. Both partners whisper count as Partner A counts 10 pennies into 5-groups (1 cent, 2 cents, etc.). Partner B changes 10 cents for 1 dime and says, "10 cents equals 1 dime." Students count on, "11 cents, 12 cents, 13 cents, etc., replacing the second set of 10 pennies with a dime and saying, "20 cents equals 2 dimes." Then, Partners A and B switch roles.

Application Problem (5 minutes)

Ted has 4 boxes of 10 pencils. How many pencils does he have altogether?

Note: This problem applies the concept development from Lesson 1 of counting by tens. As students depict this problem with a drawing, circulate and notice students who are counting all, counting on, or counting by tens. During the Debrief, students will represent the number 40 using a place value chart.

Concept Development (31 minutes)

Materials: (T) Hide Zero cards (from G1–M1–Lesson 38 and
G1–M3–Lesson 2), chart paper (S) 4 ten-sticks from
personal math toolkit (from G1–M4–Lesson 1),
personal white board with place value chart insert

NOTES ON MULTIPLE
MEANS OF
REPRESENTATION:

The familiarity of the Hide Zero cards
from Module 3 allows for an easy
transition to the use of the place value
chart for students. Just as some
students have needed to use various
tools for more support, allow the Hide
Zero cards and place value chart to be
used throughout the module as
needed.

Students sit at their desks with their materials.

T: (Show 17 using Hide Zero cards.) When I pull apart
these Hide Zero cards, 17 will be in two parts. What
will they be?

S: 10 and 7.

T: (Pull apart 17 into 10 and 7.) You are right! Show me
17 using your linking cubes.

S: (Show 1 ten-stick and 7 extra cubes. If students count out 17 cubes and break them apart
separately, ask them to try to make as many tens as they can.)

T: How many tens, or ten-sticks, do you have?

S: 1 ten.

T: How many extra ones do you have?

S: 7 extra ones.

Repeat the process following the suggested sequence: 27, 37, 23, and 32.

T: (Show 17 with Hide Zero cards and linking cubes again. Make a blank t-chart on the chart paper.) I
can write 1 ten here in this chart (write 1 on the left side of the t-chart, which will become the tens
place). How many extra ones?

S: 7 ones.

T: Point to where you think I should write 7.

S: (Point to the second column.)

T: (Write 7 in the ones place.)

T: (Point to the 1 in the tens place.) What does this 1 stand for? Show me with
your cubes.

S: (Hold up a ten-stick.) 1 ten!

T: I can write *tens* here because this 1 stands for 1 *ten*. (Label the place value
chart with *tens*.)

T: Point to the set of cubes that tells us what this 7 stands for.

S: (Point to 7 loose cubes.) 7 ones!

T: I can write *ones* here because this 7 stands for…

S: 7 ones.

T: (Point to the place value chart.) Look at our new chart, which is called a **place value chart**. What is 1
ten and 7 ones?

Lesson 2:   Use the place value chart to record and name tens and ones within a
Date: two-digit number.
              9/20/13

4.A.16

S: 17.

T: The Say Ten way?

S: 1 ten 7.

T: Looking at the cubes in front of you, how many tens and ones are in 17?

S: 1 ten 7 ones.

T: Before we go on to other numbers, let's make a drawing to show 17.

Repeat the process using the following sequence: 27, 37, 14, 24, 34, 13, 31, 30, 12, 21, and 20.

For the first two numbers (27 and 37), have students represent the number with their linking cubes, 5-group column drawings, and place value chart. For the remaining numbers, have students use only their linking cubes and place value chart. Making pictorial representations will be inefficient as the numbers get bigger.

Problem Set (10 minutes)

Students should do their personal best to complete the Problem Set within the allotted 10 minutes. For some classes, it may be appropriate to modify the assignment by specifying which problems they work on first.

Student Debrief (10 minutes)

Lesson Objective: Use the place value chart to record and name tens and ones within a two-digit number.

The Student Debrief is intended to invite reflection and active processing of the total lesson experience.

Invite students to review their solutions for the Problem Set. They should check work by comparing answers with a partner before going over answers as a class. Look for misconceptions or misunderstandings that can be addressed in the Debrief. Guide students in a conversation to debrief the Problem Set and process the lesson.

You may choose to use any combination of the questions below to lead the discussion.

- How many tens and how many ones are in the number 29? What amount is greater, 2 tens or 9 ones? Explain your thinking. Use your cubes and your place value chart.

- Look at Problem 18. How did you complete your place value chart? Explain your thinking.

- What new math tool did we use to show how many tens and ones in a number? (**Place value chart**.) How does the place value chart help us? (It helps us see numbers taken apart into tens and ones.)

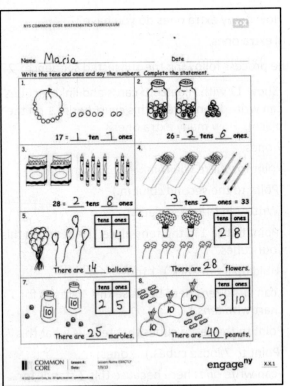

Lesson 2: Use the place value chart to record and name tens and ones within a two-digit number.

Date: 9/20/13

4.A.1

- How did the Application Problem connect to today's lesson? How would you write the answer in a place value chart?

Exit Ticket (3 minutes)

After the Student Debrief, instruct students to complete the Exit Ticket. A review of their work will help you assess the students' understanding of the concepts that were presented in the lesson today and plan more effectively for future lessons. You may read the questions aloud to the students

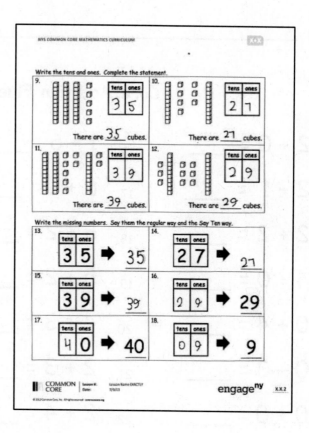

Lesson 2:   Use the place value chart to record and name tens and ones within a two-digit number.

Date: 9/20/13

4.A.18

Core Addition Fluency Review

1. $2 + 0 =$ ___
2. $2 + 1 =$ ___
3. $2 + 2 =$ ___
4. $4 + 0 =$ ___
5. $0 + 4 =$ ___
6. $0 + 3 =$ ___
7. $0 + 0 =$ ___
8. $3 + 1 =$ ___
9. $1 + 3 =$ ___
10. $1 + 4 =$ ___
11. $1 + 5 =$ ___
12. $5 + 1 =$ ___
13. $1 + 7 =$ ___
14. $7 + 1 =$ ___
15. $1 + 8 =$ ___

16. $1 + 6 =$ ___
17. $6 + 1 =$ ___
18. $6 + 2 =$ ___
19. $5 + 2 =$ ___
20. $4 + 3 =$ ___
21. $2 + 3 =$ ___
22. $2 + 4 =$ ___
23. $4 + 2 =$ ___
24. $3 + 2 =$ ___
25. $9 + 1 =$ ___
26. $8 + 2 =$ ___
27. $7 + 2 =$ ___
28. $7 + 3 =$ ___
29. $6 + 3 =$ ___
30. $6 + 4 =$ ___

31. $5 + 3 =$ ___
32. $3 + 5 =$ ___
33. $3 + 4 =$ ___
34. $3 + 3 =$ ___
35. $4 + 4 =$ ___
36. $5 + 4 =$ ___
37. $4 + 6 =$ ___
38. $2 + 7 =$ ___
39. $2 + 8 =$ ___
40. $2 + 5 =$ ___
41. $5 + 5 =$ ___
42. $4 + 5 =$ ___
43. $2 + 6 =$ ___
44. $3 + 6 =$ ___
45. $3 + 7 =$ ___

COMMON CORE | Lesson 2: Use the place value chart to record and name tens and ones within a two-digit number.
Date: 9/20/13

4.A.1

Name _____   Date _____

Write the tens and ones and say the numbers. Complete the statement.

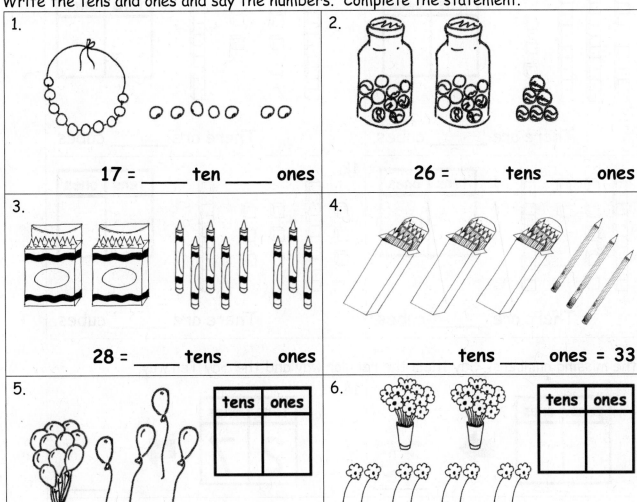

1.

17 = _____ ten _____ ones

2.

26 = _____ tens _____ ones

3.

28 = _____ tens _____ ones

4.

_____ tens _____ ones = 33

5.

tens	ones

There are _____ balloons.

6.

tens	ones

There are _____ flowers.

7.

tens	ones

There are _____ marbles.

8.

tens	ones

There are _____ peanuts.

COMMON CORE

Lesson 2:   Use the place value chart to record and name tens and ones within a
two-digit number.
Date: 9/20/13

4.A.20

Write the tens and ones. Complete the statement.

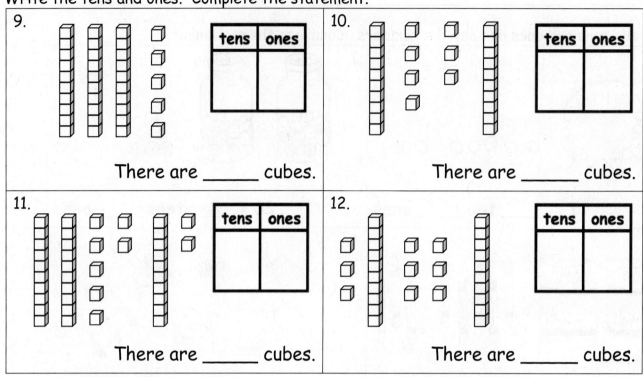

9. There are _____ cubes.

10. There are _____ cubes.

11. There are _____ cubes.

12. There are _____ cubes.

Write the missing numbers. Say them the regular way and the Say Ten way.

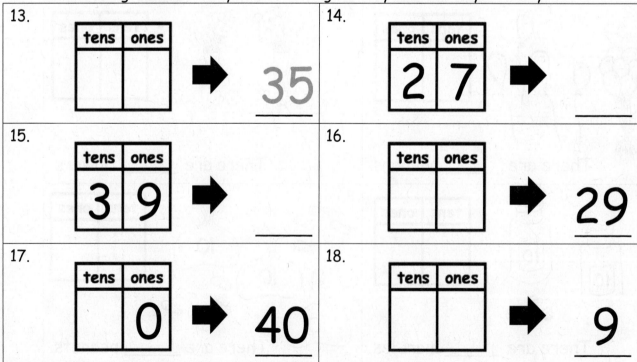

13.

tens	ones

➡ 35

14.

tens	ones
2	7

➡ ____

15.

tens	ones
3	9

➡ ____

16.

tens	ones

➡ 29

17.

tens	ones
	0

➡ 40

18.

tens	ones

➡ 9

Lesson 2: Use the place value chart to record and name tens and ones within a two-digit number.

Date: 9/20/13

4.A.

Name _____   Date _____

Match the picture to the place value chart that shows the correct tens and ones.

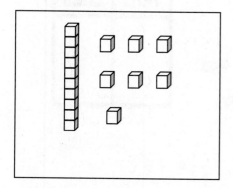

tens	ones
4	0

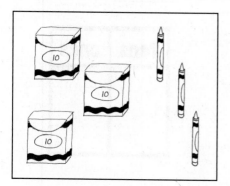

tens	ones
1	7

tens	ones
3	3

Name _____   Date _____

Write the tens and ones and complete the statement.

1.

tens	ones

There are _____ straws.

2.

tens	ones

There are _____ peanuts.

3.

tens	ones

There are _____ strawberries.

4.

tens	ones

There are _____ beads.

5.

tens	ones

There are _____ apples.

6.

tens	ones

There are _____ carrots.

COMMON CORE | **Lesson 2:** | Use the place value chart to record and name tens and ones within a two-digit number.
| **Date:** | 9/20/13

4.A.

Write the tens and ones. Complete the statement.

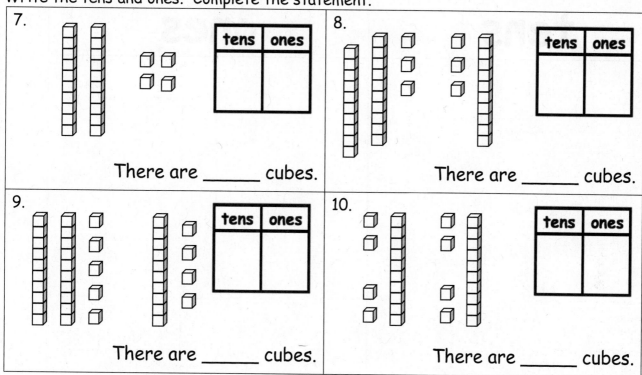

7.

tens	ones

There are _____ cubes.

8.

tens	ones

There are _____ cubes.

9.

tens	ones

There are _____ cubes.

10.

tens	ones

There are _____ cubes.

Write the missing numbers. Say them the regular way and the Say Ten way.

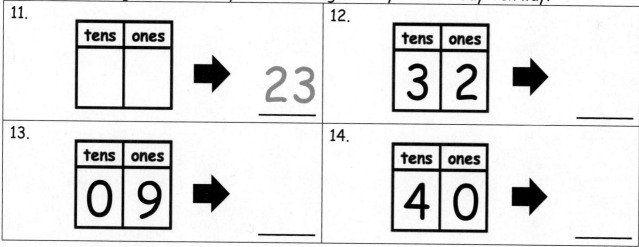

11.

tens	ones

➡ 23
   _____

12.

tens	ones
3	2

➡ _____

13.

tens	ones
0	9

➡ _____

14.

tens	ones
4	0

➡ _____

15. Choose a number less than 40. Make a math drawing to represent it and fill in the number bond and place value chart.

tens	ones

Lesson 2: Use the place value chart to record and name tens and ones within a two-digit number.

Date: 9/20/13

4.A.24

tens	ones

Lesson 2: Use the place value chart to record and name tens and ones within a two-digit number.

Date: 9/20/13

4.A.

Lesson 3

Objective: Interpret two-digit numbers as either tens and some ones or as all ones.

Suggested Lesson Structure

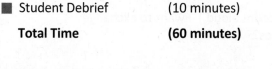

■ Application Problem	(5 minutes)
■ Fluency Practice	(12 minutes)
■ Concept Development	(33 minutes)
■ Student Debrief	(10 minutes)
Total Time	**(60 minutes)**

Application Problem (5 minutes)

Sue is writing the number 34 on a place value chart. She can't remember if she has 4 tens and 3 ones or 3 tens and 4 ones. Use a place value chart to show how many tens and ones are in 34. Use a drawing and words to explain this to Sue.

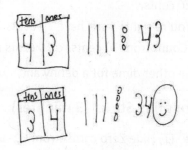

Note: This problem invites children to write or discuss their understanding of tens and ones, based on their learning from Lesson 2. For students who find it challenging to create written explanations, have them share orally with a partner and use drawings to support their thinking. During the Debrief, students will also share other interpretations of 34.

Fluency Practice (12 minutes)

- Core Addition Fluency Review **1.OA.6**   (5 minutes)
- Dime Exchange **1.NBT.5**   (4 minutes)
- Magic Counting Sticks **1.NBT.2**   (3 minutes)

Core Addition Fluency Review (5 minutes)

Materials: (S) Core Addition Fluency Review from G1–M4–Lesson 2

Note: This activity assesses students' progress toward mastery of the required addition fluency for first graders. Since this is the second day students are doing this activity, encourage students to remember how many problems they answered yesterday and celebrate improvement.

Lesson 3:	Interpret two-digit numbers as either tens and some ones or as all ones.	
Date:	9/20/13	**4.A.26**

Students complete as many problems as they can in three minutes. Choose a counting sequence for early finishers to practice on the back of their papers. When time runs out, read the answers aloud so students can correct their work and celebrate improvement.

Dime Exchange (4 minutes)

Materials: (T) 20 pennies and 2 dimes

Note: This activity provides students practice with recognizing pennies and dimes and identifying their values. This fluency activity is necessary in order to prepare students to utilize coins as abstract representations of tens and ones in G1–M1–Lesson 6.

T: (Lay out 2 dimes.) What coins do you see?

S: 2 dimes.

T: Let's count by tens to see how much money I have. (Students count aloud.) I want to exchange 1 dime for some pennies. What is the correct number of pennies?

S: 10 pennies.

T: (Replace a dime with 10 pennies in 5-group formation.) How much money do I have now?

S: 20 cents.

T: You're right! I still have 20 cents. Count back with me.

S: (Count from 20 cents to 10 cents removing 1 penny at a time.)

Change the other dime for a penny and students count from 10 cents to 0 cents.

Magic Counting Sticks (3 minutes)

Materials: (T) Hide Zero cards (from G1–M1–Lesson 38)

Note: This activity reviews the concept of ten as a unit and as 10 ones, which will prepare students for today's lesson.

T: (Divide students into partners and assign Partners A and B. Show 13 with Hide Zero cards.) How many tens are in 13?

S: 1 ten.

T: (Point to the 1 in 13.) Partner A, show 1 ten with your magic counting sticks. (Partner A holds up a bundled ten.) How many ones should Partner B show?

S: 3 ones.

T: (Point to the 3.) Partner B, show 3 ones. 1 ten and 3 ones is 13. Partner A, open up your ten. How many fingers do you have?

S: 10 fingers.

T: (Take apart the Hide Zero cards to show 10 and 3.) 10 fingers + 3 fingers is?

S: 13 fingers.

Alternate partners and repeat with other teen numbers.

Lesson 3:	Interpret two-digit numbers as either tens and some ones or as all ones.
Date:	9/20/13

4.A.

Concept Development (33 minutes)

Materials: (T) Hide Zero cards (from G1–M1– Lesson 38), personal math toolkit of 4 ten-sticks (S) Personal
math toolkit of 4 ten-sticks

Students gather in the meeting area in a semi-circle formation.

T: Show me your magic counting sticks. Wriggle them in the air. Now show me 1 ten.

S: (Clasp their hands together.)

T: Show me 10 ones.

S: (Unclasp hands and show individual fingers.)

T: How can we show 34 using our magic counting sticks?

S: We can't. We only have 10 magic sticks. → We need more people to show 34. → We need 4
people—3 people to show 3 tens, 1 more person to show 4 extra ones.

T: Great idea! (Call up four volunteers.) Show us 34.

S: (Three students clasp their hands together while the last student on the right facing the class shows
4 fingers.)

T: How many tens and ones make up 34?

S: 3 tens and 4 ones.

T: How many ones is the number 34 made of?

S: I see 3 tens and 4 ones. So there are just 4 ones. → I see 34 ones. Each ten is made of 10 ones. So I
counted on by tens to get to 30, and I counted by ones to get to 34.

T: I heard some students say that there are 4 ones. Think again. If we *only* use ones to make 34, how
many will it take? Open up your hands to show your fingers, volunteers!

S: (The first three students unclasp their hands and show all fingers.)

T: How many ones make up 34?

S: 34 ones.

T: How many ones is the same as 3 tens 4 ones?

S: 34 ones.

T: Let's count to check. How should we count?

S: We can count the fingers by ones. → Let's count them by tens first. That will be much faster.

T: Great idea. Let's count by grouping the 10 ones. Start with Student A. How many ones are here?

S: 10 ones.

T: Keep counting!

S: 20 ones, 30 ones, 34 ones.

T: Great. Let's do some more. (Call up three volunteers.) Show me 27 *ones*.

S: (Show individual fingers.)

T: If you are able to make a ten, clasp your hands.

S: (Two students clasp hands.)

COMMON CORE™   Lesson 3:   Interpret two-digit numbers as either tens and some ones or as all
ones.
Date: 9/20/13

4.A.28

T: 27 ones is the same as how many tens and ones?

S: 2 tens and 7 ones.

T: How many ones?

S: 27 ones!

Repeat the process using the following sequence: 37, 14, 24, 34, 13, 31, 10, and 40.

When students demonstrate solid understanding with the finger work, move on to representing the numbers with Hide Zero cards.

T: (Show 24 using Hide Zero cards.) How many tens and ones make up 24?

S: 2 tens 4 ones.

T: How many ones are in 2 tens? (Pull apart 24 into 20 and 4.)

S: 20 ones.

T: How many extra ones are there?

S: 4 ones.

T: How many ones is the same as 2 tens and 4 ones?

S: 24 ones.

T: How many tens and ones is the same as 24 ones? (Put 24 back together.)

S: 2 tens 4 ones.

Repeat the process using the following sequence: 13, 23, 16, 26, 36, 29, 20 and 30 using Hide Zero cards. For the first two or three, have students work with a partner to represent the number with their linking cubes, first with as many tens as possible, and then decomposed into all ones. Support students in seeing that there are the same number of cubes and connecting this with the mathematical idea that, for instance, 1 ten 3 ones is the same amount as 13 ones.

Problem Set (10 minutes)

Note: For completing today's Problem Set, have students say the number and the sentence for each problem. This will allow students to hear themselves reading numbers in different ways.

Students should do their personal best to complete the Problem Set within the allotted 10 minutes. For some classes, it may be appropriate to modify the assignment by

NOTES ON MULTIPLE MEANS OF ACTION AND EXPRESSION:

By introducing each number in a different way, students are held accountable for understanding place value no matter how the number is presented. Doing it this way can be a challenge for some students, so make sure that students who need information presented a specific way are still getting the information they need.

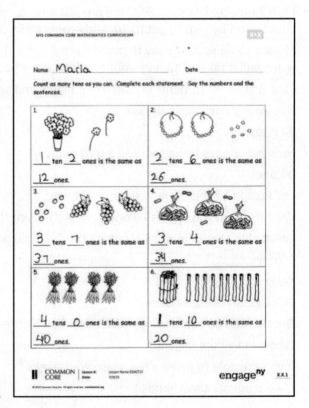

Lesson 3: Interpret two-digit numbers as either tens and some ones or as all ones.

Date: 9/20/13

4.A

specifying which problems they work on first. Some problems do not specify a method for solving. Students solve these problems using the RDW approach used for Application Problems.

Student Debrief (10 minutes)

Lesson Objective: Interpret two-digit numbers as either tens and some ones or as all ones.

The Student Debrief is intended to invite reflection and active processing of the total lesson experience.

Invite students to review their solutions for the Problem Set. They should check work by comparing answers with a partner before going over answers as a class. Look for misconceptions or misunderstandings that can be addressed in the Debrief. Guide students in a conversation to debrief the Problem Set and process the lesson.

You may choose to use any combination of the questions below to lead the discussion.

- Look at Problem 6. What is your solution? How are both of these answers correct?
- Look at Problem 10. Explain how 4 tens is the same as 40 ones. You may use linking cubes or the place value chart to support your thinking.
- Look at Problem 12. What are the different ways we can make 29?
- Student A says 2 tens and 9 ones only has 9 ones. Do you agree? Why or why not? How can you help them understand their mistake?
- Look at your Application Problem. Share your work and explain your thinking with a partner. If we counted in all ones, how many ones are in 34?

Exit Ticket (3 minutes)

After the Student Debrief, instruct students to complete the Exit Ticket. A review of their work will help you assess the students' understanding of the concepts that were presented in the lesson today and plan more effectively for future lessons. You may read the questions aloud to the students.

COMMON CORE

Lesson 3:   Interpret two-digit numbers as either tens and some ones or as all ones.
Date: 9/20/13

4.A.30

Name _____   Date _____

Count as many tens as you can. Complete each statement. Say the numbers and the sentences.

1.	2.
_____ ten _____ ones is the same as _____ones.	_____ tens _____ ones is the same as _____ones.
3.	4.
_____ tens _____ ones is the same as _____ones.	_____ tens _____ ones is the same as _____ones.
5.	6.
_____ tens _____ ones is the same as _____ones.	_____ ten _____ ones is the same as _____ones.

Lesson 3: Interpret two-digit numbers as either tens and some ones or as all ones.
Date: 9/20/13

4.A

Match.

7. | 3 tens 2 ones |

29 ones

8.

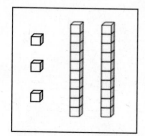

tens	ones
1	7

40 ones

23 ones

9. | 37 ones |

32 ones

10. | 4 tens |

17 ones

11.

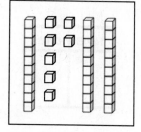

12. | 9 ones 2 tens |

Fill in the missing numbers.

13. **15** ➡️

tens	ones

➡️ _____ ones

14. _____ ➡️ _____ tens _____ ones ➡️ 39 ones

COMMON
CORE™

Lesson 3: Interpret two-digit numbers as either tens and some ones or as all ones.

Date: 9/20/13

4.A.32

Name _____   Date _____

1.

_____ tens _____ ones is the same

as _____ ones.

2.

_____ tens _____ ones is the same

as _____ ones.

tens	ones

3. **27** ➡ | tens | ones | ➡ _____ ones

Name _____ Date _____

Count as many tens as you can. Complete each statement. Say the numbers and the sentences.

1.	2.
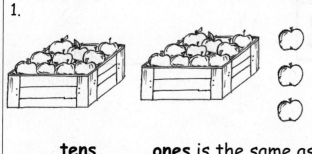	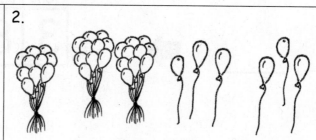
_____ tens _____ ones is the same as _____ones.	_____ tens _____ ones is the same as _____ones.
3.	4.
	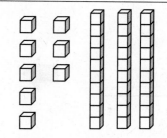
_____ tens _____ ones is the same as _____ones.	_____ tens _____ ones is the same as _____ones.

Fill in the missing numbers.

tens	ones
2	9

5. _____ ➡ | tens | ones | ➡ _____ ones

COMMON CORE™

Lesson 3:   Interpret two-digit numbers as either tens and some ones or as all ones.

Date: 9/20/13

4.A.34

6.   **34** ➡ _____ tens _____ ones ➡ _____ ones

7.   _____ ➡

tens	ones
3	8

➡ _____ ones

8.   _____ ➡ 9 ones 3 tens ➡ _____ ones

9.   _____ ➡ _____ ones _____ tens ➡ **40** ones

10. Choose at least one number less than 40. Draw the number in three ways:

As grapes:	In a number bond:	In the place value chart:
	⋀	tens | ones

Lesson 3:   Interpret two-digit numbers as either tens and some ones or as all ones.

Date: 9/20/13

4.A.

Lesson 4

Objective: Write and interpret two-digit numbers as addition sentences that combine tens and ones.

Suggested Lesson Structure

■ Fluency Practice   (12 minutes)
  Application Problem   (5 minutes)
  Concept Development   (33 minutes)
■ Student Debrief   (10 minutes)
  Total Time   **(60 minutes)**

Fluency Practice (12 minutes)

- Subtraction with Cards **1.OA.6**   (5 minutes)
- Dime Exchange **1.NBT.2**   (5 minutes)
- 10 More **1.NBT.5**   (2 minutes)

Subtraction with Cards (5 minutes)

Materials: (S) 1 pack of numeral cards 0–10 per set of partners (from G1–M1–Lesson 36)

Note: This review fluency strengthens students' abilities to subtract within 10, which is a required core fluency for Grade 1.

Students combine their numeral cards and place them face down between them. Each partner flips over two cards and subtracts the smaller number from the larger one. The partner with the smallest difference keeps the cards played by both players. If the differences are equal, the cards are set aside and the winner of the next round keeps the cards from both rounds. The player with the most cards at the end of the game wins.

Dime Exchange (5 minutes)

Materials: (S) 10 pennies and 2 dimes per pair

Note: This fluency activity is necessary in order to prepare students to utilize coins as abstract representations of tens and ones in G1–M1–Lesson 6. If there are not enough coins to do this activity in pairs, it may be done as a teacher-directed activity.

Students work in pairs. Partner A begins with 2 dimes. Partner B begins with 10 pennies. Partner A whisper-counts as she lays 2 dimes, "10 cents, 20 cents." Partner B exchanges 1 dime for 10 pennies, lays them out in 5-groups, and says "1 dime is equal to 10 pennies." Students whisper-count as Partner A takes away 1 penny

Lesson 4:   Write and interpret two-digit numbers as addition sentences that
              combine tens and ones.   4.A.36
Date: 9/20/13

at a time (20 cents, 19 cents, etc.). When they get to 10, they exchange the dime for 10 pennies and whisper-count to 0. Partners A and B switch roles and repeat.

10 More (2 minutes)

Note: This fluency activity reviews adding 10 to a single-digit number, which will prepare students for today's lesson.

T: What's 10 more than 5?
S: 15.
T: Say 15 the Say Ten way.
S: Ten 5.
T: Say it as an addition sentence, starting with 5.
S: 5 + 10 = 15.
T: Say the addition sentence, starting with 10.
S: 10 + 5 = 15.

Repeat, beginning with other numbers between 0 and 10.

Application Problem (5 minutes)

Lisa has 3 boxes of 10 crayons and 5 extra crayons. Sally has 19 crayons.
Sally says she has more crayons, but Lisa disagrees. Who is right?

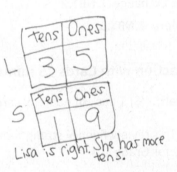

Note: In this problem, students use what they learned in Lesson 3 about interpreting a two-digit number in terms of tens and ones and apply this to a problem involving a comparison of two quantities. To decide which is larger, students really only need to compare how many tens Lisa and Sally each have.
Note: Be sure to note which students understand and which don't understand that Sally has a larger number of ones than Lisa does but that Lisa still has a larger amount of crayons because she has more tens.

Concept Development (33 minutes)

Materials: (T) 40 linking cubes, chart paper with a place value chart, Hide Zero cards (from G1–M3–Lesson 2), piece of blank paper to cover sections (S) personal math toolkit of 4 ten-sticks (from G1–M4–Lesson 1), personal white board with the place value chart template insert (from G1–M4–Lesson 2), numeral cards (from G1–M1–Lesson 36)

Students gather in the meeting area in a semi-circle formation with their personal white boards. The toolkits of 4 ten-sticks are at their individual desks or tables.

T: (Lay out 3 ten-sticks and 7 ones using linking cubes on the floor.) Say this number as tens and ones.
S: 3 tens 7 ones.

Lesson 4:	Write and interpret two-digit numbers as addition sentences that combine tens and ones.	4.A.
Date:	9/20/13	

T: Which is the same as the number...

S: 37!

T: (Fill in the place value chart.) 3 is the **digit** in the tens place. 7 is the digit in the ones place. (Point to each digit in the chart.)

T: On your board, make a number bond that shows the tens and the ones.

S: (Take apart 37 into 30 and 7.)

T: (Record the number bond on the chart.) Write as many addition sentences as you can that use your number bond.

$$30 + 7 = 37$$
$$7 + 30 = 37$$
$$37 = 30 + 7$$
$$37 = 7 + 30$$

7 more than 30 is 37.
30 more than 7 is 37.

Circulate and ensure that students are only using the three numbers from this bond: 37, 30, and 7. If students begin writing subtraction sentences, remind them of the directions. You may choose to challenge some students to consider subtraction sentences, but these sentences will not be addressed during the course of the lesson.

T: Give me a number sentence that matches this number bond. Start with the part that represents the tens. (Record on the chart as students answer.)

S: 30 + 7 = 37.

T: Start your number sentence with the ones. (Record on the chart.)

S: 7 + 30 = 37.

T: 37 is the same as? (Write 37 = and complete the number sentence as students answer.)

S: 30 plus 7.

T: This time start with the ones. 37 is the same as? (Write 37 = and complete the number sentence.)

S: 7 plus 30.

T: Talk to your partner. What do you notice about the addends in all of these number sentences?

S: There is one that tells how many tens there are and the other tells how many ones there are. → You can switch the addends around and the total is still the same. → That was true with smaller numbers, too! → The bigger number also tells how many ones are in the tens.

T: Great. (Point to 7.) 7 more than 30 is? Say the whole sentence.

S: 7 more than 30 is 37. (Record on the chart.)

T: (Point to 30.) 30 more than 7 is? Say the whole sentence.

S: 30 more than 7 is 37. (Record on the chart.)

NOTES ON MULTIPLE MEANS OF EXPRESSION:

Students may need additional support with the language of "___ is the same as ___," "___ is ___ more than ___," etc. Insert a sentence frame into their personal white board, and allow the student to fill in the blanks. Pointing to each word and number as it is read can provide a bridge between the concrete and the abstract.

Repeat the process following the suggested sequence: 18, 28, 38, 12, 21, 23, 32, 30 and 40. When appropriate, switch to modeling with Hide Zero cards and have students write their responses on their boards. Use different language to elicit a variety of answers for each number: (e.g., 18 is the same as...; 10 plus 8 is...; 8 more than 10 is...; 10 more than 8 is....)

Lesson 4:   Write and interpret two-digit numbers as addition sentences that combine tens and ones.

Date: 9/20/13

4.A.38

For the remainder of time, have partners play Combine Tens and Ones. Leave the chart for 37 up on the board as a reference to support students.

NOTES ON
MULTIPLE MEANS OF
ENGAGEMENT:

When playing games with your students modeling how the game is played is very important. Oral instructions alone are not going to help all of your class understand how the game is played. Have two students demonstrate Partner A and Partner B roles so that all students see and hear the way the game is played.

- Prepare two decks by combining numeral cards 0 through 9 from both players. The first deck is comprised of 1 set of digits 1 to 3. The rest of the cards are in the second deck.

- Pick a card from the first deck. This number is placed in the tens place on the place value chart (e.g., 2 is drawn and placed in the tens place).

- Pick a card from the second deck. This number is placed in the ones place on the place value chart (e.g., 7 is drawn and placed in the ones place).

- Partner A and B make a number bond decomposing the number into tens and ones.

- Partner A writes two addition number sentences (e.g., $20 + 7 = 27$; $7 + 20 = 27$; $27 = 20 + 7$; $27 = 7 + 20$).

- Partner B writes 1 *more than* statement that combines tens and ones (e.g., 20 more than 7 is 27; 7 more than 20 is 27; 27 is 7 more than 20; 27 is 20 more than 7).

- Switch roles for the next set of cards drawn.

Problem Set (10 minutes)

Students should do their personal best to complete the Problem Set within the allotted 10 minutes. For some classes, it may be appropriate to modify the assignment by specifying which problems they work on first. Some problems do not specify a method for solving. Students solve these problems using the RDW approach used for Application Problems.

Student Debrief (10 minutes)

Lesson Objective: Write and interpret two-digit numbers as addition sentences that combine tens and ones.

The Student Debrief is intended to invite reflection and active processing of the total lesson experience.

Invite students to review their solutions for the Problem Set. They should check work by comparing answers with a partner before going over answers as a class. Look for

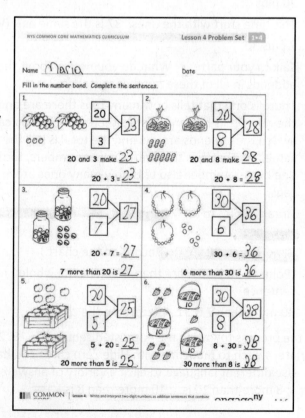

Lesson 4: Write and interpret two-digit numbers as addition sentences that combine tens and ones.
Date: 9/20/13

4.A.

misconceptions or misunderstandings that can be addressed in the Debrief. Guide students in a conversation to debrief the Problem Set and process the lesson.

You may choose to use any combination of the questions below to lead the discussion.

- How can solving Problem 1 help you solve Problem 2?

- How did you solve Problem 5? Is it easier for you to start with the ones first or tens first?

- Look at Problem 15. Explain why the answer is not 23. Write the number in a place value chart. Which digit is in the tens place? Which digit is in the ones place?

- Based on our work today, what do you think the word **digit** means? (Digits are the symbols 0–9 that can be used to create any number. 32 is a two-digit number. The numeral 3 is the digit in the tens place, and the numeral 2 is the digit in the ones place.)

- When you played Combine Tens and Ones, did you ever pick a 0 card? What did you write for your number sentences and number bond?

- Look at your Application Problem. Share your thinking with a partner. How many crayons does Lisa have? Write the number of crayons Lisa has using two number sentences, as we did during today's lesson.

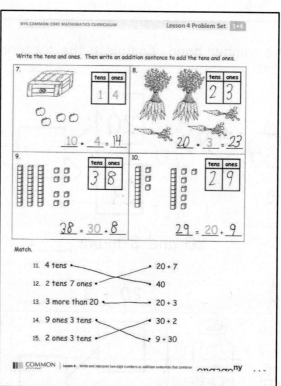

Exit Ticket (3 minutes)

After the Student Debrief, instruct students to complete the Exit Ticket. A review of their work will help you assess the students' understanding of the concepts that were presented in the lesson today and plan more effectively for future lessons. You may read the questions aloud to the students.

COMMON CORE™

Lesson 4:   Write and interpret two-digit numbers as addition sentences that combine tens and ones.
Date: 9/20/13

4.A.40

© 2013 Common Core, Inc. All rights reserved. commoncore.org

Name _____ Date _____

Fill in the number bond. Complete the sentences.

1.

20 and 3 make _____.

20 + 3 = _____

2.
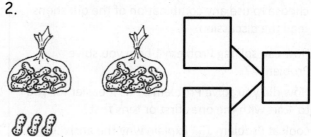

20 and 8 make _____.

20 + 8 = _____

3.
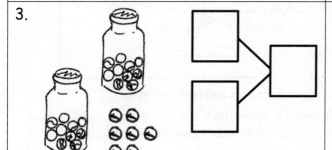

20 + 7 = _____

7 more than **20** is _____.

4.
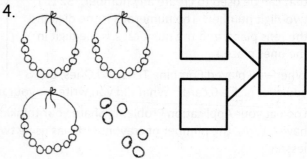

30 + 6 = _____

6 more than **30** is _____.

5.
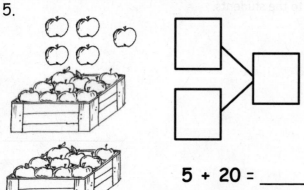

5 + 20 = _____

20 more than **5** is _____.

6.
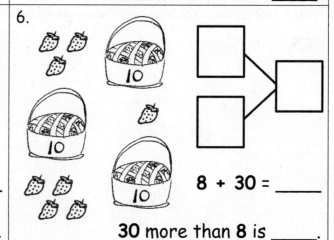

8 + 30 = _____

30 more than **8** is _____.

COMMON CORE

Lesson 4: Write and interpret two-digit numbers as addition sentences that combine tens and ones.

Date: 9/20/13

4.A.

Write the tens and ones. Then write an addition sentence to add the tens and ones.

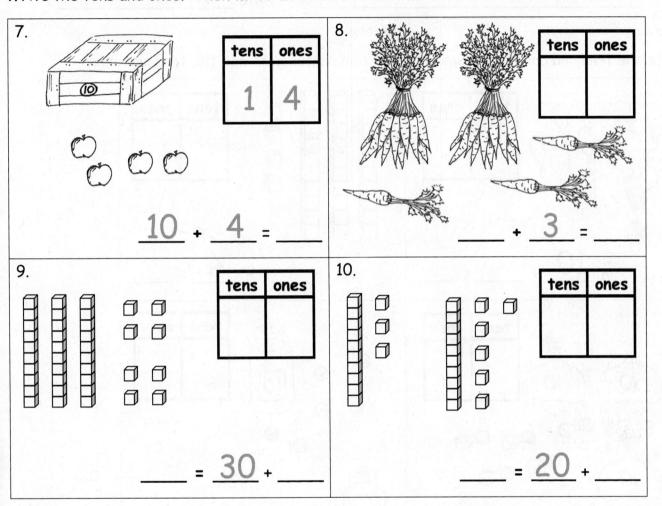

7.

tens	ones
1	4

__10__ + __4__ = ____

8.

tens	ones

____ + __3__ = ____

9.

tens	ones

____ = __30__ + ____

10.

tens	ones

____ = __20__ + ____

Match.

11. 4 tens •   • 20 + 7

12. 2 tens 7 ones •   • 40

13. 3 more than 20 •   • 20 + 3

14. 9 ones 3 tens •   • 30 + 2

15. 2 ones 3 tens •   • 9 + 30

Name _____   Date _____

Write the tens and ones. Then write an addition sentence to add the tens and ones.

1.

tens	ones

__10__ + _____ = _____

2.

tens	ones

_____ + __4__ = _____

3.

tens	ones

_____ = __30__ + _____

4.

tens	ones

_____ = __6__ + _____

COMMON CORE™

Lesson 4:   Write and interpret two-digit numbers as addition sentences that combine tens and ones.

Date: 9/20/13

4.A.

Name _____ Date _____

Fill in the number bond or write the tens and ones. Complete the addition sentences.

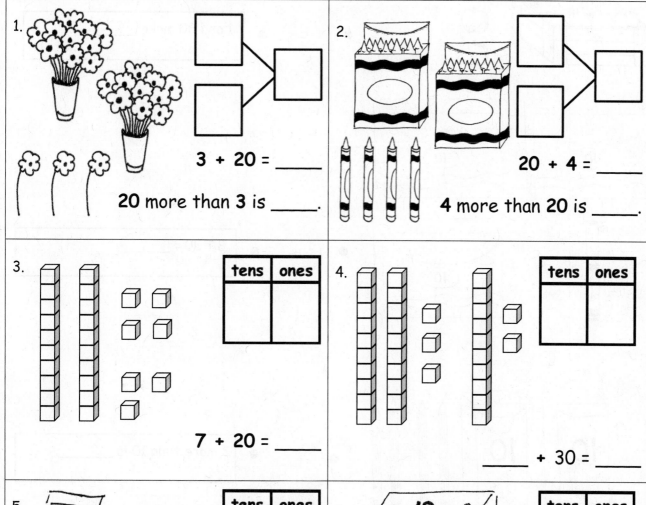

1.

$3 + 20 =$ ____

20 more than 3 is ____.

2.

$20 + 4 =$ ____

4 more than 20 is ____.

3.

tens	ones

$7 + 20 =$ ____

4.

tens	ones

____ $+ 30 =$ ____

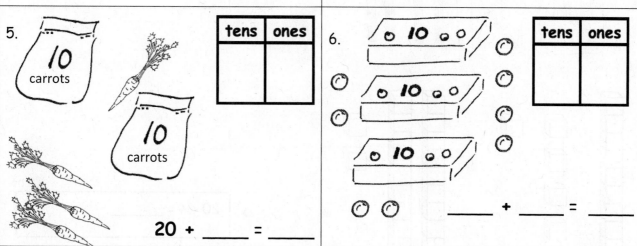

5.

tens	ones

10 carrots

10 carrots

$20 +$ ____ $=$ ____

6.

tens	ones

10

10

10

____ $+$ ____ $=$ ____

Lesson 4:   Write and interpret two-digit numbers as addition sentences that combine tens and ones.

Date: 9/20/13

4.A.44

Match the pictures with the words.

7.

● ● $\boxed{\text{1 and 30 make _____.}}$

8.

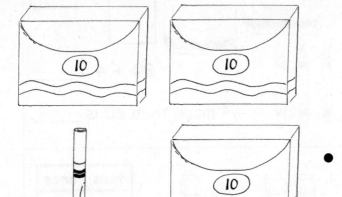

● ● $\boxed{\text{8 + 30 = _____.}}$

9.

● ● $\boxed{\text{2 more than 10 is _____.}}$

10.

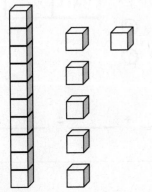
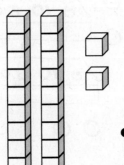

● ● $\boxed{\text{20 + 4 = _____.}}$

COMMON CORE **Lesson 4:** Write and interpret two-digit numbers as addition sentences that combine tens and ones.
Date: 9/20/13

4.A.

Lesson 5

Objective: Identify 10 more, 10 less, 1 more, and 1 less than a two-digit number.

Suggested Lesson Structure

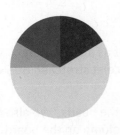

■ Fluency Practice   (10 minutes)
■ Application Problem   (5 minutes)
■ Concept Development   (35 minutes)
■ Student Debrief   (10 minutes)
   Total Time   **(60 minutes)**

Fluency Practice (10 minutes)

▪ Sprint: 10 More, 10 Less Review **1.OA.6**   (10 minutes)

Sprint: 10 More, 10 Less Review (10 minutes)

Materials: (S) 10 More, 10 Less Review Sprint

Note: This review Sprint provides practice with addition and subtraction within 20 and prepares students to extend this skill for numbers to 40 in today's lesson.

Application Problem (5 minutes)

Lee has 4 pencils and buys 10 more. Kiana has 17 pencils and loses 10 of them. Who has more pencils now? Use drawings, words, and number sentences to explain your thinking.

Note: This problem gives students a chance to add and subtract 10 using their own methods. At this point in the year, students should feel quite comfortable adding and subtracting 10 with numbers within 20. Circulate and notice students' understanding and link this to today's lesson, as students notice ways to more quickly add and subtract 10 to and from larger numbers.

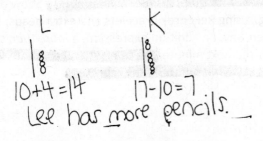

© 2013 Common Core, Inc. All rights reserved. **commoncore.org**

Concept Development (35 minutes)

Materials: (T) 4 Rekenrek bracelets stretched into a straight line (first used in G1–M1–Lesson 8), 5 additional red beads, 5 additional white beads, 4 ten-sticks, 2 pieces of chart paper with two pairs of place value charts as shown (S) Personal math toolkit of 4 ten-sticks of linking cubes, personal white board with double place value charts template

Students sit at their desks with all materials.

T: (Show the Rekenrek bracelet stretched out as a vertical line.) When we made drawings to show this Rekenrek bracelet stretched out, we called it a…

S: 5-group column!

T: You're right! We drew 10 circles showing the beads. We also drew a line through it to show there are 10 circles or beads. (Draw a 5-group column on the board.)

T: (Place 4 individual beads next to the Rekenrek bracelet.) How many beads are there?

S: 14 beads.

T: Say an addition sentence that represents how many beads there are, starting with 10.

S: 10 + 4 = 14.

T: Draw the number of beads using 5-group columns.

S: (Draw one 5-group column and four beads.)

T: (Add two more Rekenrek bracelets representing 34.) How many beads are here now? Let's count.

S/T: (Point to each bracelet as you count by tens and then to each bead for the last four beads.) 10, 20, 30. (Pause.) 31, 32, 33, 34.

T: Draw the number of beads using 5-group columns. (Give 10 seconds to draw.) Your time is up!

S: I didn't have enough time to draw all 34 beads!

T: Wow, drawing 34 beads would take us a long time! Let me show you a shortcut to drawing tens. Watch how quickly I can represent 34. (Draw 3 quick tens and 4 circles.)

T: Now, you try drawing 34 using quick tens.

S: (Draw.)

T: We call each of these lines a **quick ten**. How do you think it got its name?

S: It's a line that holds 10 beads. → It represents a ten, so we don't have to draw all the beads! → It's so quick to draw a ten now!

Have students practice representing numbers with quick tens for two minutes. Show or call out using numbers from 11 to 40 in varied ways (e.g., using Rekenrek bracelets and extra beads, ten-sticks and extra linking cubes, place value chart, the Say Ten way, an addition expression, a *more than* statement, and a number bond with two parts filled in). For the next minute, the teacher and students switch roles. The teacher draws quick tens and the students say what number they represent.

Lesson 5:   Identify 10 more, 10 less, 1 more, and 1 less than a two-digit number.
Date: 9/20/13

4.A.

T: Draw 15.

S: (Draw a quick ten and 5 circles.)

T: How many tens and ones are there?

S: 1 ten and 5 ones.

T: (Write 15 on the double place value chart template.)

T: Show me 1 more than 15.

S: (Draw 1 more circle.)

T: What is 1 more than 15? Say the whole sentence.

S: 1 more than 15 is 16. (Write 16 on the place value chart.)

T: So, from 15 to 16, we added 1 more. (Draw an arrow from the first place value chart to the second and write + 1 above the arrow.)

T: Look at the place value chart. What changed and what didn't? Turn and talk to your partner about why this is so.

S: The tens didn't change. They both stayed as 1 ten because we only added 1 more. → The ones changed from 5 to 6 because we added 1 more. 6 is 1 more than 5. → To figure out 1 more, I just have to add 1 more to the number in the ones place!

T: Great thinking! Show me 15 with your drawing again.

S: (Show 15.)

T: (Write 15 on a new place value chart.) Now, how can you show *10* more than 15? (Draw an arrow and write + 10 above it.) Turn and talk to your partner and then show with your cubes.

S: Just draw one more quick ten!

T: That's an efficient way to show 10 more! Let's have everyone show 10 more this way, drawing just one more quick ten. What is 10 more than 15? Say the whole sentence.

S: 10 more than 15 is 25.

T: I'm about to write the new number on the place value chart to show 10 more than 15. Talk to your partner about what you think will change and what will remain the same?

S: The tens changed this time from 1 ten to 2 tens because we added 10 more. → The ones didn't change because we just added a ten-stick. → We could add 10 extra ones, but once you get 10 we make them into a ten-

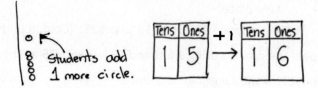
Students add 1 more circle.

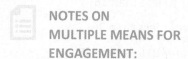

NOTES ON MULTIPLE MEANS FOR ENGAGEMENT:

Some students may not be able to imagine adding or subtracting a ten at this point. Support these students with all of the materials used in the lesson and give them plenty of practice. Their path to abstract thinking may be a little longer than those of other students.

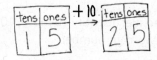
Students add 1 more quick ten.

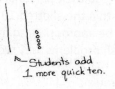

NOTES ON MULTIPLE MEANS OF ENGAGEMENT:

Other students in your class may be able to visualize adding and subtracting ones and tens. Since these students have moved from concrete to abstract thinking, challenge them by giving problems adding or subtracting 2 ones/tens or 3 ones/tens.

COMMON CORE

Lesson 5:   Identify 10 more, 10 less, 1 more, and 1 less than a two-digit number.
Date: 9/20/13

4.A.48

MP.6

stick, so why bother? We can add a ten quickly. → I just have to add 1 more to the number in the tens place!

T: We added 10 more to 15 to get 25. (Complete the second place value chart with 2 and 5.)

Repeat the process using *1 less* and *10 less* with 35 as shown to the right.

Then follow the suggested sequence:

- 1 more/10 more than 14
- 1 less/10 less than 16
- 1 more/1 less than 36
- 10 more/10 less than 38
- 1 more/1 less than 32
- 10 more/10 less than 23
- 1 more than 29
- 1 less than 30

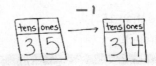

Problem Set (10 minutes)

Students should do their personal best to complete the Problem Set within the allotted 10 minutes. For some classes, it may be appropriate to modify the assignment by specifying which problems they work on first.

Student Debrief (10 minutes)

Lesson Objective: Identify 10 more, 10 less, 1 more, and 1 less than a two-digit number.

The Student Debrief is intended to invite reflection and active processing of the total lesson experience.

Invite students to review their solutions for the Problem Set. They should check work by comparing answers with a partner before going over answers as a class. Look for misconceptions or misunderstandings that can be addressed in the Debrief. Guide students in a conversation to debrief the Problem Set and process the lesson.

You may choose to use any combination of the questions below to lead the discussion.

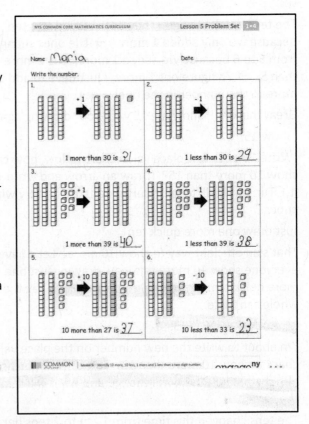

- Look at Problem 11. What is 10 less than 26? Which digit changed when you went from 26 to 16?
- Look at Problem 12. What is 1 less than 26? Which digit changed when you went from 26 to 25?

Lesson 5:   Identify 10 more, 10 less, 1 more, and 1 less than a two-digit number.
Date: 9/20/13

4.A.

- Look at Problem 9. In what ways did the pictures change from the starting number to the end number? Explain why this is so. Which digit changed? What happened to the digits when you went from 29 to 30? Why is this so? Is this similar to and different from our other problems?

- What does the word *digit* mean?

- Look at your solution to Problem 14. What changed in the number? Even though we added 1 more in Problem 9 and made 1 less in Problem 14, why did the numbers in both the tens and the ones change?

- What new math drawing did we use to work more efficiently? (**Quick ten** drawings.)

- How did the Application Problem connect to today's lesson?

Exit Ticket (3 minutes)

After the Student Debrief, instruct students to complete the Exit Ticket. A review of their work will help you assess the students' understanding of the concepts that were presented in the lesson today and plan more effectively for future lessons. You may read the questions aloud to the students.

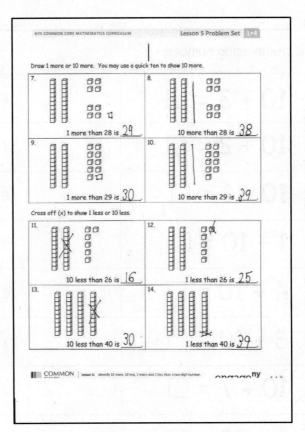

COMMON CORE

Lesson 5:   Identify 10 more, 10 less, 1 more, and 1 less than a two-digit number.
Date: 9/20/13

4.A.50

A

Number correct: _____

Name _____   Date _____

*Write the missing number.

1	10 + 3 = ☐	16	10 + ☐ = 11
2	10 + 2 = ☐	17	10 + ☐ = 12
3	10 + 1 = ☐	18	5 + ☐ = 15
4	1 + 10 = ☐	19	4 + ☐ = 14
5	4 + 10 = ☐	20	☐ + 10 = 17
6	6 + 10 = ☐	21	17 - ☐ = 7
7	10 + 7 = ☐	22	16 - ☐ = 6
8	8 + 10 = ☐	23	18 - ☐ = 8
9	12 - 10 = ☐	24	☐ - 10 = 8
10	11 - 10 = ☐	25	☐ - 10 = 9
11	10 - 10 = ☐	26	1 + 1 + 10 = ☐
12	13 - 10 = ☐	27	2 + 2 + 10 = ☐
13	14 - 10 = ☐	28	2 + 3 + 10 = ☐
14	15 - 10 = ☐	29	4 + ☐ + 3 = 17
15	18 - 10 = ☐	30	☐ + 5 + 10 = 18

B

Number correct:

Name _____   Date _____

*Write the missing number.

1	10 + 1 = ☐	16	10 + ☐ = 10
2	10 + 2 = ☐	17	10 + ☐ = 11
3	10 + 3 = ☐	18	2 + ☐ = 12
4	4 + 10 = ☐	19	3 + ☐ = 13
5	5 + 10 = ☐	20	☐ + 10 = 13
6	6 + 10 = ☐	21	13 - ☐ = 3
7	10 + 8 = ☐	22	14 - ☐ = 4
8	8 + 10 = ☐	23	16 - ☐ = 6
9	10 - 10 = ☐	24	☐ - 10 = 6
10	11 - 10 = ☐	25	☐ - 10 = 8
11	12 - 10 = ☐	26	2 + 1 + 10 = ☐
12	13 - 10 = ☐	27	3 + 2 + 10 = ☐
13	15 - 10 = ☐	28	2 + 3 + 10 = ☐
14	17 - 10 = ☐	29	4 + ☐ + 4 = 18
15	19 - 10 = ☐	30	☐ + 6 + 10 = 19

Lesson 5:   Identify 10 more, 10 less, 1 more, and 1 less than a two-digit number.
Date: 9/20/13

Name _____   Date _____

Write the number.

1. 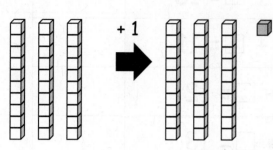 1 more than 30 is _____.	2. 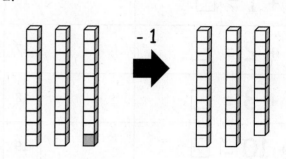 1 less than 30 is _____.
3. 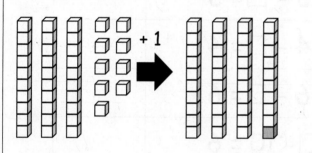 1 more than 39 is _____.	4. 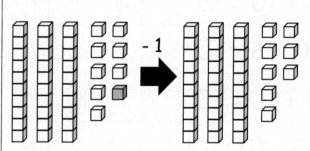 1 less than 39 is _____.
5. 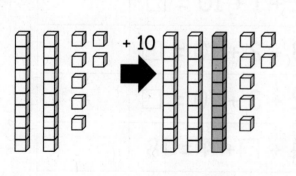 10 more than 27 is _____.	6. 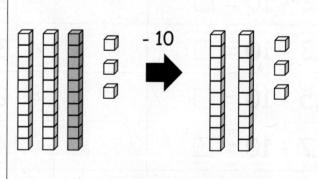 10 less than 33 is _____.

COMMON CORE™   Lesson 5:   Identify 10 more, 10 less, 1 more, and 1 less than a two-digit number.
Date: 9/20/13

4.A.

Draw 1 more or 10 more. You may use a quick ten to show 10 more.

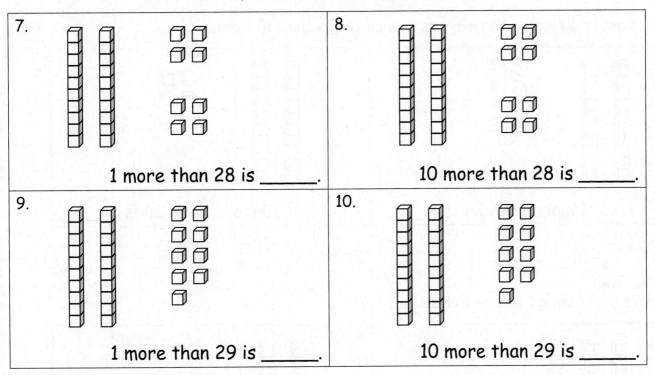

7.

1 more than 28 is _____.

8.

10 more than 28 is _____.

9.

1 more than 29 is _____.

10.

10 more than 29 is _____.

Cross off (x) to show 1 less or 10 less.

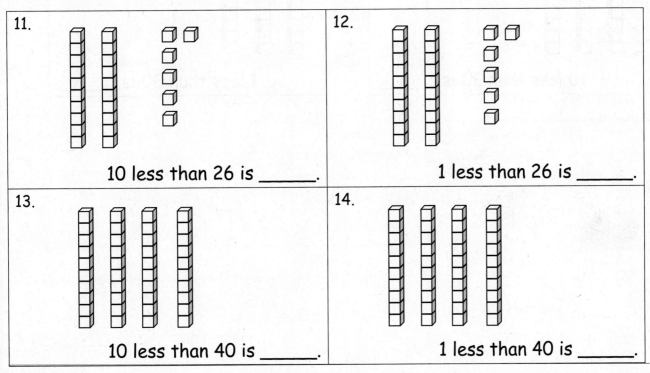

11.

10 less than 26 is _____.

12.

1 less than 26 is _____.

13.

10 less than 40 is _____.

14.

1 less than 40 is _____.

COMMON CORE   Lesson 5:   Identify 10 more, 10 less, 1 more, and 1 less than a two-digit number.
Date: 9/20/13

4.A.54

Name _____   Date _____

Draw 1 more or 10 more. You may use a quick ten to show 10 more.

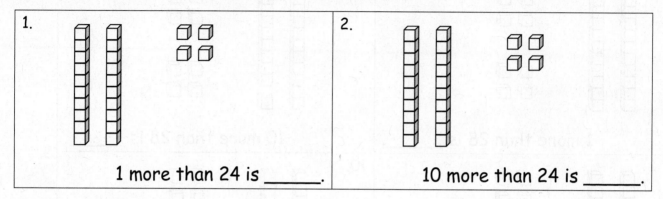

1 more than 24 is _____.

10 more than 24 is _____.

Cross off (x) to show 1 less or 10 less.

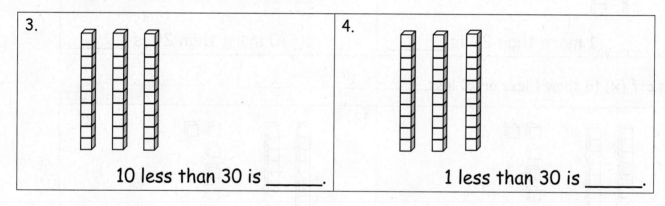

10 less than 30 is _____.

1 less than 30 is _____.

COMMON CORE™   Lesson 5:   Identify 10 more, 10 less, 1 more, and 1 less than a two-digit number.
Date: 9/20/13

4.A.

Name _____ Date _____

Draw quick tens and ones to show the number. Then draw 1 more or 10 more.

1. 1 more than 38 is _____.	2. 10 more than 38 is _____.
3. 1 more than 35 is _____.	4. 10 more than 35 is _____.

Draw quick tens and ones to show the number. Cross off (x) to show 1 less or 10 less.

5. 10 less than 23 is _____.	6. 1 less than 23 is _____.
7. 10 less than 31 is _____.	8. 1 less than 31 is _____.

Lesson 5:   Identify 10 more, 10 less, 1 more, and 1 less than a two-digit number.
Date: 9/20/13

4.A.56

Match the words to the picture that shows the right amount.

9.

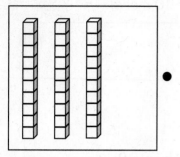

•   • 1 less than 30.

10.

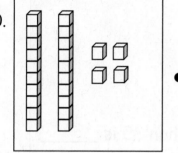

•   • 1 more than 23 is 24.

11.

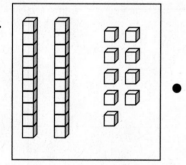

•   • 10 less than 36.

12.

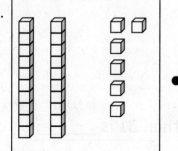

•   • 10 more than 20.

COMMON CORE™

Lesson 5:   Identify 10 more, 10 less, 1 more, and 1 less than a two-digit number.
Date: 9/20/13

4.A.1

tens	ones

tens	ones

   Lesson 5:   Identify 10 more, 10 less, 1 more, and 1 less than a two-digit number.   4.A.58

    Date: 9/20/13

Lesson 6

Objective: Use dimes and pennies as representations of tens and ones.

Suggested Lesson Structure

■ Fluency Practice   (5 minutes)
■ Application Problem   (5 minutes)
■ Concept Development (40 minutes)
■ Student Debrief   (10 minutes)
  Total Time   **(60 minutes)**

Fluency Practice (5 minutes)

- Quick Tens **1.NBT.2**   (3 minutes)
- Count Coins **1.NBT.2**   (2 minutes)

Quick Tens (3 minutes)

Materials: (T) Variety of materials to show tens and ones (e.g., 100-bead Rekenrek, linking cubes with ten-sticks and extra cubes, place value chart

Note: This fluency activity reinforces place value, as quick tens are an abstract representation of the unit ten.

Show and say numbers from 11 to 40 in varied ways for two minutes. Students draw the number with quick tens and circles (in 5-group columns). Use the materials listed above to show numbers. Choose different ways to say the numbers:

- The Say Ten way
- As an addition expression
- As a *more than* statement
- As a number bond with two parts filled in

For the next minute, represent numbers using quick tens and ones. Students say the numbers aloud.

Count Coins (2 minutes)

Materials: (T) 10 pennies and 4 dimes

Note: This fluency activity provides practice with recognizing pennies and dimes and counting with abstract representations of tens and ones, which will prepare them for today's lesson.

Lay out 2 dimes. Students count up from 20 by ones as you lay out 10 pennies into 5-groups. Repeat, this

COMMON CORE   Lesson 6:   Use dimes and pennies as abstract representations of tens and ones.
                  Date: 9/20/13

4.A.5

time changing the 10 pennies for another dime when you get to 40.

Application Problem (5 minutes)

Sheila has 3 bags of 10 pretzels and 9 extra pretzels. She gives 1 bag to a friend. How many pretzels does she have now?

Extension: John has 19 pretzels. How many more pretzels does he need to have as many as Sheila does now?

Note: Depending on students' strategies for solving, students may subtract in quantities larger than the grade level standard of within 20. Some students may subtract 1 bag from 3 bags as their method for solving, while others may recognize that sharing 1 bag of 10 pretzels means that they have to find what number is 10 less than 39. In the Debrief, students will model the quantity and use place value charts to demonstrate their method for solving.

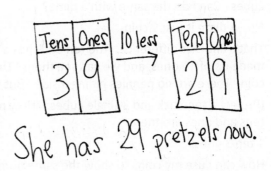

Concept Development (40 minutes)

Materials: (T) Personal math toolkit with 4 ten-sticks of linking cubes, 4 dimes and 10 pennies, projector
(S) 4 dimes and 10 pennies, personal white board with coin charts and place value charts template

Students gather in the meeting area with their personal math toolkits in a semi-circle formation.

- T: (Lay down a ten-stick on the floor.) How many ones, or individual cubes, are in a ten-stick?
- S: 10 ones.
- T: (Lay down 10 individual cubes into 5-groups next to the ten-stick.) What is the same or different about these two groups of cubes?
- S: They are different because one of them is a ten and the other is 10 ones. → They are the same amount. The ten-stick is made up of 10 cubes. The 10 ones are also made of 10 cubes. → If you put 10 ones together, they'll become a ten-stick.
- T: You are right! They are worth the same amount; they have the same **value**. Also, they are both *made* of *10* cubes. (Lay down a dime, underneath the ten-stick.) How many pennies have the same value as one dime?
- S: 10 pennies.
- T: (Lay down 10 pennies into 5-groups next to the dime, directly below the 10 individual cubes.) What is the same or different about these two groups of coins?
- S: A dime is 10 cents. 10 pennies are worth 10 cents. → The dime is

only made of 1 coin. The pennies group is made up of 10 coins. → The coins are different.

T: Great observations! So 1 ten-stick has the same value as 10 individual cubes. And 1 dime has the same value as?

S: 10 pennies!

T: I can take a ten-stick and break it apart into 10 individual cubes. Can I do the same with a dime?

S: No. A dime is just 1 coin.

T: That's another difference. The ten-stick has a value of 10 ones and we can see why. It's actually made up of 10 ones, and we can see them. The dime has the same value as 10 pennies but it's just 1 coin. There are no pennies hiding inside. But it still has the same value as 10 pennies.

T: (Project a ten-stick and 3 single cubes.) How many tens and ones are there?

S: 1 ten 3 ones.

T: How can I use my coins to show the same number as the cubes? Show 1 ten 3 ones with your coins, then share with your partner.

Students discuss as the teacher circulates. Be sure to address any misconceptions while you circulate. Some students may want to put down 13 pennies but won't be able to since each student is only given 10 pennies.

NOTES ON MULTIPLE MEANS OF ENGAGEMENT:

Remember to adjust lesson structure to suit specific learning needs. Some of your students may have more success working with a partner since this lesson calls for a great deal of counting and manipulation of materials.

MP.7

T: I noticed that some students wanted to lay down 13 pennies but found that they didn't have enough. What can we do to help?

S: Use 1 dime for 1 ten, then use 3 pennies for 3 ones.

T: Great idea! It's just like using the ten-stick to represent 1 ten. (Choose a student volunteer to show 1 dime and 3 pennies, directly below the linking cubes.)

Repeat the process using the suggested sequence: 15, 18, 28, 38, 31, 13, 40, and 39.

T: (Show 39 cents with 3 dimes and 9 pennies.)

T: How many dimes?

S: 3 dimes.

T: (Fill in the dimes and pennies place value chart.) How many pennies?

S: 9 pennies.

T: (Fill in the dimes and pennies place value chart.) How many tens?

S: 3 tens.

T: (Fill in the tens and ones place value chart.) How many

NOTES ON MULTIPLE MEANS OF REPRESENTATION:

Dimes are an abstract representation of tens, particularly because they are smaller than pennies, rather than ten times the size of a penny. For students who are struggling with grasping quantities of tens and ones, continue to use linking cubes or bundled straws, which can more visually present the comparative quantities.

Lesson 6: Use dimes and pennies as abstract representations of tens and ones.
Date: 9/20/13

4.A.6

ones?

S: 9 ones.

T: (Fill in the tens and ones place value chart.) What is the value of 3 dimes and 9 pennies?

S: 39 cents.

T: Give a number sentence to show the total of 39 cents by adding your dimes and pennies.

S: 30 cents + 9 cents = 39 cents.

Repeat the process using the following sequence: 1 dime and 4 pennies, 1 dime and 5 pennies, 2 dimes and 5 pennies, 3 dimes, 6 pennies and 3 dimes, and 2 dimes and 8 pennies. In addition, have students use the place value chart on their personal white boards to write down the value of these coins. Be sure to flip the coins in order for the students to become familiar with both heads and tails.

Give students 1 minute to study their 4 dimes and 10 pennies, noticing similarities and differences of these coins.

T: Show 15 cents.

S: (Show 1 dime 5 pennies.)

T: Now, show me 1 more penny and write how much you have in place value chart.

S: (Add a penny and write 16.)

T: So, what is 1 more than 15? Say in a whole sentence.

S: 1 more than 15 is 16.

Repeat the process using the same number for 10 more, 1 less, and 10 less. For further practice, you may use the following suggested sequence: 3 tens 5 ones, 27, 1 ten 9 ones, 31, and 1 ten 3 ones. When appropriate, have students move on to drawing instead of using the coins as shown.

Note: As students are sharing their work with coins remind them to use the unit, cents. Have students add their dimes and pennies to their personal math toolkit.

Problem Set (10 minutes)

Students should do their personal best to complete the Problem Set within the allotted 10 minutes. For some classes, it may be appropriate to modify the assignment by specifying which problems they work on first.

Student Debrief (10 minutes)

Lesson Objective: Use dimes and pennies as abstract representations of tens and ones.

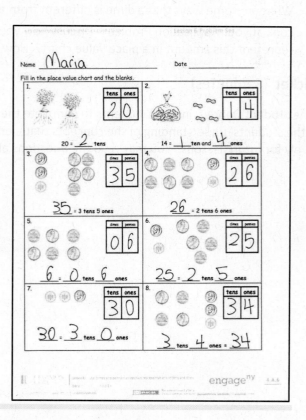

Lesson 6:   Use dimes and pennies as abstract representations of tens and ones.
Date: 9/20/13

4.A.62

The Student Debrief is intended to invite reflection and active processing of the total lesson experience.

Invite students to review their solutions for the Problem Set. They should check work by comparing answers with a partner before going over answers as a class. Look for misconceptions or misunderstandings that can be addressed in the Debrief. Guide students in a conversation to debrief the Problem Set and process the lesson.

You may choose to use any combination of the questions below to lead the discussion.

- Look at Problem 2. If you were to show that amount with dimes and pennies, how many of each coin would you use?

- Look at Problems 3 and 6. How is Problem 6 different from Problem 3? What is different about the amount shown in the pictures?

- Look at Problems 13 and 14. What did you cross off in 13? What did you cross off in 14? Why did you cross off a different coin in each problem?

- How are the tools that represent 1 ten different from one another? (Project the ten-stick and the dime.)

- What are some ways that a dime is different from a penny?

- Look at your Application Problem. Discuss how you solved it with a partner. How could you represent this amount in a place value chart? How is this problem connected to today's lesson?

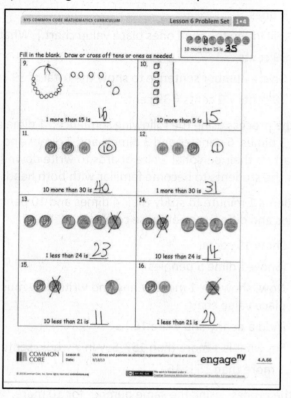

Exit Ticket (3 minutes)

After the Student Debrief, instruct students to complete the Exit Ticket. A review of their work will help you assess the students' understanding of the concepts that were presented in the lesson today and plan more effectively for future lessons. You may read the questions aloud to the students.

COMMON CORE

Lesson 6:   Use dimes and pennies as abstract representations of tens and ones.
Date: 9/20/13

4.A.

Name _____ Date _____

Fill in the place value chart and the blanks.

1.

tens	ones

20 = _____ tens

2.

tens	ones

14 = _____ ten and _____ones

3.

dimes	pennies

_____ = 3 tens 5 ones

4.

dimes	pennies

_____ = 2 tens 6 ones

5.

dimes	pennies

_____ = _____ tens _____ ones

6.

dimes	pennies

_____ = _____ tens _____ ones

7.

tens	ones

_____ = _____ tens _____ ones

8.

tens	ones

_____ tens _____ ones = _____

10 more than 25 is __35__

Fill in the blank. Draw or cross off tens or ones as needed.

9. 1 more than 15 is _____.	**10.** 10 more than 5 is _____.
11. 10 more than 30 is _____.	**12.** 1 more than 30 is _____.
13. 1 less than 24 is _____.	**14.** 10 less than 24 is _____.
15. 10 less than 21 is _____.	**16.** 1 less than 21 is _____.

 Lesson 6: Use dimes and pennies as abstract representations of tens and ones.
Date: 9/20/13

4.A.

Name _____   Date _____

Fill in the blank. Draw or cross off tens or ones as needed.

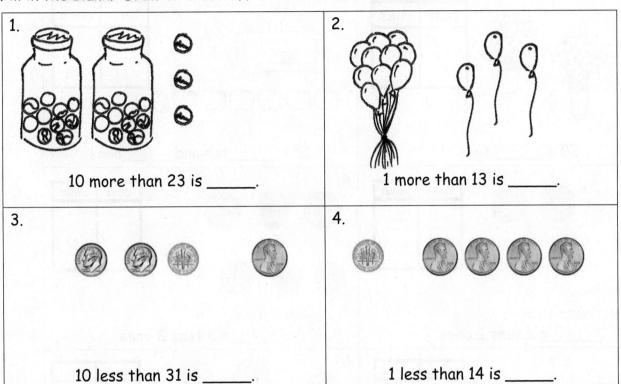

1.

10 more than 23 is _____.

2.

1 more than 13 is _____.

3.

10 less than 31 is _____.

4.

1 less than 14 is _____.

Name _____ Date _____

Fill in the place value chart and the blanks.

1.		2.	

1.

tens	ones

30 = _____ tens

2.

tens	ones

17 = _____ ten and _____ ones

3.

dimes	pennies

_____ = 2 tens 2 ones

4.

dimes	pennies

_____ = 3 tens 3 ones

5.

dimes	pennies

_____ = _____ tens _____ ones

6.

dimes	pennies

_____ = _____ tens _____ ones

7.

tens	ones

_____ = _____ tens _____ ones

8.

tens	ones

_____ tens _____ ones = _____

COMMON CORE

Lesson 6: Use dimes and pennies as abstract representations of tens and ones.
Date: 9/20/13

4.A.

10 more than 25 is **35**

Fill in the blank. Draw or cross off tens or ones as needed.

9.

1 more than 12 is _____.

10.

10 more than 3 is _____.

11.

10 more than 22 is _____.

12.

1 more than 22 is _____.

13.

1 less than 39 is _____.

14.

10 less than 39 is _____.

15.

10 less than 33 is _____.

16.

1 less than 33 is _____.

Lesson 6:   Use dimes and pennies as abstract representations of tens and ones.
Date: 9/20/13

4.A.68

dimes	pennies

tens	ones

COMMON CORE | Lesson 6: | Use dimes and pennies as abstract representations of tens and ones.
Date: | 9/20/13

4.A

Topic B

Comparison of Pairs of Two-Digit Numbers

1.NBT.3, 1.NBT.1, 1.NBT.2

Focus Standard:	1.NBT.3	Compare two two-digit numbers based on meaning of the tens and ones digits, recording the results of comparisons with the symbols >, =, and <.
Instructional Days:	4	
Coherence -Links from:	G1–M2	Introduction to Place Value Through Addition and Subtraction Within 20
-Links to:	G2–M3	Place Value, Counting, and Comparison of Numbers to 1,000

Topic B begins with Lesson 7, where students identify the greater or lesser of two given numbers. They first work with concrete materials whereby they build each quantity (**1.NBT.2**) and find the greater or the lesser number through direct comparison. They progress to the more abstract comparison of numerals using their understanding of place value to identify the greater or lesser value. Students begin with comparing numbers such as 39 and 12, where the number of both units in the greater number is more than in the smaller number. They then compare numbers such as 18 and 40, where they must realize the place of the 4 explains the greater value of 40. 4 tens is greater than 8 ones.

In Lesson 8, students continue to practice comparing, with the added layer of saying the comparison sentence from left to right. First, they order a group of numerals, so that they are reading the set from least to greatest and then greatest to least, always reading from left to right. Then, as students compare two quantities or numerals, they place an *L* below the lesser quantity and a *G* below the greater quantity. When they read, they simply say the first numeral, the comparison word under the numeral, and then the second numeral. This prepares students for using the symbols in later lessons.

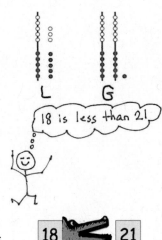

The topic closes with Lessons 9 and 10, where students use the comparison symbols >, =, and < to compare pairs of two-digit numbers (**1.NBT.3**). In Lesson 9, students focus on the quantity that is greater, as they use the alligator analogy to "eat" and identify the amount that's greater. Within this same lesson, students use the alligator analogy to then identify the amount that is less. Lastly, in Lesson 10, students write the appropriate mathematical symbol to compare two numerals and then apply their knowledge of reading from left to right. For example, 18 < 40 is read as "18 is less than 40."

A Teaching Sequence Towards Mastery of Comparison of Pairs of Two-Digit Numbers

Objective 1: Compare two quantities, and identify the greater or lesser of the two given numerals.
(Lesson 7)

Objective 2: Compare quantities and numerals from left to right.
(Lesson 8)

Objective 3: Use the symbols >, =, and < to compare quantities and numerals.
(Lessons 9–10)

Lesson 7

Objective: Compare two quantities, and identify the greater or lesser of the two given numerals.

Suggested Lesson Structure

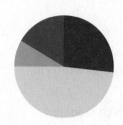

■ Fluency Practice	(16 minutes)
■ Application Problem	(5 minutes)
■ Concept Development	(29 minutes)
■ Student Debrief	(10 minutes)
Total Time	**(60 minutes)**

Fluency Practice (16 minutes)

- 1 More/Less, 10 More/Less **1.NBT.5**   (6 minutes)
- Sprint: +1, −1, +10, −10 **1.NBT.5**   (10 minutes)

1 More/Less, 10 More/Less (6 minutes)

Materials: (S) Kit with 40 linking cubes, 4 dimes, 10 pennies, personal white board with large place value chart insert

Note: This activity provides practice with both proportional (linking cubes) and non-proportional (coins) representations of tens and ones. Students review the connection between place value and adding or subtracting ten or one.

    T: Show 20 cubes. Add 1. Say the addition sentence, starting with 20.
    S: 20 + 1 = 21.
    T: Add 10. Say the addition sentence, starting with 21.
    S: 21 + 10 = 31.
    T: Subtract 1. Say the subtraction sentence, starting with 31.
    S: 31 − 1 = 30.
    T: Show 39. Add 1. Say the addition sentence, starting with 39.
    S: 39 + 1 = 40.

Continue adding or subtracting 10 or 1, choosing different start numbers within 40 as appropriate. After three minutes, use coins instead of linking cubes. When using coins, be careful not to ask students to subtract 1 from a multiple of 10, as students have not yet learned to subtract by decomposing a dime into 10 pennies.

Lesson 7:	Compare two quantities, and identify the greater or lesser of the two given numerals.
Date:	9/20/13

4.B.3

Sprint: +1, −1, +10, −10 (10 minutes)

Materials: (S) +1, −1, +10, −10 Sprint

Note: This Sprint reviews the concepts taught in G1–M1–Lesson 5 and supports students' understanding of place value.

Application Problem (5 minutes)

Benny has 4 dimes. Marcus has 4 pennies. Benny said, "We have the same amount of money!" Is he correct? Use drawings or words to explain your thinking.

Note: This problem enables a teacher to identify which students understand, or are beginning to understand, the importance of the value of a unit. The most essential understanding for this problem is for students to differentiate between the two types of coins and their values.

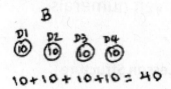

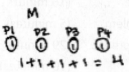

Concept Development (29 minutes)

Materials: (T) Enlarged dimes and pennies for display, place value chart (S) 5-group cards, dimes and pennies from personal math toolkit

Students gather in the meeting area with their materials.

- T: Look at the Application Problem. Whose coins have a **greater** total value?
- S: Benny's do! → 40 cents is more than 4 cents. (Teacher writes *greater* under the 4 dimes and circles this side of the work.)
- T: Correct. The word greater means more. 40 is more than 4. 40 is greater than 4.
- T: How could you describe 4 (circle Marcus' pennies with your finger) compared to 40? 4 is...?
- S: Smaller than 40. → Less than 40. → Fewer than 40.
- T: Yes, we would say 4 is *less* than 40. Let's compare some more numbers. Let's find the greater number in each pair of numbers.

NOTES ON MULITPLE MEANS OF ENGAGEMENT:

Challenge advanced students with more questions about the 4 pennies and 4 dimes such as:

- How much money do the boys have together?
- How many more cents does Benny have than Marcus?
- Do you know of any other combinations of coins that could make 40 cents?

Lesson 7: Compare two quantities, and identify the greater or lesser of the two given numerals.

Date: 9/20/13

4.B

Display the following suggested sequence of number pairs one at a time:

- 5 and 12
- 39 and 21
- 23 and 32
- 17 and 15
- 14 and 40
- 30 and 13
- 1 ten 9 ones and 2 tens 1 one
- 3 tens 1 one and 1 ten 3 ones

Note: 17 and 15 above is first example in which the ones place must be considered to compare the numbers; it will be discussed in the Debrief.

Use ten-sticks or quick ten drawings. Each time, ask students to explain how they know which number is greater. Encourage students to use the language of tens and ones as they compare the tens and the ones in each number.

Repeat the process, next finding the number that is less in each pair.

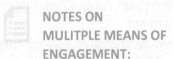

NOTES ON MULITPLE MEANS OF ENGAGEMENT:

Some students may have difficulty comparing numbers that have similar digits such as 12 and 21, or numbers that sound similar, such as 14 and 40 or 13 and 30. Use linking cubes along with the place value chart so students can see the comparison with manipulatives.

T: (Display 28 and 38 in place value charts.) Which number is greater?

S: 38!

T: Look at the place value charts. Do you look at the tens place or the ones place to help you find the greater number? Turn and talk with a partner.

S: There is an 8 in the ones place for both numbers. → You look at the tens place first though.

T: (Point to each digit while explaining.) Yes, 3 tens is greater than 2 tens. 38 is greater than 28.

T: (Display 29 and 32 in place value charts.) Which number is greater?

S: 32!

T: Look at the place value charts. 9 is a lot bigger than either of the digits in 32. Does that mean 29 is greater than 32? Turn and talk to your partner.

S: We still have to look at the tens place first. Tens are bigger than ones. → There are only 2 tens in 29 and there are 3 tens in 32. The tens place is where you have to look.

T: (Point to each digit while explaining.) Yes, 3 tens is greater than 2 tens. Let's remember the *value* of the digits when comparing!

Comparison with Cards Game

Partner A and Partner B

1. Each partner turns over two cards.
2. Add the two numbers together and find the total.
3. Partner A says a sentence to compare the totals using the words *greater than* or *equal to*.

Lesson 7: Compare two quantities, and identify the greater or lesser of the two given numerals.

Date: 9/20/13

4.B.5

4. The partner with the greater total wins the cards. (If the totals are equal, leave the cards until the next round when one student does have a greater total.)

5. Repeat with Partner B making the comparison statement.

After the first minute of play, change the rules so that the person with the total that is *less* wins the cards. Partners should use the words *less than* when comparing the cards during this round. Alternate between the two rules for four minutes. At the five-minute mark, change the rules so that if the totals are *equal*, the game is over. Have students save one pair of cards to compare with a partner during the debrief using a place value chart.

Problem Set (10 minutes)

Students should do their personal best to complete the Problem Set within the allotted 10 minutes. For some classes, it may be appropriate to modify the assignment by specifying which problems they work on first.

Student Debrief (10 minutes)

Lesson Objective: Compare two quantities, and identify the greater or lesser of the two given numerals.

The Student Debrief is intended to invite reflection and active processing of the total lesson experience.

Invite students to review their solutions for the Problem Set. They should check work by comparing answers with a partner before going over answers as a class. Look for misconceptions or misunderstandings that can be addressed in the Debrief. Guide students in a conversation to debrief the Problem Set and process the lesson.

You may choose to use any combination of the questions below to lead the discussion.

▪ In Problem 3 did you look at the tens or the ones to compare? Why?

▪ Look at your Problem Set with a partner and find an example where you needed to look at the ones place to compare.

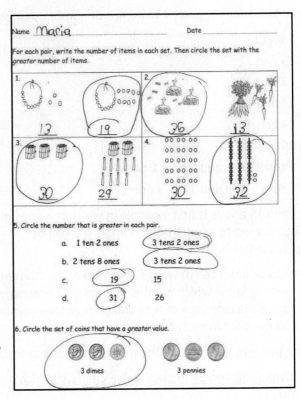

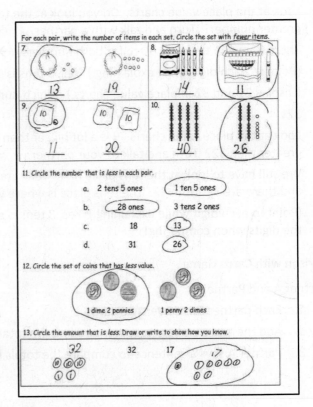

COMMON CORE

Lesson 7:   Compare two quantities, and identify the greater or lesser of the two given numerals.

Date: 9/20/13

4.B

- How are dimes and pennies similar to tens and ones?

- Look at Problem 4. Was this pair more difficult for you to compare? Why?

- The numeral in the tens place we can call a digit. The numeral in the ones place can also be called a digit. Look at the pair of numbers in Problem 5(d) and identify the digit in the tens place and the digit in the ones place for both numbers.

- Take out the cards you kept from today's Comparison with Cards Game. What is the total of each pair of cards? Write your total in a place value chart on your personal white board and compare with your partner.

- Share your answer to today's Application Problem with a partner. Restate your answer using the words **greater** or *less*.

Exit Ticket (3 minutes)

After the Student Debrief, instruct students to complete the Exit Ticket. A review of their work will help you assess the students' understanding of the concepts that were presented in the lesson today and plan more effectively for future lessons. You may read the questions aloud to the students.

Lesson 7:   Compare two quantities, and identify the greater or lesser of the two
given numerals.

Date: 9/20/13

4.B.7

A

Name _____   Date _____

*Write the missing number. Pay attention to the addition or subtraction sign.

1	$5 + 1 = \square$	16	$29 + 10 = \square$
2	$15 + 1 = \square$	17	$9 + 1 = \square$
3	$25 + 1 = \square$	18	$19 + 1 = \square$
4	$5 + 10 = \square$	19	$29 + 1 = \square$
5	$15 + 10 = \square$	20	$39 + 1 = \square$
6	$25 + 10 = \square$	21	$40 - 1 = \square$
7	$8 - 1 = \square$	22	$30 - 1 = \square$
8	$18 - 1 = \square$	23	$20 - 1 = \square$
9	$28 - 1 = \square$	24	$20 + \square = 21$
10	$38 - 1 = \square$	25	$20 + \square = 30$
11	$38 - 10 = \square$	26	$27 + \square = 37$
12	$28 - 10 = \square$	27	$27 + \square = 28$
13	$18 - 10 = \square$	28	$\square + 10 = 34$
14	$9 + 10 = \square$	29	$\square - 10 = 14$
15	$19 + 10 = \square$	30	$\square - 10 = 24$

COMMON CORE™

Lesson 7:   Compare two quantities, and identify the greater or lesser of the two
              given numerals.
Date: 9/20/13

4.

B

Number correct: _____

Name _____   Date _____

*Write the missing number. Pay attention to the addition or subtraction sign.

1	4 + 1 = ☐		16	28 + 10 = ☐	
2	14 + 1 = ☐		17	9 + 1 = ☐	
3	24 + 1 = ☐		18	19 + 1 = ☐	
4	6 + 10 = ☐		19	29 + 1 = ☐	
5	16 + 10 = ☐		20	39 + 1 = ☐	
6	26 + 10 = ☐		21	40 - 1 = ☐	
7	7 - 1 = ☐		22	30 - 1 = ☐	
8	17 - 1 = ☐		23	20 - 1 = ☐	
9	27 - 1 = ☐		24	10 + ☐ = 11	
10	37 - 1 = ☐		25	10 + ☐ = 20	
11	37 - 10 = ☐		26	22 + ☐ = 32	
12	27 - 10 = ☐		27	22 + ☐ = 23	
13	17 - 10 = ☐		28	☐ + 10 = 39	
14	8 + 10 = ☐		29	☐ - 10 = 19	
15	18 + 10 = ☐		30	☐ - 10 = 29	

Name _____   Date _____

For each pair, write the number of items in each set. Then circle the set with the *greater* number of items.

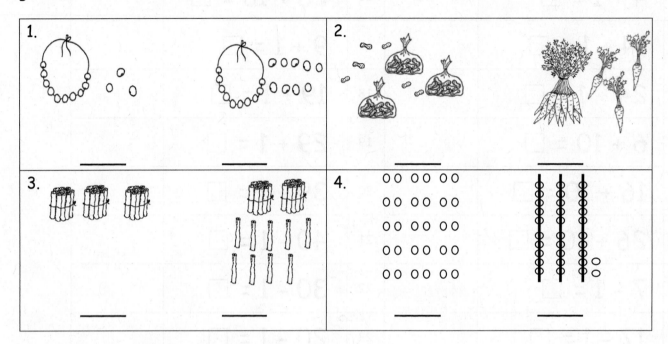

5. Circle the number that is *greater* in each pair.

    a.   1 ten 2 ones   3 tens 2 ones

    b.   2 tens 8 ones   3 tens 2 ones

    c.   19   15

    d.   31   26

6. Circle the set of coins that have a *greater* value.

        3 dimes   3 pennies

 COMMON CORE™   Lesson 7:   Compare two quantities, and identify the greater or lesser of the two
                                       given numerals.
                     Date: 9/20/13

4.B

For each pair, write the number of items in each set. Circle the set with *fewer* items.

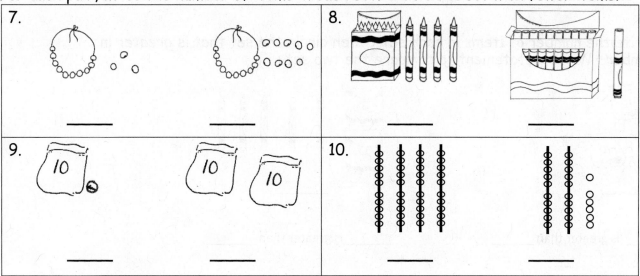

7. _____   _____

8. _____   _____

9. _____   _____

10. _____   _____

11. Circle the number that is *less* in each pair.

   a.   2 tens 5 ones   1 ten 5 ones

   b.   28 ones   3 tens 2 ones

   c.   18   13

   d.   31   26

12. Circle the set of coins that has *less* value.

   1 dime 2 pennies   1 penny 2 dimes

13. Circle the amount that is *less*. Draw or write to show how you know.

   32   17

Name _____   Date _____

1. Write the number of items in each set. Then circle the set that is *greater* in number. Write a statement to compare the two sets.

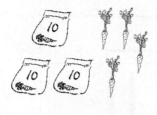   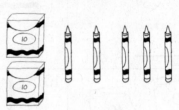

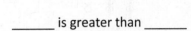

_____   _____

_____ is greater than _____   _____ is greater than _____

2. Write the number of items in each set. Then circle the set that is *less* in number. Say a statement to compare the two sets.

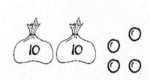   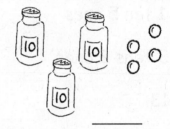

_____   _____

_____ is less than _____   _____ is less than _____

3. Circle the set of coins that has a greater value.

4. Circle the set of coins that has less value.

	Lesson 7:	Compare two quantities, and identify the greater or lesser of the two given numerals.	
	Date:	9/20/13	

4.E

Name _____   Date _____

Write the number and circle the set that is *greater* in each pair. Say a statement to compare the two sets.

1.

2.

Circle the number that is *greater* for each pair.

3.
3 tens 8 ones	3 tens 9 ones

4.
25	35

Write the number and circle the set that is *less* in each pair. Say a statement to compare the two sets.

5.

6.

Circle the number that is *less* for each pair.

7.
2 tens 7 ones	3 tens 7 ones

8.
22	29

9. Circle the set of coins that has *less* value.

10. Circle the set of coins that has *greater* value.

4.B.13

Katelyn and Johnny are playing comparison with cards. They have recorded the totals for each round. For each round, circle the total that won the cards and write the statement. The first one is done for you.

ROUND 1 - The total that is the **greater** wins.

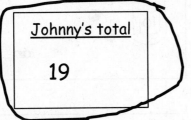

Katelyn's total	Johnny's total
16	19

19 is greater than 16.

ROUND 2 - The total that is **less** wins.

Katelyn's total	Johnny's total
27	24

_____

ROUND 3- the total that is **greater** wins.

Katelyn's total	Johnny's total
32	22

_____

ROUND 4- the total that is **less** wins.

Katelyn's total	Johnny's total
29	26

_____

If Katelyn's total is 39 and Johnny's total has 3 tens 9 ones, who would win the game? Draw a math drawing to explain how you know.

tens	ones

Lesson 7: Compare two quantities, and identify the greater or lesser of the two given numerals.

Date: 9/20/13

4.B.15

Lesson 8

Objective: Compare quantities and numerals from left to right.

Suggested Lesson Structure

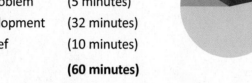

- ■ Fluency Practice   (13 minutes)
- ■ Application Problem   (5 minutes)
- ■ Concept Development   (32 minutes)
- ■ Student Debrief   (10 minutes)
- **Total Time**   **(60 minutes)**

Fluency Practice (13 minutes)

- Subtraction with Cards **1.OA.6**   (5 minutes)
- Core Subtraction Fluency Review **1.OA.6**   (5 minutes)
- Beep Counting by Ones and Tens **1.OA.5, 1.NBT.3**   (3 minutes)

Subtraction with Cards (5 minutes)

Materials: (S) 1 pack of numeral cards 0–10 per set of partners (from G1–M1–Lesson 36)

Note: This activity reviews yesterday's lesson and provides practice with subtraction within 10. Students' fluency with these facts will be assessed after this game.

Students combine their numeral cards and place them face down between them. Each partner flips over two cards and subtracts the smaller number from the larger one. The partner with the smallest difference says a *less than* sentence and keeps the cards played by both players. If both players have the same difference, each partner flips two more cards and the player with the smaller difference says a *less than* sentence and keeps all the cards. The player with the most cards at the end of the game wins.

Core Subtraction Fluency Review (5 minutes)

Materials: (S) Core Subtraction Fluency Review

Note: This subtraction review sheet contains the majority of subtraction facts within 10 (excluding some –0 and –1 facts), which are part of the required core fluency for Grade 1. Consider using this sheet to monitor progress towards mastery.

Students complete as many problems as they can in three minutes. Choose a counting sequence for early finishers to practice on the backs of their papers. When time runs out, read the answers aloud so students can correct their work. Encourage students to remember how many they got correct today so they can try to improve their scores on future Core Subtraction Fluency Reviews.

Beep Counting by Ones and Tens (3 minutes)

Say a series of three numbers but replace one of the numbers with the word *beep* (e.g., 1, 2, 3, beep). When signaled, students say the number that was replaced by the word *beep* in the sequence. Scaffold number sequences, beginning with easy sequences and moving to more complex ones. Choose sequences that count forward and backward by ones and tens within 40.

Suggested sequence type: 10, 11, 12, beep; 20, 21, 22, beep; 20, 19, 18, beep; 30, 29, 28 beep; 0, 10, 20, beep; 1, 11, 21, beep; 40, 30, 20, beep; 39, 29, 19, beep. Continue with similar sequences, changing the sequential placement of the beep.

Application Problem (5 minutes)

Anton picked 25 strawberries. He picked some more strawberries. Then he had 35 strawberries.

a. Use a place value chart to show how many more strawberries Anton picked.

b. Write a statement comparing the two amounts of strawberries using one of these phrases: *greater than, less than,* or *equal to.*

Note: In this *add to with change unknown* problem, students are now asked to use their understanding of place value to identify how many more strawberries Anton picked and to compare the beginning and ending quantities.

Concept Development (32 minutes)

Materials: (T) Comparison cards (S) Comparison cards, personal white boards, ten-sticks and coins from personal math toolkit

Note: For this lesson, use the word side of the comparison cards. The symbol side will be used in future lessons.

Project the following two sequences on the board, both of which were used in today's Beep Counting: 10, 11, 12, 13 and 40, 30, 20, 10

T: You said these numbers during fluency. What is different about them?

S: One set goes up and one set goes down. → One we count up by ones and one set we count down by tens.

T: What do you mean it *goes up*?

NOTES ON
MULTIPLE MEANS OF
REPRESENTATION:

Be sure your English Language Learners understand the word *compare.* Remind students about comparing the length of objects as they learned about in Module 3 and show some concrete examples. Help students make the connection between comparing length and comparing numbers.

COMMON CORE™ Lesson 8: Compare quantities and numerals from left to right.
Date: 9/20/13

4.B.17

S: The numbers get bigger.

T: Let's use our math language to explain that. Who remembers the words we used yesterday when we were comparing two numbers?

S: Greater than. → Less than. → Equal to.

T: Are you saying this number (point to 10) is less than or greater than 11 (point to 11)?

S: Less than.

T: What about the next numbers? 11 is…

S: Less than 12.

T: Let's say the whole sequence and use the comparison words as we compare each number in the set.

S/T: (Continue pointing to each number.) 10 is less than 11. 11 is less than 12. 12 is less than 13.

T: When we compare numbers using words, we read from left to right, just like when we are reading a sentence in a book or when we are reading a number sentence.

T: 40, 30, 20, 10 is in a different order. Turn to your partner and discuss which word we will use when comparing them. Remember we start with 40.

S: (Discuss.) Greater than!

T: Let's read the whole sequence, using greater than to compare the number pairs as we go.

S/T: 40 is greater than 30. 30 is greater than 20. 20 is greater than 10.

T: Today, we are reading left to right when we compare numbers. (Distribute comparison cards to students. Write 13 and 23 on the board.) Partner A (seated on the left), show 13 with your ten-sticks. Partner B, show 23 with your ten-sticks. Find the card with the comparison words that show how your number compares to your partner's number and put it under your ten-sticks.

S: (Partners place cubes and cards.)

T: I see these cards under your numbers. (Write *less than* under 13 and *greater than* under 23.) To read this from left to right, we would say 13 is….?

S: Less than 23!

T: Yes, less than. Let's move the less than card between our numbers. We'll read together. (Move card between 13 and 23.)

S/T: 13 is less than 23.

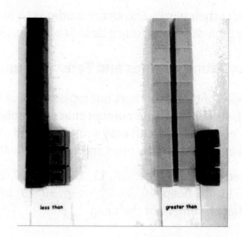

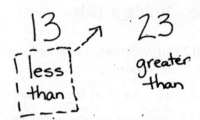

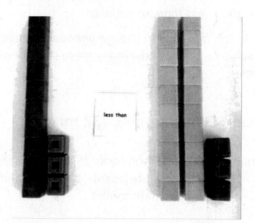

NOTES ON MULTIPLE MEANS OF ACTION AND EXPRESSION:

Some students may still need concrete models after others are ready to move on. When moving to using numbers only, ask the students who need more concrete supports to be the class helper by modeling the numbers with linking cubes.

Repeat the process with the following suggested sequence: 15 and 19, 21 and 19, 3 tens 5 ones and 2 tens 8 ones, 21 and 31, 18 and 9, 38 and 12, and 27 and 19. Move quickly to quick ten drawings or no visual supports as appropriate for the group of students. Grouping students by readiness levels will make this easier.

T: Does anyone else notice something interesting about which card we have been using when we read the comparison from left to right?

S: We always use Partner A's card!

T: Do we even *need* Partner B's card to say our comparison sentence?

S: No!

T: Ok, switch spots so that we can use Partner B's card. (Partners switch spaces so that Partner B is sitting on the left.)

Repeat the process with the following suggested sequence: 14 and 17, 3 tens and 2 tens, 2 tens 9 ones and 3 tens, 24 and 38, and 34 and 28. This time, only Partner B should use the comparison cards, since it has been determined that only the comparison card on the left gets moved into the middle to read the comparison sentence.

T: (Leave 34 and 28 on display.) Which digit in each number did you look at first to compare them?

S: We looked at the digit in the tens place!

T: Why do we look at the tens place first when we compare two numbers? Turn and talk to your partner.

S: The digit 3 in 34 stands for 30. The digit 2 in 24 stands for 20. 30 is greater than 20. Even if there were 9 ones that's still less than a ten.

T: (Write the multiples of 10 from 0 to 40 across the board, with space in between the numbers. Write the following five numbers above the sequence: 29, 38, 7, 14, 24.) If I want to place these numbers into this set of numbers, *in order*, where would they go? Where would I put 29?

S: In front of the 30. It's less than 30. (Write 29 between 20 and 30.)

T: Where would I put 38?

S: Between 30 and 40. It's greater than 30 and less than 40. (Write 38 between 30 and 40. Continue with this process until all the numbers are placed.)

T: (Leave this sequence on the board. Write the numbers 40, 30, 20, 10, 0 on the board with space in between the numbers.) Let's put those same numbers in order into *this* set.

T: Where does 29 go now?

S: Between the 30 and 20. 29 is less than 30. It's greater than 20. (Continue having students place the numbers in order in the sequence.)

T: Let's read the first sequence we made, starting on the...

> **NOTES ON MULTIPLE MEANS OF REPRESENTATION:**
>
> Highlight the critical vocabulary for English language learners as you teach the lesson by showing objects as a visual as you say the words. Vocabulary in this lesson that you will want to highlight is *in order, in front of, before,* and *between*. Without understanding these words, English language learners will have difficulty placing numbers into the tens sequence.

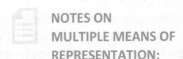

29, 38, 7, 14, 24

0   10   20   30   40

COMMON CORE | Lesson 8: | Compare quantities and numerals from left to right.
Date: | 9/20/13

4.B.19

S: Left!

S/T: (Point to the numbers as students read the sequence.) 0 is less than 7. 7 is less than 10. (Continue on.)

T: What will we say when we are comparing the numbers in the second set?

S: Greater than!

S/T: (Point to the numbers as students read the sequence.) 40 is greater than 38. 38 is greater than 30. (Continue on.)

Problem Set (10 minutes)

In this Problem Set, students wil be ordering numbers from least to greatest and greatest to least, it would be helpful to review the meaning of the words least and greatest to prepare students to answer these questions. Students should do their personal best to complete the Problem Set within the allotted 10 minutes. For some classes, it may be appropriate to modify the assignment by specifying which problems they work on first.

Student Debrief (10 minutes)

Lesson Objective: Compare quantities and numerals from left to right.

The Student Debrief is intended to invite reflection and active processing of the total lesson experience.

Invite students to review their solutions for the Problem Set. They should check work by comparing answers with a partner before going over answers as a class. Look for misconceptions or misunderstandings that can be addressed in the Debrief. Guide students in a conversation to debrief the Problem Set and process the lesson.

You may choose to use any combination of the questions below to lead the discussion.

- Look at Problem 2. Use math drawings, materials or place value charts to prove your solution for 36 _____ 3 tens 6 ones.

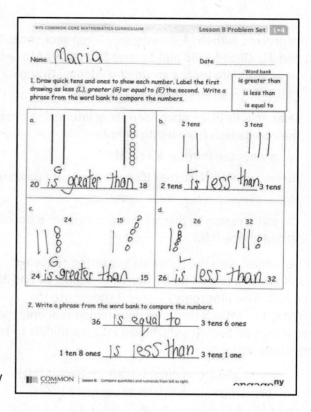

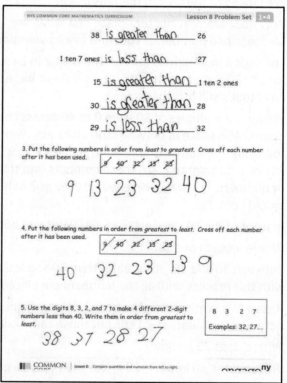

COMMON CORE | Lesson 8: Compare quantities and numerals from left to right.
Date: 9/20/13

4.B.

- How did Problem 3 help you solve Problem 4? What is the same about these two problems? What is different?

- Rewrite your statement for the Application Problem using only numbers and the phrase *greater than* or *less than* to compare the two sets of strawberries. Start with Anton's amount of strawberries.

- Share your solution to Problem 5 with your partner. Did you have the same solution? If your solutions were different explain how they could both be correct.

Exit Ticket (3 minutes)

After the Student Debrief, instruct students to complete the Exit Ticket. A review of their work will help you assess the students' understanding of the concepts that were presented in the lesson today and plan more effectively for future lessons. You may read the questions aloud to the students.

Name _____   Date _____

Core Subtraction Fluency Review

1. 8 - 0 = ____
2. 8 – 1 = ____
3. 7 - 7 = ____
4. 3 - 3 = ____
5. 3 - 2 = ____
6. 4 - 2 = ____
7. 5 - 2 = ____
8. 5 - 3 = ____
9. 9 - 2 = ____
10. 8 - 2 = ____
11. 7 - 2 = ____
12. 4 - 4 = ____
13. 4 - 3 = ____
14. 5 - 4 = ____
15. 8 - 3 = ____

16. 9 - 3 = ____
17. 10 - 3 = ____
18. 10 - 4 = ____
19. 10 - 2 = ____
20. 10 – 8 = ____
21. 10 - 7 = ____
22. 10 - 6 = ____
23. 6 - 6 = ____
24. 7 - 7 = ____
25. 7 - 6 = ____
26. 8 - 8 = ____
27. 8 - 7 = ____
28. 9 - 9 = ____
28. 9 - 8 = ____
30. 10 - 9 = ____

31. 5 - 5 = ____
32. 6 - 5 = ____
33. 7 - 5 = ____
34. 8 - 5 = ____
35. 8 - 4 = ____
36. 10 - 5 = ____
37. 9 - 5 = ____
38. 9 - 4 = ____
39. 6 - 3 = ____
40. 6 - 4 = ____
41. 7 - 3 = ____
42. 7 - 4 = ____
43. 8 - 6 = ____
44. 9 - 6 = ____
45. 9 - 7 = ____

COMMON CORE™

Lesson 8:   Compare quantities and numerals from left to right.
Date: 9/20/13

4.B.

Name _____ Date _____

Word Bank

| is greater than |
| is less than |
| is equal to |

1. Draw quick tens and ones to show each number. Label the first drawing as *less (L), greater (G),* or *equal to (E)* the second. Write a phrase from the word bank to compare the numbers.

a.

20 _____ 18

b.   2 tens   3 tens

2 tens _____ 3 tens

c.   24   15

24 _____ 15

d.   26   32

26 _____ 32

2. Write a phrase from the word bank to compare the numbers.

36 _____ 3 tens 6 ones

1 ten 8 ones _____ 3 tens 1 one

Lesson 8:   Compare quantities and numerals from left to right.
Date: 9/20/13

4.B.23

38 _____ 26

1 ten 7 ones _____ 27

15 _____ 1 ten 2 ones

30 _____ 28

29 _____ 32

3. Put the following numbers in order from *least* to *greatest*. Cross off each number after it has been used.

    | 9 | 40 | 32 | 13 | 23 |

4. Put the following numbers in order from *greatest* to *least*. Cross off each number after it has been used.

    | 9 | 40 | 32 | 13 | 23 |

5. Use the digits 8, 3, 2, and 7 to make 4 different two-digit numbers less than 40. Write them in order from *greatest* to *least*.

    | 8 | 3 | 2 | 7 |

    Examples: 32, 27….

COMMON CORE™ | Lesson 8: | Compare quantities and numerals from left to right.
Date: | 9/20/13

4.B.

Name _____   Date _____

Write the numbers in order from *greatest* to *least*.

```
            40
  39               29
        30
```

_____ _____ _____ _____

Complete the sentence frames using the phrases from the word bank to compare the two numbers.

Word Bank

| is greater than |
| is less than |
| is equal to |

17 _____ 24

23 _____ 2 tens 3 ones

29 _____ 20

Name _____   Date _____

Word Bank

is greater than
is less than
is equal to

1. Draw the numbers using quick tens and circles. Use the phrases from the word bank to complete the sentence frames to compare the numbers.

20 30	14 22
20 _____ 30	14 _____ 22
15 1 ten 5 ones	39 29
15 _____ 1 ten 5 ones	39 _____ 29
31 13	23 33
31 _____ 13	23 _____ 33

2. Circle the numbers that are *greater* than 28.

32   29   2 tens 8 ones   4 tens   18

3. Circle the numbers that are *less* than 31.

29   3 tens 6 ones   3 tens   13   3 tens 9 ones

4. Write the numbers in order from *least* to *greatest*.

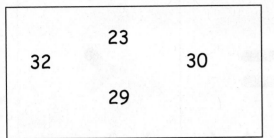

_____ _____ _____ _____

Where would the number 27 go in this order? Use words or rewrite the numbers to explain.

5. Write the numbers in order from *greatest* to *least*.

	40	
13		30
	31	

_____ _____ _____ _____

Where would the number 23 go in this order? Use words or rewrite the numbers to explain.

6. Use the digits 9, 4, 3, and 2 to make 4 different two-digit numbers less than 40. Write them in order from *least* to *greatest*.

| 9 | 3 | 4 | 2 |

Examples: 34, 29....

COMMON CORE   Lesson 8:   Compare quantities and numerals from left to right.
Date: 9/20/13

4.B.27

Comparison cards, p. 1. Print double-sided on cardstock. Distribute each of the three cards to students.

>	<	=	<
>	<	=	>
>	<	=	=
>	<	=	

Comparison cards, p. 2. Print double-sided on cardstock. Distribute each of the three cards to students.

less than	equal to	less than	greater than
greater than	equal to	less than	greater than
equal to	equal to	less than	greater than
	equal to	less than	greater than

COMMON CORE™

Lesson 8:   Compare quantities and numerals from left to right.
Date: 9/20/13

4.B.29

Lesson 9

Objective: Use the symbols >, =, and < to compare quantities and numerals.

Suggested Lesson Structure

■ Fluency Practice   (14 minutes)

■ Application Problem   (5 minutes)

■ Concept Development   (31 minutes)

■ Student Debrief   (10 minutes)

   Total Time   **(60 minutes)**

Fluency Practice (14 minutes)

- Core Subtraction Fluency Review **1.OA.6**   (5 minutes)
- Digit Detective **1.NBT.2**   (4 minutes)
- Sequence Sets of Numbers **1.NBT.3**   (5 minutes)

Core Subtraction Fluency Review (5 minutes)

Materials: (S) Core Subtraction Fluency Review from G1–M4–Lesson 8

Note: This activity assesses students' progress toward mastery of the required addition fluency for first graders. Since this is the second day students are doing this activity, encourage students to remember how many problems they answered yesterday and celebrate improvement.

Students complete as many problems as they can in three minutes. Choose a counting sequence for early finishers to practice on the back of their papers. When time runs out, read the answers aloud so students can correct their work and celebrate improvement.

Digit Detective (4 minutes)

Materials: (T/S) Personal white boards with place value chart insert (from G1–M4–Lesson 2)

Note: This activity reviews the term digit and relates it to place value.

Write a number on your personal white board, but do not show students.

    T: The digit in the tens place is 2. The digit in the ones place is 3. What's my number? (Snap.)

    S: 23.

    T: What's the value of the 2? (Snap.)

Lesson 9:   Use the symbols >, =, and < to compare quantities and numerals.
Date: 9/20/13

4.B.

S: 20.

T: What's the value of the 3? (Snap.)

S: 3.

Repeat sequence with a ones digit of 2 and a tens digit of 3.

T: The digit in the tens place is 1 more than 2. The digit in the ones place is 1 less than 2. What's my number? (Snap.)

S: 31.

T: The digit in the ones place is equal to 8 – 4. The digit in the tens place is equal to 9 – 7. What's my number? (Snap.)

S: 24.

As with the above example, begin with easy clues and gradually increase the complexity. Give students the option to write the digits on their place value chart as you say the clues.

Sequence Sets of Numbers (5 minutes)

Materials: (S) Personal white boards

Note: This activity reviews yesterday's lesson.

Write sets of four numbers within 40 (e.g., 23, 13, 32, 22). Students write and read the numbers from least to greatest, then from greatest to least. Ask questions such as the following:

- How could you use the words *greater than* or *less than* to compare 32 and 23?
- What number has the same digit in the tens place and ones place?
- Which two numbers have the same digit in the tens place?
- Which two numbers have the same digit in the ones place?
- Which number is less than 23?

Continue with similar questions and different sets of numbers.

Suggested sets: 13, 11, 31, 1; 17, 27, 21, 12; 38, 18, 25, 35; etc.

Application Problem (5 minutes)

Carl has a collection of rocks. He collects 10 more rocks. Now he has 31 rocks. How many rocks did he have in the beginning?

a.   Use place value charts to show how many rocks Carl had at the beginning.

b.   Write a statement comparing how many rocks Carl started and ended with, using one of these phrases: *greater than, less than, equal to.*

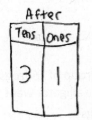

Carl had 21 rocks at the beggining.
21 is less than 31.

Note: In this *add to with start unknown* problem, students are asked to mentally determine what number is 10 less than 31. For struggling students, a place value chart and/or manipulatives would be helpful.

Concept Development (31 minutes)

Materials: (T) Alligator A and B pictures (double-sided), comparison cards (from G1–M4–Lesson 8) (S) Comparison cards (from G1–M4–Lesson 8), personal white boards

Note: When comparing numbers, most students tend to express the comparison by starting with the greater number, regardless of the order of the numbers on the page. For instance, if the numbers 3 and 30 were displayed on the board, students may say 30 is greater than 3. The statement is true, even though the student was not comparing from left to right. The best support we can give students is to affirm their true remark, and ask them to now compare the numbers starting with the one on the left, pointing to the 3. Examples of this are embedded in the dialogue below.

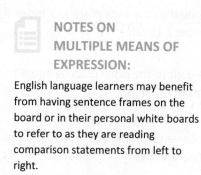

NOTES ON
MULTIPLE MEANS OF
EXPRESSION:

English language learners may benefit from having sentence frames on the board or in their personal white boards to refer to as they are reading comparison statements from left to right.

_____ is greater than _____.

_____ is less than _____.

As they become more familiar with reading the statement, remove the sentence frame.

Gather students in the meeting area with their materials.

T: (Project or draw a group of 2 frogs and a group of 10 frogs with enough room in between the groups to place the alligator picture.) Here is an alligator. He is *really* hungry. Notice his open mouth. (Trace the shape of the mouth with your finger.) Would this hungry alligator rather eat 2 frogs for dinner, or eat 10 frogs for dinner?

S: 10 frogs!

T: Why would he rather eat the group of 10 frogs?

S: 10 frogs is more than 2 frogs! → 10 is greater than 2!

T: Yes, terrific. What would we say if we started comparing the numbers from the left, starting with the number 2?

S: 2 is less than 10. (Place Alligator A, between the frogs, showing the alligator facing the group of 10 frogs.)

T: (Project or draw a group of 15 frogs and a group of 10 frogs in the same manner.) Which group of frogs will the hungry alligator want to eat this time?

S: The group of 15 frogs!

T: Why?

S: 15 frogs is greater than 10 frogs.

T: Show or explain how you know that.

S: 15 is made of 1 ten and 5 ones. That's more than just 1 ten. → I can show it with my ten-sticks! See? 1 ten and 5 ones is more than 1 ten.

Lesson 9: Use the symbols >, =, and < to compare quantities and numerals.
Date: 9/20/13

4.B.3

T: (Draw bond under 15 to show 10 and 5. Turn the card over to Alligator B to show the alligator facing the 15 frogs.)

T: Now I will post only numbers. We'll continue to compare them and decide which number the alligator would prefer.

Repeat the process from above with the following suggested sequence of numbers:

- 1 ten and 1 ten 6 ones
- 30 and 20
- 4 tens and 3 tens 8 ones
- 39 and 32
- 14 and 40
- 23 and 32

When appropriate, you may want to use the alligator cards and cover up the words *greater than* and *less than* to encourage students to rely on using just the symbols.

With each pair of numbers, encourage students to explain their reasoning. Ask the students to express each number in tens and ones, comparing the tens and the ones in each number as they explain why one number is greater than or less than the other number.

T: Now it's your turn to do this with a partner. Take out your comparison cards. Hold up the card that says *less than*.

S: (Hold up *less than* card, showing the words.)

T: Turn the card over. The wavy water lines should be at the bottom of your card. You will see a *part* of the alligator's mouth. If you'd like, use a yellow colored pencil to add some teeth to your alligator's mouth. (Demonstrate by adding teeth on the teacher comparison card. In tomorrow's lesson students will erase teeth.)

Repeat this process for the *greater than* card.

T: Now we're ready to play Compare It!

T: Each of you will write a number from 0 to 40 on your board, without showing your partner. When you are both ready, put them down next to each other. For the first round, Partner A uses her cards to put the alligator picture between the boards, always having the alligator's mouth open to the greater number. Then Partner B will read the expression from left to right. Each round will last one minute. The object of the game is to see how many different comparisons you can make within each round. You can use tally marks to keep track.

NOTES ON MULTIPLE MEANS OF ACTION AND EXPRESSION:

As students are completing their Problem Set, encourage them to quietly read each expression as they circle their answer. This will allow you to hear which students are reading the expressions correctly and support those who may need it.

At the end of the first round, have partners use Partner B's cards. Alternate for each round until the students have played for four minutes. During that time, circulate and notice which students are successful and which students may need more support. Encourage students to make the game more challenging by varying how

 Lesson 9: Use the symbols >, =, and < to compare quantities and numerals.
Date: 9/20/13

4.B.33

they represent the number, using quick tens, place value charts, and writing the numbers as tens and ones. Grouping students by readiness levels will facilitate this opportunity to differentiate.

Problem Set (10 minutes)

Students should do their personal best to complete the Problem Set within the allotted 10 minutes. For some classes, it may be appropriate to modify the assignment by specifying which problems they work on first.

Student Debrief (10 minutes)

Lesson Objective: Use the symbols >, =, and < to compare quantities and numerals.

The Student Debrief is intended to invite reflection and active processing of the total lesson experience.

Invite students to review their solutions for the Problem Set. They should check work by comparing answers with a partner before going over answers as a class. Look for misconceptions or misunderstandings that can be addressed in the Debrief. Guide students in a conversation to debrief the Problem Set and process the lesson.

You may choose to use any combination of the questions below to lead the discussion.

- Compare your answer to Problem 4(a) with your partner's. Did you and your partner come up with the same answer? Can there be *more* than one answer? Are there other problems that can have more than one answer? Why?

- Compare your answer to Problem 4(j) with your partner's. Did you and your partner come up with the same answer? Can there be only *one* answer. Are there other problems that can only have one answer? Why?

- What new math symbols did we use today to compare different numbers? (> for greater than, < for less than.)

- Look at your statement to today's Application Problem. Rewrite your statement using only numbers and a symbol.

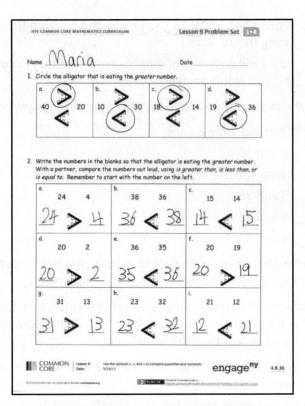

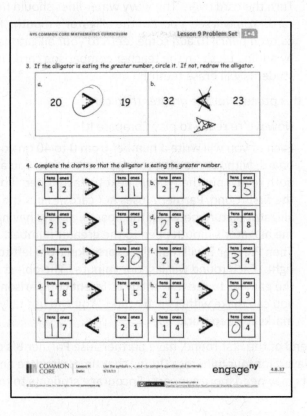

Lesson 9:   Use the symbols >, =, and < to compare quantities and numerals.
Date: 9/20/13

4.B.3

Exit Ticket (3 minutes)

After the Student Debrief, instruct students to complete the Exit Ticket. A review of their work will help you assess the students' understanding of the concepts that were presented in the lesson today and plan more effectively for future lessons. You may read the questions aloud to the students.

Lesson 9:   Use the symbols >, =, and < to compare quantities and numerals.
Date: 9/20/13

4.B.35

Name _____   Date _____

1. Circle the alligator that is eating the *greater* number.

a.	b.	c.	d.
40 20	10 30	18 14	19 36

2. Write the numbers in the blanks so that the alligator is eating the *greater* number. With a partner, compare the numbers out loud, using *is greater than, is less than, or is equal to*. Remember to start with the number on the left.

a. 24 4	b. 38 36	c. 15 14
___ > ___	___ < ___	___ < ___
d. 20 2	e. 36 35	f. 20 19
___ > ___	___ < ___	___ > ___
g. 31 13	h. 23 32	i. 21 12
___ > ___	___ < ___	___ < ___

COMMON CORE   Lesson 9:   Use the symbols >, =, and < to compare quantities and numerals.
Date: 9/20/13

4.B.

3. If the alligator is eating the *greater* number, circle it. If not, redraw the alligator.

a.

20   >   19

b.

32   <   23

4. Complete the charts so that the alligator is eating the *greater* number.

a.

tens	ones
1	2

>

tens	ones
1	

b.

tens	ones
2	7

>

tens	ones
2	

c.

tens	ones
2	5

>

tens	ones
	5

d.

tens	ones
	8

<

tens	ones
3	8

e.

tens	ones
2	1

>

tens	ones
2	

f.

tens	ones
2	4

<

tens	ones
	4

g.

tens	ones
1	8

>

tens	ones
	5

h.

tens	ones
2	1

>

tens	ones
	9

i.

tens	ones
	7

<

tens	ones
2	1

j.

tens	ones
1	4

>

tens	ones
	4

Name _____ Date _____

1. Write the numbers in the blanks so that the alligator is eating the greater number. Read the number sentence, using *is greater than, is less than,* or *is equal to.* Remember to start with the number on the left.

a. 12 10	b. 22 24	c. 17 25
___ > ___	___ < ___	___ > ___

d. 13 3	e. 27 28	f. 30 21
___ > ___	___ > ___	___ < ___

g. 12 21	h. 31 13	i. 32 23
___ > ___	___ < ___	___ < ___

Name _____ Date _____

1. Write the numbers in the blanks so that the alligator is eating the greater number.
   Read the number sentence, using *is greater than, is less than,* or *is equal to.*
   Remember to start with the number on the left.

   a.
   10   20

   ___ > ___

   b.
   15   17

   ___ < ___

   c.
   24   22

   ___ > ___

   d.
   29   30

   ___ > ___

   e.
   39   38

   ___ < ___

   f.
   39   40

   ___ < ___

2. Complete the charts so that the gator is eating the *greater* number.

   a.
tens	ones
1	8
   >
tens	ones
1	

   b.
tens	ones
2	4
   <
tens	ones
	3

   c.
tens	ones
   >
tens	ones

   d.
tens	ones
2	3
   >
tens	ones
	2

   e.
tens	ones
   <
tens	ones

   f.
tens	ones
1	7
   >
tens	ones
	7

COMMON CORE

Lesson 9:   Use the symbols >, =, and < to compare quantities and numerals.
Date: 9/20/13

4.B.39

Compare each set of numbers by matching to the correct alligator or phrase to make a true number sentence. Check your work by reading the sentence from left to right.

3.

16	17

31	23

35	25

is *less* than

12	21

22	32

is *greater* than

29	30

39	40

COMMON CORE

Lesson 9: Use the symbols >, =, and < to compare quantities and numerals.
Date: 9/20/13

4.B

Alligator template, double-sided on cardstock for the teacher.

greater than

Alligator template, double-sided on cardstock for the teacher.

less than

COMMON CORE™ | Lesson 9: | Use the symbols >, =, and < to compare quantities and numerals.
Date: | 9/20/13

4.B.

Lesson 10

Objective: Use the symbols >, =, and < to compare quantities and numerals.

Suggested Lesson Structure

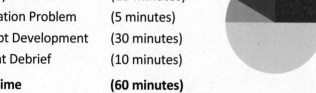

- ■ Fluency Practice   (15 minutes)
- ■ Application Problem   (5 minutes)
- ■ Concept Development   (30 minutes)
- ■ Student Debrief   (10 minutes)
- **Total Time**   **(60 minutes)**

Fluency Practice (15 minutes)

- Sprint: Number Sequences Within 40 **1.NBT.3**   (10 minutes)
- Digit Detective **1.NBT.3**   (5 minutes)

Sprint: Number Sequences Within 40 (10 minutes)

Materials: (S) Number Sequences Within 40 Sprint

Note: In this Sprint, students recognize forward and backward counting patterns. As with all Common Core Sprints, the sequence progresses from simple to complex, with the final quadrant being the most challenging. The last four problems of this particular Sprint involve counting by twos, a second grade standard. First grade students who complete enough problems to encounter this challenge may use their understanding of the relationship between counting and addition to solve these problems (**1.OA.5**).

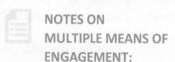

NOTES ON MULTIPLE MEANS OF ENGAGEMENT:

Connect learning to areas of interest. Students who enjoy writing can be given the challenge to write their own Application Problem using tens and ones. Practicing their writing skills during math is a great cross-curricular activity. Students can also present their problem to the class to solve.

Digit Detective (5 minutes)

Materials: (T/S) Personal boards with place value chart insert (G1–M1–Lesson 2)

Note: This activity was conducted as teacher-directed fluency in the previous lesson. Today, students practice in partners and compare their numbers using inequality symbols.

Students work in partners. Each student writes a number from 0 to 40 in their place value chart but does not show their partner. Partners then can either tell which digit is in each place or give addition or subtraction clues about the digits. Partners guess each other's numbers and then write and say an inequality sentence

Lesson 10:	Use the symbols >, =, and < to compare quantities and numerals.
Date:	9/20/13

4.B.43

comparing them. Circulate and ask questions to encourage students to realize that their inequality sentences may be different, but may both be true (e.g., 14 < 37 and 37 > 14).

Application Problem (5 minutes)

Elaine had 19 blueberries and ate 10. Mike had 13 and picked 7. Compare Elaine and Mike's blueberries after Elaine ate some and Mike picked some more.

a. Use words and pictures to show how many blueberries each person has.

b. Use the term *greater than* or *less than* in your statement.

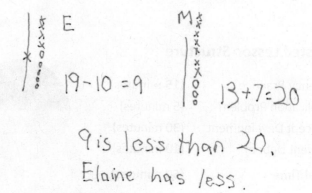

Note: In this problem, students apply several elements from their previous learning, such as mentally adding 10 and using comparative language. During the debrief, students will write the number sentence using the proper comparative symbol. If the challenge of wielding both Elaine and Mike feels too much for your students, invite them to work in pairs and let one student be Mike, the other Elaine.

Concept Development (30 minutes)

Materials: (T) Alligator template (from G1–M4–Lesson 9), comparison cards (from G1–M4–Lesson 8), projector (S) Comparison cards (from G1–M4–Lesson 8), erasers, personal white boards

Gather students in the meeting area with their materials.

T: (Project 28 and 37 in place value charts.) Which number would the hungry alligator want to eat?

S: 37!

T: (Place the *greater than* alligator symbol.) Why?

S: 37 is greater than 28. → There are more tens in 37 than in 28. → The digit 3 in 37 shows there are more tens in 37 than there are in 28.

T: Today, we will use math symbols to compare numbers. You just said that 37 is greater than 28. (Hold up the *greater than* card with the symbol side showing.) I will use this math symbol to make the number sentence 37 is greater than 28. (Tape card below the alligator and rewrite the numbers on either side of the symbol.)

T: What do you notice is similar between the alligator and the math symbol? Turn and talk with a partner.

NOTES ON MULTIPLE MEANS OF ENGAGEMENT:

A few students should keep the teeth on their alligators while the rest of the class removes their teeth. This will help the class see that the symbols are the same with or without teeth. The students who initially keep their teeth can be those who may need additional support reading the statements correctly. At some point during the lesson, switch the job to other students to support movement towards greater independence.

COMMON CORE

Lesson 10:   Use the symbols >, =, and < to compare quantities and numerals.
Date: 9/20/13

4.B

S: The symbol looks like the alligator's mouth. → The symbol is open on the side that the alligator likes to eat.

T: We call this symbol the *greater than* sign.

T: (Project 15 and 18 in place value charts.) Can you figure out the symbol we will use between these numbers? Talk with a partner.

S: (Share quickly.) The *less than* sign!

T: We need to place the *less than sign*, because 15 is *less than* 18. What does this sign look like? Draw it in the air. (Students draw in the air.)

T: Yes, it looks like this. (Draw or tape the *less than* symbol between 15 and 18.) How did you know?

S: It is like the alligator's mouth. It should be opened toward the greater number. → The smaller end points at the smaller number. → The open part is toward the greater number.

T: Today, let's erase the teeth we made on our comparison cards and try to use the math symbol to make true number sentences like the two we just made.

T: We will play Compare It! again today. We need someone to remind us of the rules.

S: We play with a partner. Each of us writes a number from 0 to 40 on our board, without showing our partner. When we are both ready, we put them down next to each other. For the first round, Partner A uses the cards to put the symbol between the boards.

T: Today, Partner B then reads the true number sentence that you made. Remember that we always read the number sentences from left to right. (Demonstrate with the number sentence on the board.)

At the end of the first round, have partners use Partner B's cards. Alternate for each round until the students have played for four minutes. During that time, circulate and notice which students are successful and which students may need more support. Encourage students to make the game more challenging by varying how they represent the number, using quick tens, place value charts, and writing the numbers as tens and ones.

Problem Set (10 minutes)

Students should do their personal best to complete the Problem Set within the allotted 10 minutes. For some classes, it may be appropriate to modify the assignment by specifying which problems they work on first.

Student Debrief (10 minutes)

Lesson Objective: Use the symbols >, =, and < to compare quantities and numerals.

The Student Debrief is intended to invite reflection and active processing of the total lesson experience.

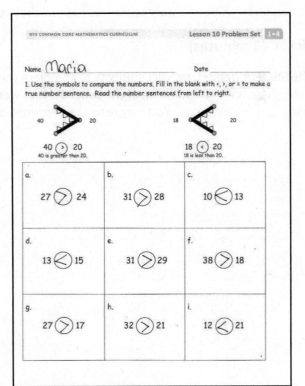

COMMON CORE   Lesson 10:   Use the symbols >, =, and < to compare quantities and numerals.

Date: 9/20/13   4.B.45

© 2013 Common Core, Inc. All rights reserved. commoncore.org

Invite students to review their solutions for the Problem Set. They should check work by comparing answers with a partner before going over answers as a class. Look for misconceptions or misunderstandings that can be addressed in the Debrief. Guide students in a conversation to debrief the Problem Set and process the lesson.

You may choose to use any combination of the questions below to lead the discussion.

- Look at Problems 1(a) and 1(b). How was the way in which you solved 1(a) different from how you solved 1(b)? Explain your thinking.

- Look at Problem 2(f). How are the numbers the same? How are they different? Compare the digit 2 in each number. How does changing the position of the digit change the value of the number?

- What are some different ways you can remember each of the symbols?

- Look at the Application Problem. How did you find the answer? Use the symbols from today's lesson to write a number sentence that matches your statement.

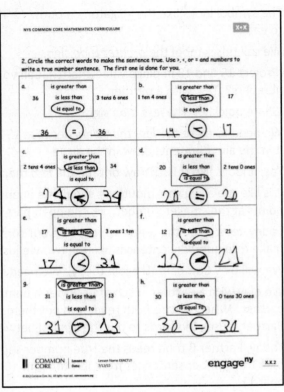

Exit Ticket (3 minutes)

After the Student Debrief, instruct students to complete the Exit Ticket. A review of their work will help you assess the students' understanding of the concepts that were presented in the lesson today and plan more effectively for future lessons. You may read the questions aloud to the students.

A

Number correct: _____

Name _____ Date _____

*Write the missing number in the sequence.

1	0, 1, 2, ___		16	15, ___, 13, 12	
2	10, 11, 12, ___		17	___, 24, 23, 22	
3	20, 21, 22, ___		18	6, 16, ___, 36	
4	10, 9, 8, ___		19	7, ___, 27, 37	
5	20, 19, 18, ___		20	___, 19, 29, 39	
6	40, 39, 38, ___		21	___, 26, 16, 6	
7	0, 10, 20, ___		22	34, ___, 14, 4	
8	2, 12, 22, ___		23	___, 20, 21, 22	
9	5, 15, 25, ___		24	29, ___, 31, 32	
10	40, 30, 20, ___		25	5, ___, 25, 35	
11	39, 29, 19, ___		26	___, 25, 15, 5	
12	7, 8, 9, ___		27	2, 4, ___, 8	
13	7, 8, ___, 10		28	___, 14, 16, 18	
14	17, ___, 19, 20		29	8, ___, 4, 2	
15	15, 14, ___, 12		30	___, 18, 16, 14	

COMMON CORE   Lesson 10:   Use the symbols >, =, and < to compare quantities and numerals.
Date: 9/20/13

B

Number correct: _____

Name _____ Date _____

*Write the missing number in the sequence.

1	1, 2, 3, ___	16	13, ___, 11, 10
2	11, 12, 13 ___	17	___, 22, 21, 20
3	21, 22, 23 ___	18	5, 15, ___, 35
4	10, 9, 8, ___	19	4, ___, 24, 34
5	20, 19, 18, ___	20	___, 17, 27, 37
6	30, 29, 28, ___	21	___, 29, 19, 9
7	0, 10, 20, ___	22	31, ___, 11, 1
8	3, 13, 23, ___	23	___, 30, 31, 32
9	6, 16, 26, ___	24	19, ___, 21, 22
10	40, 30, 20, ___	25	5, ___, 25, 35
11	38, 28, 18, ___	26	___, 25, 15, 5
12	6, 7, 8, ___	27	2, 4, ___, 8
13	6, 7, ___, 9	28	___, 12, 14, 16
14	16, ___, 18, 19	29	12, ___, 8, 6
15	16, ___, 14, 13	30	___, 20, 18, 16

COMMON CORE | **Lesson 10:** Use the symbols >, =, and < to compare quantities and numerals.
Date: 9/20/13

4.B

Name _____   Date _____

1. Use the symbols to compare the numbers. Fill in the blank with <, >, or = to make a true number sentence. Read the number sentences from left to right.

40 > 20   18 < 20

40 (>) 20
40 is greater than 20.

18 (<) 20
18 is less than 20.

a.	b.	c.
27 ◯ 24	31 ◯ 28	10 ◯ 13
d.	**e.**	**f.**
13 ◯ 15	31 ◯ 29	38 ◯ 18
g.	**h.**	**i.**
27 ◯ 17	32 ◯ 21	12 ◯ 21

2. Circle the correct words to make the sentence true. Use >, <, or = and numbers to write a true number sentence. The first one is done for you.

a. 36 is greater than / is less than / (is equal to) 3 tens 6 ones 36 = 36	**b.** 1 ten 4 ones is greater than / is less than / is equal to 17 ___ ○ ___
c. 2 tens 4 ones is greater than / is less than / is equal to 34 ___ ○ ___	**d.** 20 is greater than / is less than / is equal to 2 tens 0 ones ___ ○ ___
e. 31 is greater than / is less than / is equal to 13 ___ ○ ___	**f.** 12 is greater than / is less than / is equal to 21 ___ ○ ___
g. 17 is greater than / is less than / is equal to 3 ones 1 ten ___ ○ ___	**h.** 30 is greater than / is less than / is equal to 0 tens 30 ones ___ ○ ___

Lesson 10:   Use the symbols >, =, and < to compare quantities and numerals.
Date: 9/20/13

Name _____   Date _____

Circle the correct words to make the sentence true. Use >, <, or = and numbers to write a true number sentence.

a.

29 | is greater than | 2 tens 6 ones
       | is less than |
       | is equal to |

_____ ◯ _____

b.

1 ten 8 ones | is greater than | 19
                 | is less than |
                 | is equal to |

_____ ◯ _____

c.

2 tens 9 ones | is greater than | 40
                  | is less than |
                  | is equal to |

_____ ◯ _____

d.

39 | is greater than | 4 tens 0 ones
       | is less than |
       | is equal to |

_____ ◯ _____

COMMON
CORE™

Lesson 10:   Use the symbols >, =, and < to compare quantities and numerals.
Date: 9/20/13

4.B.51

Name _____ Date _____

1. Use the symbols to compare the numbers. Fill in the blank with <, >, or = to make a true number sentence. Complete the number sentence with a phrase from the word bank.

Word bank

Word bank
is greater than
is less than
is equal to

40 > 20   18 < 20

40 ⟨ > ⟩ 20   18 ⟨ < ⟩ 20

40 is greater than 20.   18 is less than 20.

a.

17 ◯ 13

17 _____ 13

b.

23 ◯ 33

23 _____ 33

c.

36 ◯ 36

36 _____ 36

d.

25 ◯ 32

25 _____ 32

e.

38 ◯ 28

38 _____ 28

f.

32 ◯ 23

32 _____ 23

COMMON CORE™   Lesson 10:   Use the symbols >, =, and < to compare quantities and numerals.
Date: 9/20/13

4.

g.

1 ten 5 ones ⬭ 14

1 ten 5 ones _____ 14

h.

3 tens ⬭ 30

3 tens _____ 30

i.

29 ⬭ 2 tens 7 ones

29 _____ 2 tens 7 ones

j.

19 ⬭ 2 tens 3 ones

19 _____ 2 tens 3 ones

k.

3 tens 1 one ⬭ 13

3 tens 1 one _____ 13

l.

35 ⬭ 3 tens 5 ones

35 _____ 3 tens 5 ones

m.

2 tens 3 ones ⬭ 32

2 tens 3 ones _____ 32

n.

3 tens ⬭ 36

3 tens _____ 36

o.

29 ⬭ 3 tens 9 ones

29 _____ 3 tens 9 ones

p.

4 tens ⬭ 39

4 tens _____ 39

COMMON CORE™

Lesson 10:   Use the symbols >, =, and < to compare quantities and numerals.
Date: 9/20/13

4.B.53

Topic C
Addition and Subtraction of Tens

1.NBT.2, 1.NBT.4, 1.NBT.6

Focus Standard:	1.NBT.2	Understand that the two digits of a two-digit number represent amounts of tens and ones. Understand the following as special cases:
		a. 10 can be thought of as a bundle of ten ones – called a "ten."
		c. The numbers 10, 20, 30, 40, 50, 60, 70, 80, 90 refer to one, two, three, four, five, six, seven, eight, or nine tens (and 0 ones).
	1.NBT.4	Add within 100, including adding a two-digit number and a one-digit number, and adding a two-digit number and a multiple of 10, using concrete models or drawings and strategies based on place value, properties of operations, and/or the relationship between addition and subtraction; relate the strategy to a written method and explain the reasoning used. Understand that in adding two-digit numbers, one adds tens and tens, ones and ones; and sometimes it is necessary to compose a ten.
	1.NBT.6	Subtract multiples of 10 in the range 10–90 from multiples of 10 in the range 10–90 (positive or zero differences), using concrete models or drawings and strategies based on place value, properties of operations, and/or relationship between addition and subtraction; relate the strategy to a written method and explain the reasoning used.
Instructional Days:	2	
Coherence -Links from:	G1–M2	Introduction to Place Value Through Addition and Subtraction Within 20
-Links to:	G1–M6	Place Value, Comparison, Addition and Subtraction to 100
	G2–M3	Place Value, Counting, and Comparison of Numbers to 1,000

In Topic C, students pick up from their previous work with 10 more and 10 less to extend the concept to adding and subtracting multiples of 10.

In Lesson 11, students represent the addition of ten more with concrete objects and number bonds, first using the numeral and then writing as *units* of ten, as shown. After creating such number bonds for several examples, students notice that only the *unit* has changed (e.g., 3 bananas + 1 banana = 4 bananas, just as 3 tens + 1 ten = 4 tens). As students explore, they see that this relationship is present even when adding more than 1 ten. They come to realize that 2 tens + 2 tens = 4 tens, just as 2 + 2 = 4 (**1.NBT.4**). Students also explore this relationship with subtraction, seeing that 4 tens can be decomposed as 3 tens and 1 ten, and that 4 tens – 3 tens = 1 ten, just as 4 – 3 = 1 (**1.NBT.6**). Students see that the arrow is used to show the addition or subtraction of an amount, regardless of whether the number is increasing (adding) or decreasing (subtracting). This provides an important foundation for applying strategies such as the make ten strategy, described in Topic D.

In Lesson 12, students add multiples of 10 to two-digit numbers that include both tens and ones. They recognize that when tens are added to a number, the ones remain the same. Students use the cubes within their kit of 4 ten-sticks as well as the more abstract manipulatives of dimes and pennies, to explore the concept. They represent their computation in familiar ways such as number bonds, quick ten drawings, arrow notation, and by using the place value chart to organize the quantities as tens and ones.

$$26 \xrightarrow{+10} 36$$

A Teaching Sequence Towards Mastery of Addition and Subtraction of Tens

Objective 1:   Add and subtract tens from a multiple of 10.
(Lesson 11)

Objective 2:   Add tens to a two-digit number.
(Lesson 12)

Lesson 11

Objective: Add and subtract tens from a multiple of 10.

Suggested Lesson Structure

■ Fluency Practice	(12 minutes)
■ Application Problem	(5 minutes)
■ Concept Development	(33 minutes)
■ Student Debrief	(10 minutes)
Total Time	**(60 minutes)**

Fluency Practice (12 minutes)

- Compare Numbers **1.NBT.3, 1.OA.6**   (5 minutes)
- Number Bond Addition and Subtraction **1.OA.6**   (5 minutes)
- Happy Counting by Tens **1.NBT.5**   (2 minutes)

Compare Numbers (5 minutes)

Materials: (S) Personal white boards

Note: In this fluency activity, students review yesterday's lesson and use their understanding of place value to compare numbers.

Say and write sets of numbers from 0 to 40 in various ways (e.g., as numerals, as tens and ones, the Say Ten way). Students write a number sentence in the same order it is written on the board. Students then read their sentences aloud.

Suggested sets:

- 5 and 8, 15 and 18, 25 and 28
- 6 and 3, ten 6 and ten 3, 2 tens 6 and 2 tens 3
- 3 and 3, 3 tens and 3 tens, 3 tens and 3 ones
- 3 and 4, 3 tens 4 ones and 4 tens 3 ones,
  3 ones 4 tens and 4 ones 3 tens

Teacher:	Student:
5 ◯ 8	5 < 8
15 ◯ 18	15 < 18
25 ◯ 28	25 < 28

Teacher:	Student:
6 ◯ 3	6 > 3
ten 6 ◯ ten 3	16 > 13
2 tens 6 ◯ 2 tens 3	26 > 23

Number Bond Addition and Subtraction (5 minutes)

Materials: (S) Personal white boards

Note: By reviewing the relationship between addition and subtraction within 10, students will be able to approach today's problem types with familiar strategies. In today's lesson, students will make the connection that differences for multiples of 10 such as 40 – 30 can be viewed as 4 tens – 3 tens.

Write a number bond for a number between 0 and 10 with a missing part. Students write an addition and subtraction sentence to find the missing part and solve.

Happy Counting by Tens (2 minutes)

Note: Reviewing Happy Counting by Tens prepares students to recognize the efficiency of counting groups of 10 in today's lesson.

Happy Count by tens the regular way and Say Ten way from 0 to 120 (see G1-M4-Lesson 1). To really reinforce place value, try alternating between counting the regular way and the Say Ten way.

Application Problem (5 minutes)

Sharon has 3 dimes and 1 penny. Mia has 1 dime and 3 pennies. Whose amount of money has a greater value?

Note: Money is used in this problem as a way to extend place value concepts and to continue to familiarize students with coins and their value.

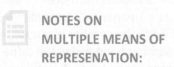

Concept Development (33 minutes)

Materials: (T) Chart paper (S) Personal white board with triple number bond/number sentence template

Students sit in the meeting area in a semi-circle formation.

- T: (Write 2 + 1 on the chart. Call up two volunteers.)
  Using your magic counting sticks, show us 2 + 1.
- S: (Student A shows 2 fingers, Student B shows 1 finger.)
- T: How many fingers are there? Say the number sentence.
- S: 2 + 1 = 3.
- T: (Complete the number sentence on the chart.)

NOTES ON MULTIPLE MEANS OF REPRESENATION:

The use of charts in the next few lessons will provide students with visual guides to use as resources in the classroom as they are learning more about place value. Some students may benefit from having a smaller version of the charts in their personal white boards or folders to refer to as needed.

Lesson 11:   Add and subtract tens from a multiple of 10.
Date: 9/20/13

4.C.4

On their boards, have students write the number sentence, use math drawings to show 2 + 1 = 3, and make a number bond as you record the information in a chart.

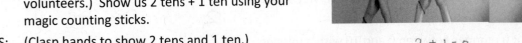

T: Let's pretend these circles stand for bananas! Say the number sentence using bananas as the unit.

S: 2 bananas + 1 banana = 3 bananas.

T: (Call for an additional volunteer to join the two volunteers.) Show us 2 tens + 1 ten using your magic counting sticks.

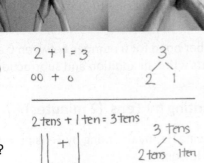

S: (Clasp hands to show 2 tens and 1 ten.)

T: (Help the first two students stand closer together to show 20.)

T: (Point to the first two students.) How many tens do we have here?

S: 2 tens.

T: (Point to the third student.) How many tens do we have here?

S: 1 ten.

T: How many tens are there in all?

S: 3 tens.

T: Say the number sentence using the unit *tens*. (If students struggle, say, "Say the number sentence starting with 2 *tens*.")

S: 2 tens + 1 ten = 3 tens.

T: (Record the number sentence on the chart.)

Have students write the number sentence, use math drawings, and make a number bond as you chart their responses as shown to the right.

Repeat the process and record the following suggested sequence on the chart: 3 tens + 1 ten, 2 tens + 2 tens, and 1 ten + 3 tens. Progress through the units from ones to bananas to tens (e.g., 3 + 1 = 4 → 3 bananas + 1 banana = 4 bananas → 3 tens + 1 ten = 4 tens). Have students write the number sentence, make math drawings, and write the number bond (using the same format from the teacher-generated chart) for each problem. These charts will be used later in this lesson.

T: (Point to the first problem on the chart.) Hmmm, how can knowing 2 + 1 = 3 help us with 2 tens + 1 ten? Turn and talk to your partner.

S: 2 tens + 1 ten = 3 tens is just like 2 + 1 = 3! → It's 2 things and 1 thing make 3 things. 2 circles and 1 circle make 3 circles. 2 bananas and 1 banana make 3 bananas. 2 tens and 1 ten make 3 tens!

**NOTES ON
MULTIPLE MEANS OF
REPRESENATION:**

Students demonstrate a true understanding of math concepts when they can apply them in a variety of situations. Some of your students may not be able to make the connection between different number bonds as seen in this lesson. Their path to abstract thinking may be a little longer than other's. Support these students with use of manipulatives and plenty of practice on their personal white boards.

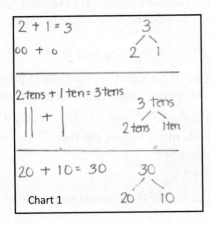

Chart 1

COMMON CORE | Lesson 11: | Add and subtract tens from a multiple of 10.
| Date: | 9/20/13

4

T: The numbers stay the same. The numbers, 2 and 1 and 3, stay the same. But the *units* change.

T: (Call up three volunteers to show 2 tens + 1 ten = 3 tens again.) Now, unbundle your magic counting sticks.

S: (Students open up their hands to show 10 fingers.)

T: (Point to the first two students.) What did 2 tens become?

S: 20.

T: (Point to the third student.) What did 1 ten become?

S: 10.

T: What is 20 + 10? Say the number sentence.

S: 20 + 10 = 30.

T: (Write the number sentence on the chart.) We'll call this the regular way, when we say 20 + 10 = 30. When we say the place value units, 2 tens plus 1 ten equals 3 tens, we call this the unit way.

T: Did we change the number of magic counting sticks when we had 2 tens + 1 ten = 3 tens?

S: No.

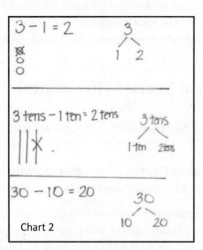

Chart 2

Elicit responses to make a number bond as the teacher charts their responses as shown on Chart 1. Have students fill in the last part of the template on their boards.

Repeat the process by revisiting the previous problems written on the charts and write them again using only numerals. For example 1 ten + 3 tens = 4 tens is now written as 10 + 30 = 40.

Next, repeat the process following the suggested sequence for solving subtraction problems as shown on Chart 2: 30 − 10, 30 − 20, 40 − 20, 40 − 40, and 40 − 0. Introduce each expression starting with ones and bananas, then tens, and finally as numerals (e.g., 2 − 1 = 1 → 2 bananas − 1 banana = 1 banana → 2 tens − 1 ten = 1 ten → 20 − 10 = 10).

T: (Write 4 tens − 3 tens on the chart.) What parts of the number bond can we fill in with these numbers?

S: 4 tens on top, with 3 tens as one of the parts. (Show the number bond with 1 ten still missing.)

T: What addition sentence can we write to match this number bond? Remember, we can say "unknown" or "mystery number" for the part we don't know yet.

S: 3 tens + "the mystery number" = 4 tens. (Record on the chart.)

T: What is the missing part?

S: 1 ten!

T: (Add the missing part to each section.) Say the subtraction sentence we created and the related addition sentence that we created.

S: 4 tens − 3 tens = 1 ten. 3 tens + 1 ten = 4 tens.

T: Let's say it the regular way too.

Lesson 11: Add and subtract tens from a multiple of 10.
Date: 9/20/13

4.C.6

S: 40 – 30 = 10. 30 + 10 = 40.

Repeat the process as needed to support students' understanding.

Problem Set (10 minutes)

Students should do their personal best to complete the Problem Set within the allotted 10 minutes. For some classes, it may be appropriate to modify the assignment by specifying which problems they work on first.

Student Debrief (10 minutes)

Lesson Objective: Add and subtract tens from a multiple of 10.

The Student Debrief is intended to invite reflection and active processing of the total lesson experience.

Invite students to review their solutions for the Problem Set. They should check work by comparing answers with a partner before going over answers as a class. Look for misconceptions or misunderstandings that can be addressed in the Debrief. Guide students in a conversation to debrief the Problem Set and process the lesson. You may choose to use any combination of the questions below to lead the discussion.

- Look at Problem 3. What simpler problem can help you solve this problem?
- How are Problems 4 and 5 related?
- Look at Problem 10. Share your solution with your partner. Did you solve the problem the same way? (Answers may vary, e.g., 1 ten – 0 tens = 1 ten, or 1 ten – 1 ten = 0 tens. Accept all possible interpretations of this picture as long as the students can support their thinking.)
- Look at Problem 12. Can you find an addition sentence and a subtraction sentence that are related?
- Use the arrow way to represent the adding and subtracting of Problem 12(a), 12(b), and 12(c).
- Explain how you solved today's Application Problem.

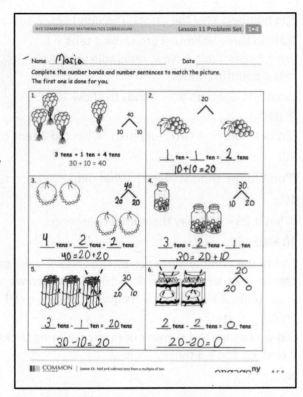

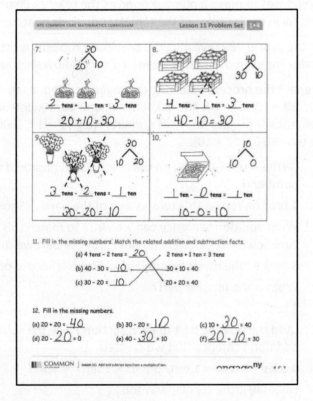

Exit Ticket (3 minutes)

After the Student Debrief, instruct students to complete the Exit Ticket. A review of their work will help you assess the students' understanding of the concepts that were presented in the lesson today and plan more effectively for future lessons. You may read the questions aloud to the students.

Name _____   Date _____

Complete the number bonds and number sentences to match the picture. The first one is done for you.

1.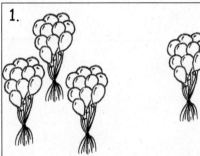

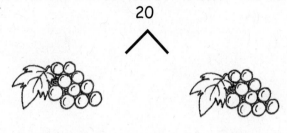
40
30   10

3 tens + 1 ten = 4 tens
30 + 10 = 40

2.
20

_____ ten + _____ ten = _____ tens

_____

3.

_____ tens = _____ tens + _____ tens

_____

4.

_____ tens = _____ tens + _____ ten

_____

5.

_____ tens - _____ ten = _____ tens

_____

6.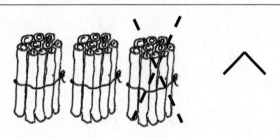

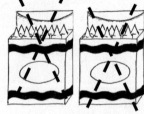

_____ tens - _____ tens = _____ tens

_____

7.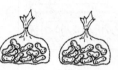

____ tens + ____ ten = ____ tens

8.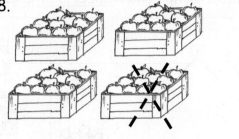

____ tens - ____ ten = ____ tens

_____

9.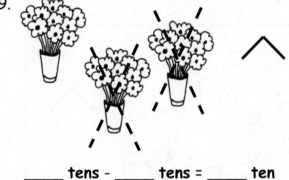

____ tens - ____ tens = ____ ten

_____

10.

____ ten - ____ tens = ____ ten

_____

11. Fill in the missing numbers. Match the related addition and subtraction facts.

   a. 4 tens – 2 tens = _____   2 tens + 1 ten = 3 tens

   b. 40 – 30 = _____   30 + 10 = 40

   c. 30 – 20 = _____   20 + 20 = 40

12. Fill in the missing numbers.

   a. 20 + 20 = _____   b. 30 – 20 = _____   c. 10 + _____ = 40

   d. 20 - _____ = 0   e. 40 - _____ = 10   f. _____ + ____ = 30

COMMON CORE | Lesson 11: | Add and subtract tens from a multiple of 10. | 4.C.10
| Date: | 9/20/13 |

Name _____ Date _____

Complete the number bonds and number sentences.

1.

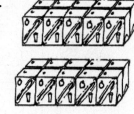

1 ten + 1 ten = _____ tens

_____ + _____ = _____ 20

2.

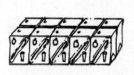

_____ tens = _____ tens + _____ ten

_____ = _____ + _____

3.

_____ tens - _____ ten = _____ tens

_____ - _____ = _____

4.

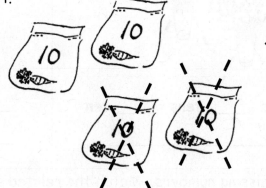

_____ tens - _____ tens = _____ tens

_____ - _____ = _____

Name _____   Date _____

Draw a number bond and complete the number sentences to match the pictures.

1.

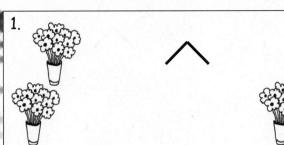

____ tens + ____ ten = ____ tens

20 + 10 = 30

2.

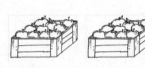

____ tens = ____ ten + ____ tens

_____

3.

____ tens - ____ ten = ____ ten

_____

4.

____ tens - ____ tens = ____ tens

_____

5.

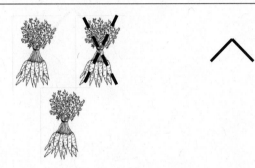

____ tens - ____ tens = ____ tens

_____

6.

____ tens + ____ tens = ____ tens

_____

Draw quick tens and a number bond to help you solve the number sentences.

7. 10 + 20 = _____	8. 30 – 10 = _____
9. 20 - 10 = _____	10. 30 + 10 = _____

Add or subtract.

11. 2 tens + 1 ten = _____   12. 20 + 20 = _____   13. 40 – 10 = _____

14. _____= 20 + 10   15. 3 tens – 2 tens = _____   16. 20 – 10 = _____

17. 10 – 10 = _____   18. _____ = 30 + 10   19. 40 – 30 = _____

Lesson 11:   Add and subtract tens from a multiple of 10.
Date: 9/20/13

4.C

Number Bond/Number Sentence Template

_____  _____ _____

_____ tens _____ tens _____ tens

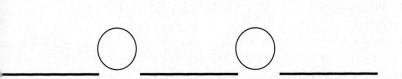

Lesson 12

Objective: Add tens to a two-digit number.

Suggested Lesson Structure

■ Fluency Practice   (15 minutes)
■ Application Problem   (5 minutes)
■ Concept Development   (30 minutes)
■ Student Debrief   (10 minutes)

Total Time   **(60 minutes)**

Fluency Practice (15 minutes)

- Sprint: Related Addition and Subtraction Within 10 **1.NBT.3, 1.OA.6** (10 minutes)
- Add and Subtract Tens Within 40 **1.OA.6, 1.NBT.2**   (3 minutes)
- Count by Tens with Coins **1.NBT.5**   (2 minutes)

Sprint: Related Addition and Subtraction Within 10 (10 minutes)

Materials: (S) Related Addition and Subtraction Within 10 Sprint

Note: This Sprint provides practice with first grade's core fluency standard, while reviewing the relationship between addition and subtraction.

Add and Subtract Tens Within 40 (3 minutes)

Materials: (S) Personal white boards

Note: This fluency activity strengthens students' understanding of the relationship between addition and subtraction while providing practice with adding and subtracting multiples of 10.

Write two related addition and subtraction sentences using 0–4 tens in unit form (e.g., 4 tens – 3 tens = ☐ tens and 3 tens + ☐tens = 4 tens). Students convert the number sentences to numeral form and solve (e.g., 40 – 30 = 10 and 30 + 10 = 40).

Count by Tens with Coins (2 minutes)

Materials: (T) 10 enlarged paper dimes and 6 enlarged paper pennies (template at end of lesson)

Note: Reviewing counting by tens prepares students to add multiples of 10 in today's lesson.

Lesson 12:   Add tens to a two-digit number.
Date: 9/20/13

4.C

Sit in a circle with students. Lay out and remove dimes to direct students to count forward and backward by tens within 100. Then lay out 6 pennies and add and remove dimes to count by tens, starting at 6 (e.g., 6, 16, 26…).

Application Problem (5 minutes)

Thomas has a box of paper clips. He used 10 of them to measure the length of his big book. There are 20 paper clips still in the box. Use the arrow way to show how many paper clips were in the box at first.

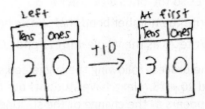

Note: This *take apart with start unknown* problem allows students to review the concept of mentally adding or subtracting 10 and using arrow notation to express their understanding. During the Debrief, students will share their thinking and notation to explain their solution. Some students may show their solution as 20 + 10 = 30 while others may solve using 30 – 10 = 20. Accept both solutions.

Concept Development (30 minutes)

Materials: (T) 4 ten-sticks, 4 dimes, and 10 pennies from personal math toolkit, double place value charts on chart paper (S) 4 ten-sticks, 4 dimes, and 10 pennies from personal math toolkit, personal white board, set of Addition and Subtraction with Cards game cards per pair of students

Note: The cards for the game Addition and Subtraction with Cards are labeled with the letter *c* to indicate that these cards correspond with the concepts taught in Topic C. Additional cards will be created in future topics with their corresponding topic letters.

Have students gather in the meeting area in a semi-circle formation with their materials.

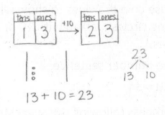

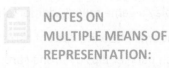

T: Using your linking cubes, show me 13.

S: (Show 1 ten-stick and 3 ones.)

T: (Point to the chart.) Let's fill out the place value chart. How many tens and ones are here?

S: 1 ten 3 ones.

T: (Write +10 above the arrow.) Do what the arrow says and show how many cubes we'll have next.

S: (Add a stick of 10.)

T: How many cubes are there now?

S: 23.

T: Say the number sentence beginning with the number of cubes we started with.

S: 13 + 10 = 23.

**NOTES ON
MULTIPLE MEANS OF
REPRESENTATION:**

Students may still struggle with coin values. With more frequent opportunities to engage with these coins and relate them to tens and ones, students will have more success making the connections.

Lesson 12:   Add tens to a two-digit number.
Date: 9/20/13

4.C.16

T: Use the quick ten drawing to show how we got 23.

S: (Draw.)

T: (Draw after the students have shown their work.) Which digit changed and which digit remained the same? Turn and talk to your partner and explain your thinking.

S: The digit in the tens place changed because we added 1 ten. We didn't touch the ones. → 1 ten more than 1 ten is 2 tens. That's why we have 2 in the tens place. We didn't add anything to the ones so the ones digit stays at 3.

T: Write the number bond that shows how we changed 13 to make 23.

S: (Write 23 as the whole with 13 and 10 as the parts.)

Continue the process following the suggested sequence where the unknown is in the sum: 16 + 10, 26 + 10, 15 + 20, and 20 + 18. Next, have students use their ten-sticks and drawings to solve problems in which the unknown appears as the change or the starting number: 13 + ___ = 23, 16 + ___ = 36, ___ + 10 = 35, and ___ + 20 = 37.

T: Show me 24 using your dimes and pennies.

S: (Show 2 dimes and 4 pennies.)

T: How many tens and ones are in 24?

S: 2 tens 4 ones.

T: (Fill in the place value chart. Write + 10 above the arrow.) Do what the arrow way says.

S: (Add 1 dime.)

T: How many tens are there now?

S: 3 tens.

T: How many ones are there?

S: 4 ones.

T: Let's use coin drawings to show what you did. (Model by using circles marked with 10 or 1 to show dimes and pennies.)

T: Say the number sentence.

S: 24 + 10 = 34.

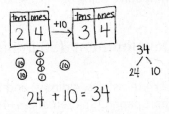

NOTES ON MULTIPLE MEANS OF REPRESENTATION:

Moving forward in small steps is what some of your students need. You may need to explicitly connect coin drawings to quick ten drawings so that students start to see the relationship between coins and quick ten drawings. Displaying a chart that shows the quick ten and coin relationship may benefit some students.

Continue the process following the suggested sequence: 15 + 10, 15 + 20, 17 + 20, 10 + 17, 20 + 14, 18 + ___ = 28, and 18 + ___ = 38.

Have students play a game called Addition and Subtraction with Cards.

1. Students place the deck of cards face down between them.

2. Each partner flips over one card, then solves the problem and says the number sentence.

3. The partner with the greater total wins the cards. (If the totals are equal, leave the cards until the next round when one student does have a greater total.)

After the first minute of play, change the rules so that the person with the total that is *less* wins the cards. Alternate between the two rules for the remaining time.

Lesson 12:	Add tens to a two-digit number.
Date:	9/20/13

4.C

Problem Set (10 minutes)

Students should do their personal best to complete the Problem Set within the allotted 10 minutes. For some classes, it may be appropriate to modify the assignment by specifying which problems they work on first.

Student Debrief (10 minutes)

Lesson Objective: Add tens to a two-digit number.

The Student Debrief is intended to invite reflection and active processing of the total lesson experience.

Invite students to review their solutions for the Problem Set. They should check work by comparing answers with a partner before going over answers as a class. Look for misconceptions or misunderstandings that can be addressed in the Debrief. Guide students in a conversation to debrief the Problem Set and process the lesson.

You may choose to use any combination of the questions below to lead the discussion.

- How is solving Problem 7 different from solving Problem 9?
- With your partner, compare the way you solved Problem 6. Which number did you draw first? Why?
- Look at Problem 11 or 12. Which coin is represented in the tens place? Which coin is represented in the ones place?
- Look at Problem 11. Explain why the ones digit didn't change from the starting number to the ending number.
- Share your answer to today's Application Problem. Explain how you found your answer.

Exit Ticket (3 minutes)

After the Student Debrief, instruct students to complete the Exit Ticket. A review of their work will help you assess the students' understanding of the concepts that were presented in the lesson today and plan more effectively for future lessons. You may read the questions aloud to the students.

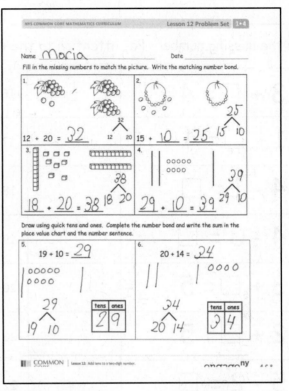

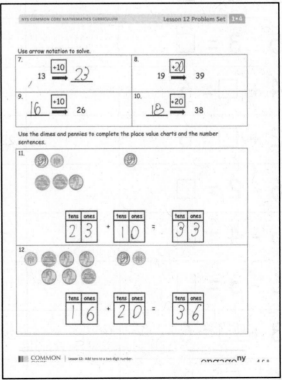

COMMON CORE

Lesson 12:   Add tens to a two-digit number.
Date: 9/20/13

4.C.18

A

Name _____   Date _____

*Write the missing number. Pay attention to the + and – signs.

1	$3 + \square = 4$		16	$3 + \square = 7$	
2	$1 + \square = 4$		17	$7 = 4 + \square$	
3	$4 - 1 = \square$		18	$7 - 4 = \square$	
4	$4 - 3 = \square$		19	$7 - 3 = \square$	
5	$3 + \square = 5$		20	$3 + \square = 8$	
6	$2 + \square = 5$		21	$8 = 5 + \square$	
7	$5 - 2 = \square$		22	$\square = 8 - 5$	
8	$5 - 3 = \square$		23	$\square = 8 - 3$	
9	$4 + \square = 6$		24	$3 + \square = 9$	
10	$2 + \square = 6$		25	$9 = 6 + \square$	
11	$6 - 2 = \square$		26	$\square = 9 - 6$	
12	$6 - 4 = \square$		27	$\square = 9 - 3$	
13	$6 - 3 = \square$		28	$9 - 4 = \square + 2$	
14	$3 + \square = 6$		29	$\square + 3 = 9 - 3$	
15	$6 - \square = 3$		30	$\square - 7 = 8 - 6$	

B

Number correct: ___

Name _____   Date _____

*Write the missing number. Pay attention to the + and – signs.

1	$4 + \square = 4$	16	$2 + \square = 7$
2	$0 + \square = 4$	17	$7 = 5 + \square$
3	$4 - 0 = \square$	18	$7 - 5 = \square$
4	$4 - 4 = \square$	19	$7 - 2 = \square$
5	$4 + \square = 5$	20	$2 + \square = 8$
6	$1 + \square = 5$	21	$8 = 6 + \square$
7	$5 - 1 = \square$	22	$\square = 8 - 6$
8	$5 - 4 = \square$	23	$\square = 8 - 2$
9	$5 + \square = 6$	24	$2 + \square = 9$
10	$1 + \square = 6$	25	$9 = 7 + \square$
11	$6 - 1 = \square$	26	$\square = 9 - 7$
12	$6 - 5 = \square$	27	$\square = 9 - 2$
13	$2 + \square = 6$	28	$9 - 3 = \square + 3$
14	$4 + \square = 6$	29	$\square + 2 = 9 - 4$
15	$6 - 4 = \square$	30	$\square - 6 = 8 - 3$

COMMON CORE™

Lesson 12:   Add tens to a two-digit number.
Date: 9/20/13

4.C.20

Name _____   Date _____

Fill in the missing numbers to match the picture. Write the matching number bond.

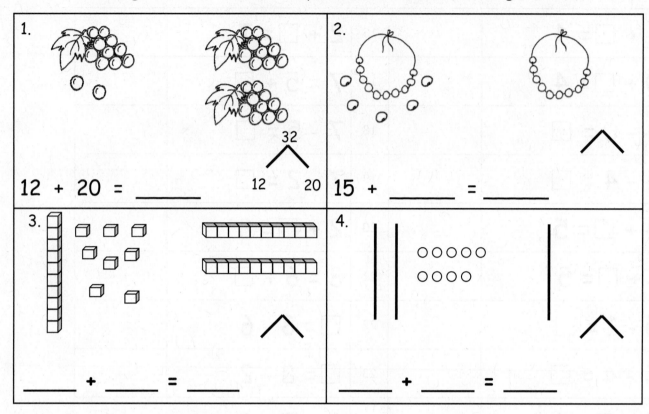

1.

12 + 20 = _____

32
12   20

2.

15 + _____ = _____

3.

_____ + _____ = _____

4.

_____ + _____ = _____

Draw using quick tens and ones. Complete the number bond and write the sum in the place value chart and the number sentence.

5.

19 + 10 = ____

tens	ones

6.

20 + 14 = ____

tens	ones

Use arrow notation to solve.

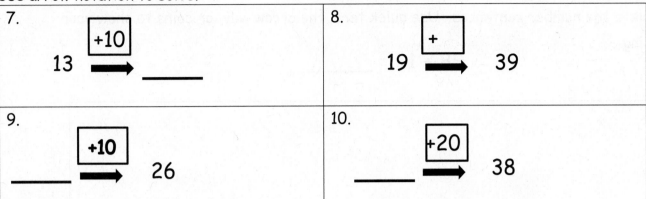

7.

```
     ┌─────┐
     │ +10 │
13   └─────┘  _____
       ───►
```

8.

```
          ┌───┐
          │ + │
19        └───┘   39
            ───►
```

9.

```
       ┌─────┐
       │ +10 │
_____ └─────┘   26
         ───►
```

10.

```
          ┌─────┐
          │ +20 │
_____    └─────┘   38
            ───►
```

Use the dimes and pennies to complete the place value charts and the number sentences.

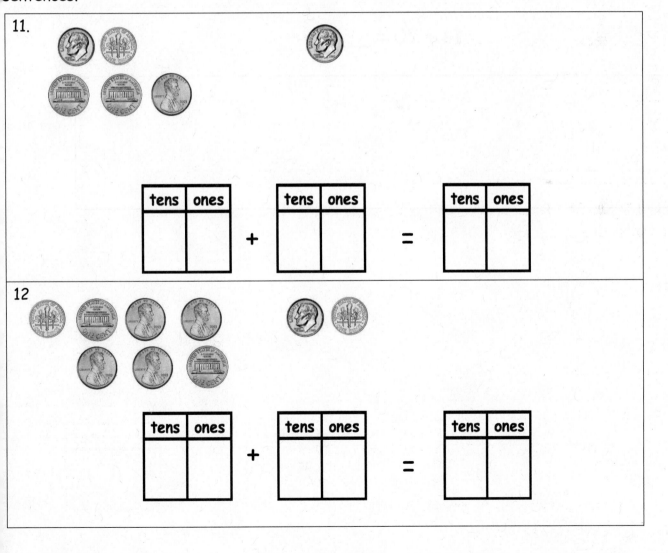

11.

tens	ones

+

tens	ones

=

tens	ones

12

tens	ones

+

tens	ones

=

tens	ones

COMMON CORE

Lesson 12:   Add tens to a two-digit number.
Date: 9/20/13

4.C.22

Name _____   Date _____

Complete the number sentences. Use quick tens, the arrow way, or coins to show your thinking.

$$28 + 10 = \underline{\quad\quad}$$

$$14 + 20 = \underline{\quad\quad}$$

Lesson 12:   Add tens to a two-digit number.
Date: 9/20/13

4.C

Name _____ Date _____

Fill in the missing numbers to match the picture. Complete the number bond to match.

1.

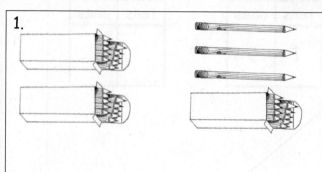

$$20 + 13 = \underline{\hspace{1cm}}$$

2.

$$17 + \underline{\hspace{1cm}} = \underline{\hspace{1cm}}$$

3.

$$\underline{\hspace{1cm}} + \underline{\hspace{1cm}} = \underline{\hspace{1cm}}$$

4.

$$\underline{\hspace{1cm}} + \underline{\hspace{1cm}} = \underline{\hspace{1cm}}$$

COMMON CORE™

Lesson 12:   Add tens to a two-digit number.
Date: 9/20/13

4.C.24

Draw using quick tens and ones. Complete the number bond and the number sentence.

5.

tens	ones
1	7

+

tens	ones
1	0

____ + ____ =

____

6.

tens	ones
1	9

+

tens	ones

____ + ____ = _39_

Use arrow notation to solve.

7.
$$19 \xrightarrow{+10} \text{\_\_\_\_}$$

8.
$$9 \xrightarrow{+30} \text{\_\_\_\_}$$

9.
$$\text{\_\_\_\_} \xrightarrow{+10} 38$$

10.
$$\text{\_\_\_\_} \xrightarrow{\boxed{+20}} 31$$

COMMON CORE   Lesson 12:   Add tens to a two-digit number.
Date: 9/20/13

4.C

Use the dimes and pennies to complete the place value charts.

11.

tens	ones

+

tens	ones

=

tens	ones

G1-M4-Topic C Flashcards

39 + 1 *c*	**30 - 1** *c*
20 + 20 *c*	**10 + 30** *c*
40 - 20 *c*	**40 - 30** *c*
30 - 20 *c*	**30 - 10** *c*

40 – 40

30 – 30

c

c

10 + 14

15 + 20

c

c

12 + 20

27 + 10

c

c

29 + 10

20 + 19

c

c

20 + 16

12 + 20

c

c

COMMON CORE™   **Lesson 12:**   Add tens to a two-digit number.
Date: 9/20/13

4.C.30

Topic D

Addition of Tens or Ones to a Two-Digit Number

1.NBT.4

Focus Standard:	1.NBT.4	Add within 100, including adding a two-digit number and a one-digit number, and adding a two-digit number and a multiple of 10, using concrete models or drawings and strategies based on place value, properties of operations, and/or the relationship between addition and subtraction; relate the strategy to a written method and explain the reasoning used. Understand that in adding two-digit numbers, one adds tens and tens, ones and ones; and sometimes it is necessary to compose a ten.
Instructional Days:	6	
Coherence -Links from:	G1–M2	Introduction to Place Value Through Addition and Subtraction Within 20
-Links to:	G1–M6	Place Value, Comparison, Addition and Subtraction to 100
	G2–M4	Addition and Subtraction Within 200 with Word Problems to 100

Topic D begins with students applying the Module 2 strategies of counting on and making ten to larger numbers, this time making a ten that is built on a structure of other tens. In Lesson 13, students use linking cubes as a concrete representation of the numbers, write a matching number sentence, and write the total in a place value chart. As they add cubes, students will see that sometimes you make a new ten, for example, 33 + 7 = 40, or 4 tens.

In Lesson 14, students use arrow notation to get to the next ten and then add the remaining amount when adding across ten. For example, when adding 28 + 6, students recognize that they started with 2 tens 8 ones and after adding 6, had 3 tens 4 ones. Students also use the bond notation from Module 2 to represent how they are breaking apart the second addend to make the ten (**1.NBT.4**).

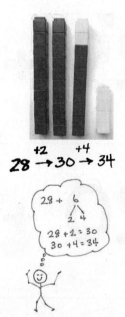

Lesson 15 provides the chance to notice the ways smaller addition problems can help with larger ones. Students add 8 + 4, 18 + 4, and 28 + 4 and notice that 8 + 4 is embedded in all three problems, which connects to their earlier work in Topic C.

Lessons 16, 17, and 18 focus on adding ones with ones or adding tens with tens. During Lesson 16, students recognize single-digit addition facts as they solve 15 + 2, 25 + 2, and 35 + 2. When adding 33 + 4, students see that they are adding 4 ones to 3 ones, while the tens remain unchanged, to make 3 tens 7 ones or 37. When adding 12 + 20, students see that they are adding 2 tens to 1 ten to make 3 tens 2 ones or 32. In both cases, one unit remains unchanged. Students work at a more abstract level by using dimes and pennies to model each addend. For instance, students model 14 cents using 1 dime and 4 pennies, and add 2 additional dimes or 2 additional pennies.

In Lesson 17, students continue working with addition of like units, and making ten as a strategy for addition. They use quick tens and number bonds as methods for representing their work.

During Lesson 18, students share and critique strategies for adding two-digit numbers. They bring to bear all of the strategies used thus far in the module, including arrow notation, quick tens, and number bonds. Projecting two correct work samples, students compare for clarity, discussing questions such as: Which drawing best shows the tens? Which drawings best help you *not* count all? Which number sentence is easiest to relate to the drawing? What is a compliment you would like to give [the student]? What is a way that [the student] might improve their work? How are [Student A]'s methods different from or the same as your partner's?

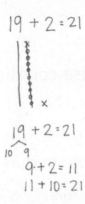

Adding ones with ones

A Teaching Sequence Towards Mastery of Addition of Tens or Ones to a Two-Digit Number
Objective 1: Use counting on and the make ten strategy when adding across a ten. (Lessons 13–14)
Objective 2: Use single-digit sums to support solutions for analogous sums to 40. (Lesson 15)
Objective 3: Add ones and ones or tens and tens. (Lessons 16–17)
Objective 4: Share and critique peer strategies for adding two-digit numbers. (Lesson 18)

Lesson 13

Objective: Use counting on and the make ten strategy when adding across a ten.

Suggested Lesson Structure

■ Application Problems	(5 minutes)
■ Fluency Practice	(12 minutes)
■ Concept Development	(33 minutes)
■ Student Debrief	(10 minutes)
Total Time	**(60 minutes)**

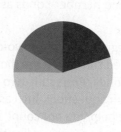

Application Problems (5 minutes)

Use linking cubes as you read, draw, and write (RDW) to solve the problems.

a. Emi had a linking cube train with 4 blue cubes and 2 red cubes. How many cubes were in her train?

b. Emi made another train with 6 yellow cubes and some green cubes. The train was made of 9 linking cubes. How many green cubes did she use?

c. Emi wants to make her train of 9 linking cubes into a train of 15 cubes. How many cubes does Emi need?

Note: Throughout Topic D, the Application Problem comes before the Fluency Practice. Each day, there are three problems, sequenced from simple to complex. Limit students' work time to five minutes. The problems are designed to pinpoint student strengths and challenges prior to Topic E, which focuses on word problems.

Take note of students who typically struggle to solve the Application Problem but who are successful with today's problems. They may need support moving from concrete to pictorial problem solving strategies. Also notice which students struggle when the position of the unknown changes.

Students should keep all Application Problems from Topic D for use during the Debriefs in Topic E.

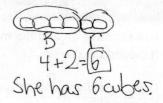

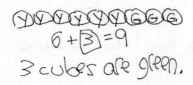

COMMON CORE

Lesson 13: Use counting on and the make ten strategy when adding across a
ten.
Date: 9/20/13

4.D.

Fluency Practice (12 minutes)

- Adding and Subtracting with Cards **1.NBT.4** (4 minutes)
- Race and Roll Addition **1.OA.6** (3 minutes)
- Core Addition Fluency Review **1.OA.6** (5 minutes)

Addition and Subtraction with Cards (4 minutes)

Materials: (S) Addition and Subtraction with Cards game cards (from G1–M4–Lesson 12)

Note: This fluency game was played during the previous lesson's Concept Development. It reviews adding and subtracting multiples of 10 within 40.

Follow the directions in G1–M4–Lesson 12's Concept Development.

Race and Roll Addition (3 minutes)

Materials: (S) 1 die for each set of partners

Note: This fluency activity reviews the grade level standard of adding within 20. Circulate as students play and informally assess which of your students are using the Level 2 strategy of counting on and which are using the Level 3 strategy of converting to an easier problem (e.g., mentally decomposing 13 and using 3 + 4 to solve 13 + 4).

All students start at 0. Partners take turns rolling a die, saying a number sentence, and adding the number rolled to the total. For example, Partner A rolls 6 and says, "0 + 6 = 6," then Partner B rolls 3 and says, "6 + 3 = 9." They continue rapidly rolling and saying number sentences until they get to 20, without going over. Partners stand when they reach 20. For example, if the partners are at 18 and roll 5, they take turns rolling until one of them rolls a 2 or rolls 1 twice, then both stand.

Core Addition Fluency Review (5 minutes)

Materials: (S) Core Addition Fluency Review from G1–M4–Lesson 2

Note: This activity assesses students' progress toward mastery of the required addition fluency for first graders. Differentiated Practice Sets can be found in G1–M4–Lesson 23, which may be helpful in supporting students towards these goals.

Students complete as many problems as they can in three minutes. Choose a counting sequence for early finishers to practice on the back of their papers. When time runs out, read the answers aloud so students can correct their work and celebrate improvement.

Lesson 13: Use counting on and the make ten strategy when adding across a ten.

Date: 9/20/13

4.D.4

Concept Development (33 minutes)

Materials: (T) 4 ten-sticks from the personal math toolkit, chart paper (S) 4 ten-sticks from the personal math toolkit, personal white board

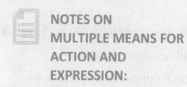

NOTES ON MULTIPLE MEANS FOR ACTION AND EXPRESSION:

Students love listening and learning from music. Find a song on iTunes about place value. One suggestion is "The Place Value Song" by Math Fiesta.

Have students sit in a meeting area in a semi-circle formation with their personal math toolkits.

T: (Show 13 as 1 ten and 3 ones using linking cubes.) How many linking cubes are there?

S: 13 linking cubes.

T: (Add 4 more linking cubes of a different color.) How many linking cubes are there now? Turn and talk to you partner about how you know.

S: There are 17 cubes. I started with 13 and counted on. Thirteeeen, 14, 15, 16, 17. → I added 3 ones and 4 ones. That makes 7 ones. 1 ten and 7 ones is 17. → 4 more than 13 is 17.

T: Nice thinking! Let's try counting on to find our solution.

S: (Point as students count.) Thirteeeen, 14, 15, 16, 17.

T: Now add the ones first. How many are in the ones place in 13?

S: 3 ones.

T: (Point to 3 cubes.) 3 ones and 4 ones is?

S: 7 ones.

T: (Snap the ones cubes together to make 7. Write 7 in the ones place in the place value chart.) How many tens do we have?

S: 1 ten.

T: (Write 1 in the tens place in the place value chart.)

T: 1 ten 7 ones is?

S: 17.

Note: Since there were no changes in tens, another option is to write 1 in the tens place first, then 7 in the ones place.

T: What are some different addition sentences we could use to put together 13 cubes and 4 cubes.

S: 13 + 4 = 17. → 10 + 7 = 17. → 10 + 3 + 4 = 17.

T: Use quick tens to draw the number of linking cubes we started with.

S/T: (Draw 1 quick ten and 3 dots for 3 ones.)

T: Draw to show the number of cubes we added to 13 using X's in 5-group column formation.

S/T: (Draw 4 X's above the 3 circles.)

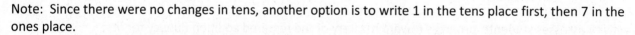

T: Say the number sentence using your drawing.

S: 13 + 4 = 17.

T: Let's use a number bond. (Write 13 + 4.) 13 cubes is 1 ten and 3 ones. (Break 13 apart into 10 and 3.) We next added 3 ones and 4 ones. Use this number bond to solve the problem on your board. Turn and talk to your partner about what you did.

S: First I added 3 and 4 and got 7. Then I added 10 and 7 and got 17.

T: Let's record how we added as two number sentences. (Write 3 + 4 = 7 and 10 + 7 = 17.) Let's solve another problem. Use your cubes to show 13.

S: (Show 1 ten-stick and 3 individual cubes in a 5-group column.)

T: Using a different color, add 7 more.

S: (Add 7 more cubes using a different color.)

T: How many cubes do you have now? Show what you did to your partner and talk about how you got the answer.

S: I put the 7 cubes next to 13 cubes. I know 3 and 7 is 10. And 10 and 10 is 20. → I stacked 7 cubes on top of the other 3. It made another ten-stick! → Now I see 2 ten-sticks. That's 20!

T: (Model with cubes.) You are right! 3 ones and 7 ones is?

S: 10 ones.

T: 10 ones is the same as?

S: 1 ten.

T: How many tens are there now? (Hold up each ten.)

S: 2 tens.

T: Where does the digit 2 go in our place value chart?

S: In the tens place.

T: (Write 2 in the tens place.) Since 3 ones and 7 ones make 1 ten, which we recorded in the tens place (point to place value chart), how many ones do we have now?

S: 0.

T: So we write 0 in the?

S: Ones place.

T: (Write 0 in the ones place.) Say the number sentence.

S: 13 + 7 = 20.

T: Draw quick tens to show the addition. Explain your drawing to your partner.

S: I framed my 7 crosses and 3 circles to show that I made a ten. → I drew a long line through my 10 ones to make it look like a quick ten.

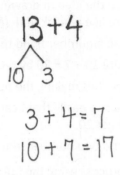

NOTES ON MULTIPLE MEANS OF REPRESENTATION:

Often students learn math concepts in an isolated fashion; although they may be able to use them with familiar problems, they do not see how to transfer their application to new situations. Be sure to incorporate math at other times in the students' day.

COMMON CORE™

Lesson 13: Use counting on and the make ten strategy when adding across a ten.

Date: 9/20/13

4.D.6

T: I love the idea of drawing a line through the new ten to make it look more like a quick ten! (Model.)

T: Make a number bond to show how you added the ones together.

S: (Write 13 + 7 = 20 by taking apart 13 into 10 and 3.)

T: How does making the number bond help you solve the problem?

S: I can see easily that I can add 3 and 7. That's 10. Then I add 10 and 10 and get 20.

T: (Write two number sentences.) Great! Now let's try some more!

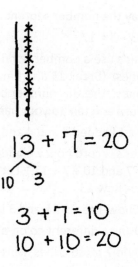

Repeat the process using the following sequence: 17 + 2, 18 + 2, 28 + 2, 23 + 6, 33 + 6, 23 + 7, and 33 + 7. As soon as possible, write the addition expression on the board and have students use quick ten math drawings and number bonds to solve rather than working with linking cubes. Some students may count on when adding 1 and 2. Counting on becomes less efficient as the second addend increases. When the second addend is larger than 3, encourage students to use Level 3 strategies such as thinking of doubles or using the make ten strategy.

Problem Set (10 minutes)

Students should do their personal best to complete the Problem Set within the allotted 10 minutes. For some classes, it may be appropriate to modify the assignment by specifying which problems they work on first.

Student Debrief (10 minutes)

Lesson Objective: Use counting on and the make ten strategy when adding across a ten.

The Student Debrief is intended to invite reflection and active processing of the total lesson experience.

Invite students to review their solutions for the Problem Set. They should check work by comparing answers with a partner before going over answers as a class. Look for misconceptions or misunderstandings that can be addressed in the Debrief. Guide students in a conversation to debrief the Problem Set and process the lesson.

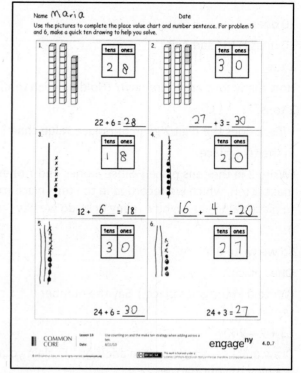

You may choose to use any combination of the questions below to lead the discussion.

- How can solving Problem 1 help you solve Problem 3?

- In Problem 9, explain why there is a 0 in the ones place in the answer when there are some ones in both addends.

- For Problem 10, a student said he has 2 tens and 10 ones. Is he right? Explain your thinking.
- What strategies did we use today to solve addition problems?
- How does your fluency work with the sums to ten help you in today's lesson?

Exit Ticket (3 minutes)

After the Student Debrief, instruct students to complete the Exit Ticket. A review of their work will help you assess the students' understanding of the concepts that were presented in the lesson today and plan more effectively for future lessons. You may read the questions aloud to the students.

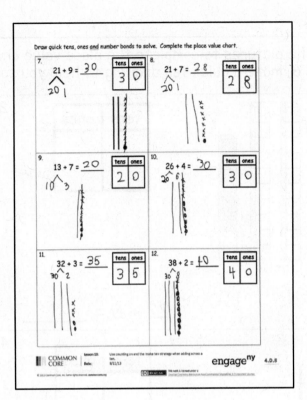

COMMON CORE

Lesson 13:   Use counting on and the make ten strategy when adding across a ten.

Date: 9/20/13

4.D.8

Name _____ Date _____

Use the pictures to complete the place value chart and number sentence. For problems 5 and 6, make a quick ten drawing to help you solve.

1.	tens | ones
22 + 6 = _____	

2.	tens | ones
_____ + 3 = _____	

3.

tens	ones

12 + _____ = _____

4.

tens	ones

_____ + _____ = _____

5.

tens	ones

24 + 6 = _____

6.

tens	ones

24 + 3 = _____

COMMON CORE™   Lesson 13:   Use counting on and the make ten strategy when adding across a ten.

Date: 9/20/13

4.D.

Draw quick tens, ones, <u>and</u> number bonds to solve. Complete the place value chart.

7.

$21 + 9 =$ _____

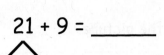

tens	ones

8.

$21 + 7 =$ _____

tens	ones

9.

$13 + 7 =$ _____

tens	ones

10.

$26 + 4 =$ _____

tens	ones

11.

$32 + 3 =$ _____

tens	ones

12.

$38 + 2 =$ _____

tens	ones

Lesson 13:   Use counting on and the make ten strategy when adding across a ten.

Date: 9/20/13

4.D.10

Name _____   Date _____

Fill in the place value chart and write a number sentence to match the picture.

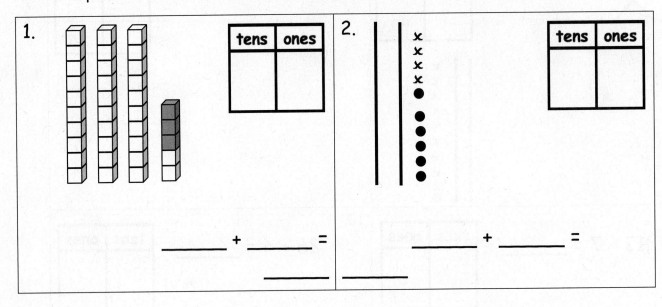

1.		tens	ones

_____ + _____ =

_____

2.		tens	ones

_____ + _____ =

_____

Draw quick tens, ones, and number bonds to solve. Complete the place value chart.

3.

33 + 6 = _____

tens	ones

4.

23 + 7 = _____

tens	ones

Name _____   Date _____

Use quick tens and ones to complete the place value chart and number sentence.

1.

tens	ones

21 + 4 = _____

2.

tens	ones

21 + 8 = _____

3.

tens	ones

25 + 4 = _____

4.

tens	ones

25 + 5 = _____

5.

tens	ones

33 + 3 = _____

6.

tens	ones

33 + 7 = _____

Lesson 13: Use counting on and the make ten strategy when adding across a
            ten.
Date: 9/20/13

4.D.12

Draw quick tens, ones, and number bonds to solve. Complete the place value chart.

7.		8.	
26 + 2 = _____	tens | ones	36 + 3 = _____	tens | ones
9.		10.	
26 + 4 = _____	tens | ones	24 + 6 = _____	tens | ones

Solve. You may draw quick tens and ones or number bonds to help.

11. a. 22 + 7 = _____   b. 22 + 8 = _____   c. 32 + 8 = _____

4.D.

Lesson 14

Objective: Use counting on and the make ten strategy when adding across
a ten.

Suggested Lesson Structure

■ Application Problems   (5 minutes)
■ Fluency Practice   (12 minutes)
■ Concept Development   (33 minutes)
■ Student Debrief   (10 minutes)
   Total Time   **(60 minutes)**

Application Problems (5 minutes)

Use linking cubes and the RDW process to solve one or more of the problems.

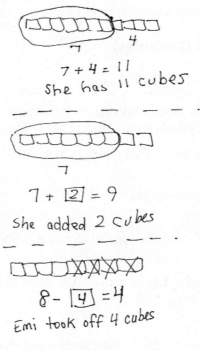

a. Emi had a linking cube train of 7 cubes. She added 4 cubes to
    the train. How many cubes are in her linking cube train?

b. Emi made another train of linking cubes. She started with 7
    cubes and added some more cubes until her train was 9 cubes
    long. How many cubes did Emi add?

c. Emi made one more train of linking cubes. It was made of 8
    linking cubes. She took some cubes off and then her train was
    4 linking cubes long. How many cubes to Emi take off?

Note: Each problem is successively more challenging. Remind children
that they are not expected to complete all three, but instead to do
their best during the five-minute time frame.

Notice which students are successful with the first problem, where the
unknown number is the result, or total, but who struggle with later
problems where the unknown number is in a different position. Keep
track of this analysis in preparation for Topic E instruction, where you
may want to select or emphasize particular problem types.

The similarity to yesterday's problems is intended to promote
perseverance and confidence for students who may be struggling with
Application Problems at this point in the year. For students who are
successful with all problems, challenge them to find the total of all the cubes used, ask how many more cubes
the first train has than the last, or encourage them to write their own additional linking cube train story.

COMMON CORE   Lesson 14:   Use counting on and the make ten strategy when adding across a
                                 ten.
                   Date: 9/20/13

4.D.14

Fluency Practice (12 minutes)

- Addition Within 40: Counting On **1.NBT.4**   (3 minutes)
- Get to 10 **1.NBT.4**   (3 minutes)
- Make Ten Addition with Partners **1.OA.6**   (6 minutes)

Addition Within 40: Counting On (3 minutes)

Note: This fluency activity reviews yesterday's lesson. Some students may count on, as they learned to do yesterday. Others may already make the connection between the single-digit addition facts and their analogous addition sentences. As always, pause to provide thinking time.

T: 5 + 2 is? (Snap.) Give me the number sentence.

S: 5 + 2 = 7.

T: 10 + 7 is? (Snap.)

S: 10 + 7 = 17.

T: 15 + 2 is? (Snap.)

S: 15 + 2 = 17.

Continue with 25 + 2 and 35 + 2. Repeat, beginning with other single-digit addition facts with sums to 10. Make sure one addend is conducive to counting on (e.g., 1, 2, or 3).

Get to 10 (3 minutes)

Materials: (T) Rekenrek

Note: In this fluency activity, students apply their knowledge of partners to ten to find analogous partners to 20, 30, and 40, which will prepare them for today's lesson.

For the first minute, say numbers from 0–10. Students say partners to ten on your snap. Then take out the Rekenrek.

T: (Show 9.) Say the number.

S: 9.

T: Give me the number sentence to make ten.

S: 9 + 1 = 10

T: (Move 1 bead to make 10. Show 19.)

T: Say the number.

S: 19.

T: Give me the number sentence to make 20.

S: 19 + 1 = 20

Suggested sequence: 29, 39; 5, 15, 25, 35; 8, 18, 28, 38; 7, 17, 27, 37; etc.

Lesson 14:   Use counting on and the make ten strategy when adding across a ten.

Date: 9/20/13

4.D.

Make Ten Addition with Partners (6 minutes)

Materials: (S) Personal white boards

Note: This fluency activity reviews how to use the Level 3 strategy of making ten to add two single-digit numbers. Students will learn how to apply this strategy when adding a one-digit number to a two-digit number in today's lesson.

- Assign partners of equal ability.
- Partners choose an addend from 1 to 10 for each other.
- On their personal boards, students add their number to 9, 8, and 7. Remind students to write the two addition sentences they learned in Module 2.

$$9 + 5 = 14$$
$$1 \wedge 4$$
$$9 + 1 = 10$$
$$10 + 4 = 14$$

$$8 + 5 = 13$$
$$2 \wedge 3$$
$$8 + 2 = 10$$
$$10 + 3 = 13$$

$$7 + 5 = 12$$
$$3 \wedge 2$$
$$7 + 3 = 10$$
$$10 + 2 = 12$$

- Partners then exchange boards and check each other's work.

> **NOTES ON MULTIPLE MEANS OF ENGAGEMENT:**
>
> Careful selection of pairs for collaborative work is essential to achieving expected outcomes. Some lessons lend themselves to groupings of students with similar skill sets while others work better when students are heterogeneously grouped. Some students would benefit from the opportunity to work independently and share with the teacher or another pair after they have completed the task.

Concept Development (33 minutes)

Materials: (T) 4 ten-sticks, chart paper (S) 4 ten-sticks from the math toolkit, personal white board

Note: During today's lesson we will be using the make ten strategy which requires students to break apart the single-digit addend, as in Module 2, whereas yesterday they broke apart the double-digit addend. This is part of how students gain confidence in flexibly using number bonds.

Have students sit in the meeting area in a semi-circle formation with their materials.

- T: (Write 19 + 3 on the chart.) How many cubes do I start with?
- S: 19 cubes. → 1 ten-stick and 9 ones. → You also need 3 ones.
- T: (Show 19 + 3 with cubes.) Turn and talk to your partner about how you can solve 19 + 3.

While students discuss, circulate and listen for sharing of both counting on and make ten strategies.

- T: (Ask student volunteers to come and share their strategies.)

Lesson 14:   Use counting on and the make ten strategy when adding across a ten.
Date: 9/20/13

4.D.16

© 2013 Common Core, Inc. All rights reserved. commoncore.org

S: I can count on. Nineteen, 20, 21, 22. → You can make another ten. 9 plus 1 more makes 10. 2 tens and then you still have 2 ones left. → 19 and 1 is 20. 20 + 2 is 22.

T: Just like we did yesterday, we can make a new ten-stick! How many more ones to make 19 get to the next ten, 20?

S: 1.

T: From where can we get the 1?

S: From the 3.

T: (Hold up 3 cubes. Break off 1 cube and complete a ten-stick.) How many tens are there now?

S: 2 tens.

T: How many ones are left?

S: 2 ones.

T: What is 2 tens and 2 ones?

S: 22.

T: 19 + 3 is?

S: 22.

T: Excellent work! Let's try some more!

> **NOTES ON MULTIPLE MEANS OF ACTION AND EXPRESSION:**
>
> Giving students an opportunity to share their thinking allows students to evaluate their process and practice. English language learners also benefit from hearing other students explain their thinking.

Have students collaborate with their partners and combine their linking cubes to find the sum for each addition expression following the suggested sequence: 18 + 4, 28 + 4, 26 + 5, 26 + 7, and 15 + 8. When appropriate, have students also draw quick tens to show how they solved the problems. (See image to the right.)

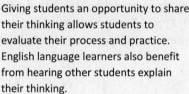

T: (Write 19 + 3 on the board again and represent the expression using linking cubes.) Let's record what we did to solve 19 + 3 using a number bond. Can we make a ten?

S: Yes.

T: How many more do we need to get to the next ten from 19? Where can we get that amount?

S: Take 1 from the 3.

T: (Ask a student volunteer to take 1 from 3 using the linking cubes.) Look at what we did with 3 in order to make the next ten. We broke 3 into...

S: 1 and 2.

T: (Make a number bond as shown to the right.) What is 19 and 1?

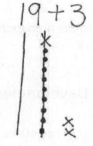

S: 20.

T: (Write 19 + 1 = 20.) 20 and 2 is...?

S: 22.

T: (Write 20 + 2 = 22.) Let's use the arrow way to record what we did. (Write 19 and model the arrow way as you talk through the notation.) We started with 19, then added 1 to make the next ten, which is 20. Then we had 2 left over. So we added 2 to 20 to get to 22.

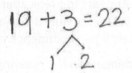

T: So 19 + 3 =?

S: 22.

Repeat the process following the suggested sequence: 29 + 3, 19 + 5, 18 + 3, 17 + 3 (use 1 arrow), 26 + 3 (use 1 arrow), 26 + 7, and 28 + 7.

When appropriate, have students choose and use only number bonds with two number sentences or the arrow way to solve instead of using the linking cubes. When sharing solutions, students should show their notations and explain their choice.

Problem Set (10 minutes)

Students should do their personal best to complete the Problem Set within the allotted 10 minutes. For some classes, it may be appropriate to modify the assignment by specifying which problems they work on first.

Student Debrief (10 minutes)

Lesson Objective: Use counting on and the make ten strategy when adding across a ten.

The Student Debrief is intended to invite reflection and active processing of the total lesson experience.

Invite students to review their solutions for the Problem Set. They should check work by comparing answers with a partner before going over answers as a class. Look for misconceptions or misunderstandings that can be addressed in the Debrief. Guide students in a conversation to debrief the Problem Set and process the lesson.

You may choose to use any combination of the questions below to lead the discussion.

- How could Problem 8 help you solve Problem 9? What smaller problem is in both Problems 8 and 9?

- With your partner, compare your work for Problem 9. Which method did you use to solve and why? How are the different methods of using quick ten drawings, the number bond, and the arrow way similar?

- How did we record the ways we added today?

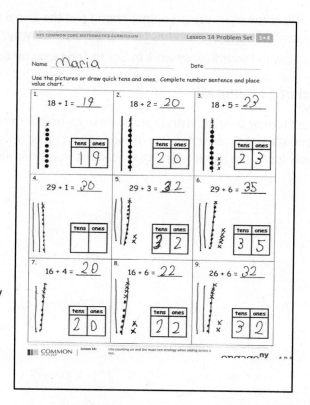

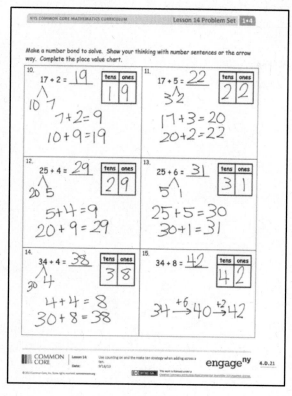

COMMON CORE™

Lesson 14:   Use counting on and the make ten strategy when adding across a ten.

Date: 9/20/13

4.D.18

© 2013 Common Core, Inc. All rights reserved. commoncore.org

- ▪ (Post the chart using a number bond and the arrow way to solve 19 + 3.) Do you notice any similarities in our number bond and the arrow way?
- ▪ How did your fluency work in Get to Ten help you during today's lesson?

Exit Ticket (3 minutes)

After the Student Debrief, instruct students to complete the Exit Ticket. A review of their work will help you assess the students' understanding of the concepts that were presented in the lesson today and plan more effectively for future lessons. You may read the questions aloud to the students.

Lesson 14: Use counting on and the make ten strategy when adding across a ten.

Date: 9/20/13

4.D.

Name _____   Date _____

Use the pictures or draw quick tens and ones. Complete the number sentence and place value chart.

1. 18 + 1 = _____ 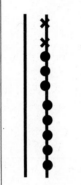 | tens | ones |	2. 18 + 2 = _____ | tens | ones |	3. 18 + 5 = _____ 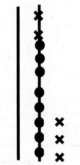 | tens | ones |
4. 29 + 1 = _____ | tens | ones |	5. 29 + 3 = _____ | tens | ones |	6. 29 + 6 = _____ | tens | ones |
7. 16 + 4 = _____ | tens | ones |	8. 16 + 6 = _____ | tens | ones |	9. 26 + 6 = _____ | tens | ones |

COMMON CORE   Lesson 14:   Use counting on and the make ten strategy when adding across a ten.
                    Date: 9/20/13

4.D.20

Make a number bond to solve. Show your thinking with number sentences or the arrow way. Complete the place value chart.

10.

$17 + 2 = $ _____

tens	ones

11.

$17 + 5 = $ _____

tens	ones

12.

$25 + 4 = $ _____

tens	ones

13.

$25 + 6 = $ _____

tens	ones

14.

$34 + 4 = $ _____

tens	ones

15.

$34 + 8 = $ _____

tens	ones

COMMON CORE

Lesson 14: Use counting on and the make ten strategy when adding across a ten.

Date: 9/20/13

4.D

Name _____   Date _____

Draw quick tens and ones. Complete number sentence and place value chart.

1.	2.	3.
17 + 1 = _____	17 + 3 = _____	17 + 6 = _____
tens | ones	tens | ones	tens | ones

Make a number bond to solve. Show your thinking with number sentences or the arrow way. Complete the place value chart.

4.		5.	
32 + 7 = _____	tens | ones	26 + 9 = _____	tens | ones

Name _____ Date _____

Use the pictures or draw quick tens and ones. Complete the number sentence and place value chart.

1.	2.	3.
15 + 3 = _____ 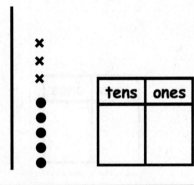	15 + 5 = _____ 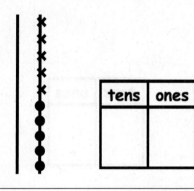	15 + 6 = _____ 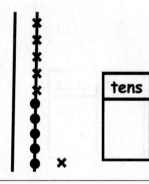
4. 28 + 2 = _____ tens | ones	5. 28 + 4 = _____ tens | ones	6. 28 + 7 = _____ tens | ones
7. 17 + 3 = _____ tens | ones	8. 17 + 7 = _____ tens | ones	9. 27 + 7 = _____ tens | ones

COMMON CORE

Lesson 14:   Use counting on and the make ten strategy when adding across a ten.

Date: 9/20/13

4.D

© 2013 Common Core, Inc. All rights reserved. commoncore.org

Make a number bond to solve. Show your thinking with number sentences or the arrow way. Complete the place value chart.

6.

$13 + 6 = $ _____

tens	ones

7.

$13 + 7 = $ _____

tens	ones

8.

$25 + 5 = $ _____

tens	ones

9.

$25 + 8 = $ _____

tens	ones

10.

$24 + 8 = $ _____

tens	ones

11.

$23 + 9 = $ _____

tens	ones

   Lesson 14:   Use counting on and the make ten strategy when adding across a ten.

Date: 9/20/13

Lesson 15

Objective: Use single-digit sums to support solutions for analogous sums to 40.

Suggested Lesson Structure

- Application Problems   (5 minutes)
- Fluency Practice   (14 minutes)
- Concept Development   (31 minutes)
- Student Debrief   (10 minutes)
  Total Time   **(60 minutes)**

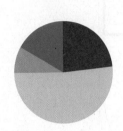

Application Problems (5 minutes)

Today, students should focus on pictorial representations. They should solve without using linking cubes. They read, draw, and write (RDW) to solve one or more of the problems.

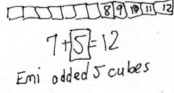

a. Emi had a linking cube train of 6 cubes. She added 3 cubes to the train. How many cubes are in her linking cube train?

b. Emi made another train of linking cubes. She started with 7 cubes and added some more cubes until her train was 12 cubes long. How many cubes did Emi add?

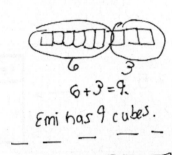

c. Emi made one more train of linking cubes. It was made of 12 linking cubes. She took some cubes off and her train became 4 linking cubes long. How many cubes did Emi take off?

Note: Continue to notice students' strengths and challenges with each problem type presented. Encourage students who seem to struggle when the linking cubes have been removed to visualize, imagine, or draw the cubes as shown in the student work to the right.

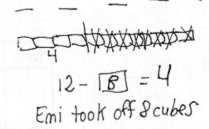

Fluency Practice (14 minutes)

- Number Bond Addition and Subtraction **1.OA.5**   (4 minutes)
- Make Ten Addition with Partners **1.OA.6**   (6 minutes)
- Add Tens **1.NBT.4**   (4 minutes)

| Lesson 15: | Use single-digit sums to support solutions for analogous sums to 40. |
| Date: | 9/20/13 |

4.

Number Bond Addition and Subtraction (4 minutes)

Materials: (S) Personal white boards

Note: This fluency activity builds a student's ability to add and subtract within 10 while reinforcing the relationship between addition and subtraction.

Write a number bond for a number between 0 and 10, with a missing part or whole. Students write an addition and a subtraction sentence with a box for the missing number in each equation. They then solve for the missing number.

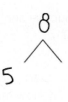

$$5 + \boxed{3} = 8$$

$$8 - 5 = \boxed{3}$$

Make Ten Addition with Partners (6 minutes)

Materials: (S) Personal white boards

Note: This fluency activity reviews how to use the Level 3 strategy of making ten to add two single-digit numbers. Reviewing the make ten strategy will prepare students for today's lesson, in which they systematically connect these problem types to analogous problems within 40 (e.g., students will make ten to solve 9 + 5 and then apply the same strategy to solve 19 + 5 and 29 + 5).

Repeat the activity from G1–M4–Lesson 14.

Add Tens (4 minutes)

Note: This fluency activity reviews adding multiples of 10, which will help prepare students for today's lesson.

T: (Flash 3 on fingers. Pause.) Add ten. The total is?
S: 13.
T: (Flash 3 again.) Add 2 tens. The total is?
S: 23.

Continue flashing numbers from 0 to 10 and instructing students to add multiples of 10. After a minute, say the multiples of 10 the regular way (e.g., 20 instead of 2 tens). For the last minute, say teen numbers and instruct students to add 10 or 2 tens or 20.

Concept Development (31 minutes)

Materials: (T) 5 ten-sticks (e.g., 4 red and 1 yellow), chart paper (S) 4 ten-sticks from the math toolkit, personal white board

Students gather in the meeting area with their materials.

T: (Show 4 red and 2 yellow cubes in a stick.) What is the addition sentence that matches the cubes?
S: 4 + 2 = 6.
T: (Record on the chart. Place a red ten-stick to the left of 4 and 2 cubes, showing 14 + 2.) How many linking cubes are there now?

S: 16.

T: What is the number sentence to add these red and yellow cubes?

S: 14 + 2 = 16.

T: (Record on the chart. Add another red ten-stick, showing 24 + 2.) How many linking cubes are there now? Say the number sentence. (Give wait time.)

S: 24 + 2 = 26.

T: (Record on the chart.) What do you think I'll do next? Turn and talk to your partner.

S: You'll add another ten-stick. → The next problem will be 34 + 2.

T: You're right. (Add another red ten-stick, showing 34 + 2.) How many linking cubes are there now? Say the number sentence. (Give wait time.)

S: 34 + 2 = 36.

T: (Record on the chart.) Many of you got the answer to these questions very quickly. Why? Turn and talk to you partner.

S: The digit in the tens place in the first addend keeps going up. The same thing is happening to the answers, too. → This reminds me of when we added only tens to a number. The ones digit stayed the same but the tens digit changed. → We're always adding 4 and 2. In every problem, the tens are changing but the ones are not because we are not touching the ones.

T: Great observations! Let's try another problem.

T: (Write and show 9 + 5 with 9 red and 5 yellow linking cubes.) Talk to your partner about how you can solve 9 + 5.

S: I can count every cube. → I can count on from 9. → I can make ten first. 10 + 4 = 14.

T: (Call up a volunteer to show 10 and 4 with linking cubes as shown to the right. Record the answer.)

T: (Add another red ten-stick and show 19 + 5.) What is the new addition problem starting with 19?

S: 19 + 5.

T: (Record on the chart.) Turn and talk to you partner about how you can figure out how many cubes there are now.

NOTES ON MULTIPLE MEANS OF REPRESENTATION:

Provide opportunities for students to practice their math facts within 10 throughout the day. Students struggling with mastery of the grade level fluency goal benefit from focused extra practice. Elicit from them which facts they find harder in order to determine that focus. Keep parents informed of these details and offer effective ways they can support the student.

$$4 + 2 = 6$$
$$14 + 2 = 16$$
$$24 + 2 = 26$$
$$34 + 2 = 36$$

S: I can see the cubes. There are 2 tens and 4 ones. That's 24. → I knew that 9 + 5 was 14. That's the simpler problem. We added 10 more to 14. That's 24.

T: The strategy of using what we already know is a very important math strategy for solving problems. (Cover 1 ten-stick with a hand.) We know that 9 + 5 = 14. 19 + 5 is just 10 more than 9 + 5. (Reveal the ten-stick.) 10 more than 14 is?

S: 24.

T: When you show 19 as tens and ones, you can easily see the simpler problem, 9 + 5. (Write the number bond for 19 as 10 and 9.)   9 + 5 is?

S: 14.

T: (Create a chart like the one shown to the right. 9 + 5 = 14.) 10 more than 14 is?

S: 24.

$$19 + 5 = 24$$
$$10 \quad 9$$
$$9 + 5 = 14$$
$$14 + 10 = 24$$

T: (Write 14 + 10 = 24. Add another red ten-stick and show 29 + 5.) Write down the new addition problem on your board starting with 29.

S: (Write 29 + 5.)

T: (Record on the chart.) Break apart 29 into tens and ones. What is the simpler problem?

S: (Make number bond with 29.) 9 + 5.

T: 9 + 5 is?

S: 14.

T: 20 more than 14 is?

S: 34.

T: 29 + 5 is?

S: 34.

$$29 + 5 = 34$$
$$20 \quad 9$$
$$9 + 5 = 14$$
$$14 + 20 = 34$$

T: Using your number bond, let's write the two number sentences that helped us solve this problem.

T/S: Write 9 + 5 = 14, 14 + 20 = 34.

T: (Create a chart as shown to the right.) Turn and talk to your partner about the patterns you notice.

S: The ones stayed the same. But the tens changed because we kept adding more tens. → Every time we add 10 more, the answer also shows 10 more. → 9 + 5 = 14 is always the simpler problem. We solved 9 + 5 which is 14 first. When we added 1 more ten, then the answer went up by 1 more ten.

$$9 + 5 = 14$$
$$19 + 5 = 24$$
$$29 + 5 = 34$$

Repeat the process and have student pairs work with their linking cubes and record their work using the following sequence:

- 5 + 4, 15 + 4, 25 + 4, 35 + 4

- 4 + 6, 14 + 6, 24 + 6, 34 + 6

- 2 + 7, 12 + 7, 22 + 7, 32 + 7

NOTES ON MULTIPLE MEANS FOR ENGAGEMENT:

Chose just right numbers in order to provide ample opportunities for students to experience success in order to build confidence in their math skills.

- 9 + 3, 19 + 3, 29 + 3
- 8 + 6, 18 + 6, 28 + 6
- 8 + 8, 18 + 8, 28 + 8
- 5 + 7, 5 + 17, 5 + 27

Next, follow the suggested sequence and have students identify the *simpler problem* before solving the given problem: 17 + 2, 19 + 2, 28 + 2, 28 + 4, 27 + 6, and 25 + 7.

Problem Set (10 minutes)

Students should do their personal best to complete the Problem Set within the allotted 10 minutes. For some classes, it may be appropriate to modify the assignment by specifying which problems they work on first.

Student Debrief (10 minutes)

Lesson Objective: Use single-digit sums to support solutions for analogous sums to 40.

The Student Debrief is intended to invite reflection and active processing of the total lesson experience.

Invite students to review their solutions for the Problem Set. They should check work by comparing answers with a partner before going over answers as a class. Look for misconceptions or misunderstandings that can be addressed in the Debrief. Guide students in a conversation to debrief the Problem Set and process the lesson.

You may choose to use any combination of the questions below to lead the discussion.

- How did looking for patterns help you solve the problems on the second page of your Problem Set?
- Look at Problems 8(a–d) and 8(i–k). In (a–d), the tens in the answers are the same as the tens in the first addend of each problem, but in (i–k), the tens in the answers do not match the tens in the first addends. Explain why this is so.

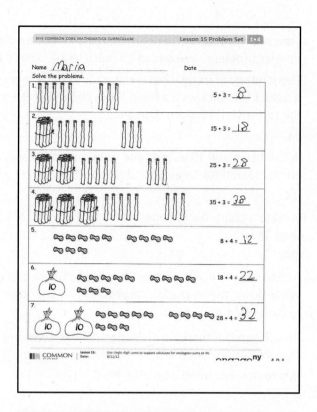

- You solved 36 + 2 easily in Problem 8(d). How can this problem help you solve 36 + 3? How can knowing 36 + 3 then help us solve 26 + 3?
- What new strategy did you learn to solve addition problems when one addend is a two-digit number?
- Look at the Application Problems and the answers from the Problem Set. Find the related addition sentence that could have helped you solve the subtraction problem.

Exit Ticket (3 minutes)

After the Student Debrief, instruct students to complete the Exit Ticket. A review of their work will help you assess the students' understanding of the concepts that were presented in the lesson today and plan more effectively for future lessons. You may read the questions aloud to the students.

Name _____ Date _____

Solve the problems.

1.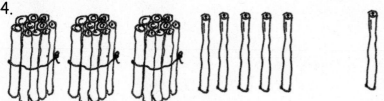

   5 + 3 = _____

2.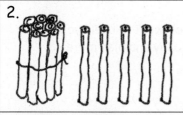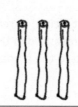

   15 + 3 = _____

3.

   25 + 3 = _____

4.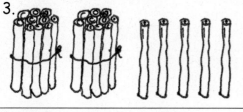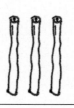

   35 + 3 = _____

5.

   8 + 4 = _____

6.

   18 + 4 = _____

7.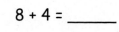

   28 + 4 = _____

8. Solve the problems.

a. 6 + 2 = _____	b. 16 + 2 = _____	c. 26 + 2 = _____	d. 36 + 2 = _____
e. 6 + 4 = _____	f. 16 + 4 = _____	g. 26 + 4 = _____	h. 36 + 4 = _____
i. 9 + 2 = _____	j. 19 + 2 = _____	k. 29 + 2 = _____	
l. 8 + 6 = _____	m. 18 + 6 = _____	n. 28 + 6 = _____	

Solve the problems. Show the 1-digit addition sentence that helped you solve.

9.   23 + 6 = _____   _____

10.   27 + 6 = _____   _____

Name _____   Date _____

1. Solve the problems.

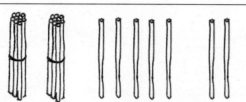

| a. | | $7 + 5 =$ _____ |

| b. | | $17 + 5 =$ _____ |

| c. | | $27 + 5 =$ _____ |

Solve the problems.

2. a. $5 + 3 =$ _____

    b. $15 + 3 =$ _____

    c. $25 + 3 =$ _____

    d. $35 + 3 =$ _____

3. a. $5 + 8 =$ _____

    b. $15 + 8 =$ _____

    c. $25 + 8 =$ _____

Name _____   Date _____

Solve the problems.

1.

   $5 + 4 = $ _____

2.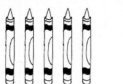

   $15 + 4 = $ _____

3.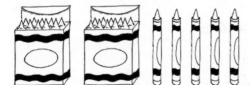

   $25 + 4 = $ _____

4.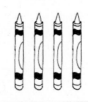

   $35 + 4 = $ _____

5.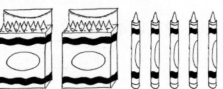

   $8 + 4 = $ _____

6.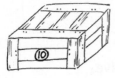

   $18 + 4 = $ _____

7.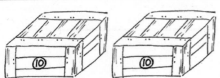

   $28 + 4 = $ _____

Lesson 15:   Use single-digit sums to support solutions for analogous sums to 40.
Date: 9/20/13

4.D.34

Use the first number sentence in each set to help you solve the other problems.

8. a. $5 + 2 =$ ___ b. $15 + 2 =$ ___ c. $25 + 2 =$ ___ d. $35 + 2 =$ ___	9. a. $5 + 5 =$ ___ b. $15 + 5 =$ ___ c. $25 + 5 =$ ___ d. $35 + 5 =$ ___
10. a. $2 + 7 =$ ___ b. $12 + 7 =$ ___ c. $22 + 7 =$ ___	11. a. $7 + 4 =$ ___ b. $17 + 4 =$ ___ c. $27 + 4 =$ ___
12. a. $8 + 7 =$ ___ b. $18 + 7 =$ ___ c. $28 + 7 =$ ___	13. a. $3 + 9 =$ ___ b. $13 + 9 =$ ___ c. $23 + 9 =$ ___

Solve the problems. Show the 1-digit addition sentence that helped you solve.

14. $24 + 5 =$ _____ _____

15. $24 + 7 =$ _____ _____

Lesson 16

Objective: Add ones and ones or tens and tens.

Suggested Lesson Structure

▇ Application Problems	(5 minutes)
▇ Fluency Practice	(9 minutes)
▇ Concept Development	(36 minutes)
▇ Student Debrief	(10 minutes)
Total Time	**(60 minutes)**

Application Problems (5 minutes)

Use the RDW process to solve one or more of the problems, without using linking cubes.

a. Emi had a linking cube train with 14 blue cubes and 2 red cubes. How many cubes were in her train?

b. Emi made another train with 16 yellow cubes and some green cubes. The train was made of 19 linking cubes. How many green cubes did she use?

c. Emi wants to make her train of 8 linking cubes into a train of 17 cubes. How many cubes does Emi need?

Note: Today, students use larger numbers to solve problems that are similar to the Application Problems used over the past few days. Notice children who were successful with the earlier set but struggled with the problem today. These students may have difficulty envisioning the relationships between the larger quantities. Encourage these students to change from empty circles to filled-in circles at the ten, as shown in the image, to help them break down and visualize the larger numbers.

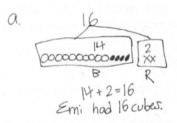

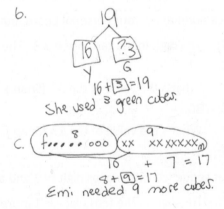

Fluency Practice (9 minutes)

▪ Analogous Addition Sentences **1.NBT.4**   (5 minutes)
▪ Digit Detective **1.NBT.2**   (4 minutes)

Analogous Addition Sentences (5 minutes)

Materials: (S) Personal white boards, dice

Note: This fluency activity reviews yesterday's lesson. Some students may wish to show their work with number bonds, while others may choose to work mentally.

Students work in partners. For struggling students, consider replacing the 6 on the die with a 0 so the sums do not cross ten.

- Step 1: Students roll a die and write the number rolled. They then make a list, adding 1 ten to their number on each new line up to 3 tens. (See diagram to the right.)
- Step 2: Students write equations, adding the number on their partner's die to each line.
- Partners exchange boards and check each other's work.

As students work, make sure to circulate and monitor students' understanding of recently introduced concepts.

STEP 1	
Partner A	Partner B
4	3
14	13
24	23
34	33

STEP 2	
Partner A	Partner B
4 + 3 = 7	3 + 4 = 7
14 + 3 = 17	13 + 4 = 17
24 + 3 = 27	23 + 4 = 27
34 + 3 = 37	33 + 4 = 37

Digit Detective (4 minutes)

Materials: (T/S) Personal white boards

Note: This activity reviews place value, which prepares students to add ones to ones or tens to tens in today's lesson. As always, pause to give students enough time to think and write before snapping.

Write a number on your personal board, but do not show students.

- T: The digit in the tens place is 3. The digit in the ones place is 1. What's my number? (Snap.)
- S: 31.
- T: What's the value of the 3? (Snap.)
- S: 30.
- T: What's the value of the 1? (Snap.)
- S: 1.

Repeat sequence with a ones digit of 3 and a tens digit of 3.

- T: The digit in the tens place is 1 more than 2. The digit in the ones place is equal to 7 – 4. What's my number? (Snap.)
- S: 33.
- T: The digit in the ones place is equal to 2 + 6. The digit in the tens place is equal to 8 – 6. What's my number? (Snap.)
- S: 28.

As with the above example, begin with easy clues and gradually increase the complexity.

Lesson 16:   Add ones and ones or tens and tens.
Date: 9/20/13

4.D.

Concept Development (36 minutes)

Materials: (T) 4 ten-sticks, 4 dimes, 10 pennies, chart paper (S) 4 ten-sticks, 4 dimes, and 10 pennies from
the math toolkit, personal white board

Students gather in the meeting area with their partners and materials.

T: (Write 16 + 2 and 16 + 20 on the board.) Using your linking cubes, Partner A, show how you would
solve 16 + 2. Partner B, show how you would solve 16 + 20.

S: (Solve.)

T: Share your work with your partner. How are they similar? How are
they different?

S: We both started with the same number, 16. → We added a
different number to 16. I added 2, but my partner added
20. → But we both added 2 more things to 16. I added 2
ones. My partner added 2 tens. → I added my 2 ones to 6
ones. My partner added his 2 tens to 1 ten.

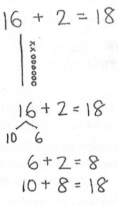

T: Excellent job comparing. Let's make quick ten drawings to
show how we can solve these problems. Start by drawing
16.

S: (Draw 16 on their personal boards.)

T: Let's add 2 ones. Should we add to the ones or to the tens?
Why?

S: To the 6 ones because we are adding 6 ones and 2 ones. →
We can add to the tens or the ones. We can do 10 + 2 = 12,
then 12 + 6 = 18. → But it's much easier to add the ones. 6
and 2 is 8. 10 and 8 is 18. → The ones!

T: You're right. Adding the ones together is much easier. Add 2 to
your ones. (Wait.) 6 ones and 2 ones is?

S: 8 ones.

T: How many tens are there?

S: 1 ten.

T: 1 ten 8 ones is?

S: 18.

T: (Make a number bond for 16.) Turn and talk to your partner about
why 16 is broken apart into 10 and 6.

S: We added 6 ones and 2 ones, so it's smart to break apart 16 into 10 and 6. → That makes it easy for
me to see the ones. → I like adding 6 + 2. It's easy for me. 10 + 6 is easy, too, 16!

T: 6 and 2 is? (Write 6 + 2 = 8 once students have answered.)

S: 8.

T: 10 and 8 is? (Write 10 + 8 = 18 once students have answered.)

**COMMON
CORE**   Lesson 16:   Add ones and ones or tens and tens.
Date: 9/20/13

4.D.38

S: 18.

T: (Point to 16 + 20.) This time, what's different?

S: Instead of adding 2 ones, we are adding 2 tens.

T: In our drawing, should we add 2 tens to the tens or the ones? Turn to your partner and explain your reason.

S: To the tens! → 1 ten + 2 tens = 3 tens. That's easy. → We can add it to the ones. But we'll have to think, "What's 16 + 20?" That's not so easy. But if we add to the tens, it's much easier. → When you see 3 ten-sticks, it's easy to see that it's 30. 30 + 6 is easy, too.

T: You are right! Adding tens to tens is much easier. Show what that looks like in your drawing. Add 20, or *2 tens*. (Wait.) How many tens are there?

S: 3 tens.

T: How many ones?

S: 6 ones.

T: 3 tens 6 ones is?

S: 36.

T: Turn and talk to your partner about breaking apart to add 2 tens to the tens first.

S: Break apart 16 into 10 and 6. → It takes out the ten that we need to add to the 2 tens. 20 and 10 is 30. Then we add 6 more to get 36.

T: Write down two number sentences to show how we add the tens first, and then the rest, to solve.

S: (Write 10 + 20 = 30 and 30 + 6 = 36.)

T: When we have an addition problem, what is a good question to ask ourselves before adding the second addend? (Point to the chart.) Think about how we solved 16 + 2 and 16 + 20.

S: Ask and decide, "Should we add to the ones or to the tens." → When you add ones to ones or tens to tens, it makes the problem easier to solve.

Repeat the process and have Student A solve 18 + 20 and Student B solve 18 + 2 using cubes and quick ten drawings and compare their work.

T: Everyone, show 18 with your cubes. (Wait.) Let's add 2. But first, we need to ask…

S: Should we add to the ones or to the tens?

T: What should we add the 2 to?

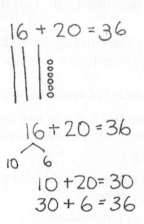

$$16 + 20 = 36$$

$$16 + 20 = 36$$
$$10 \quad 6$$
$$10 + 20 = 30$$
$$30 + 6 = 36$$

NOTES ON MULTIPLE MEANS OF REPRESENTATION:

Students below grade level might benefit from place value charts as well as concrete models to help them determine whether to add to the tens or ones.

$$18 + 2 = 20$$

$$18 + 2 = 20$$
$$10 \quad 8$$
$$8 + 2 = 10$$
$$10 + 10 = 20$$

COMMON CORE™   Lesson 16:   Add ones and ones or tens and tens.
Date: 9/20/13

4.D.

S: The ones!

T: Add 2 to the ones. (Wait.) 18 + 2 is?

S: 20.

T: Turn and share with your partner about how you got your answer.

S: I added 2 cubes to the 8 cubes. It made another ten-stick! → I now have 2 ten-sticks. 10 and 10 is 20. → 8 plus 2 equals 10, 10 plus 10 equals 20.

T: Use a quick ten drawing and a number bond to show how you added ones and ones together.

S: (Complete drawings and number bonds.)

Repeat the process as partner work following the suggested sequence:

- 17 + 20 and 17 + 2
- 19 + 1 and 19 + 10
- 15 + 20 and 15 + 2

To help students see the relationship between tens and ones and dimes and pennies, have every student use coins, coin drawings, and number bonds to solve: 14 + 2, 14 + 20, 26 + 10, and 26 + 4.

Problem Set (10 minutes)

Students should do their personal best to complete the Problem Set within the allotted 10 minutes. For some classes, it may be appropriate to modify the assignment by specifying which problems they work on first.

Student Debrief (10 minutes)

Lesson Objective: Add ones and ones or tens and tens.

The Student Debrief is intended to invite reflection and active processing of the total lesson experience.

Invite students to review their solutions for the Problem Set. They should check work by comparing answers with a partner before going over answers as a class. Look for misconceptions or misunderstandings that can be addressed in the Debrief. Guide students in a conversation to debrief the Problem Set and process the lesson.

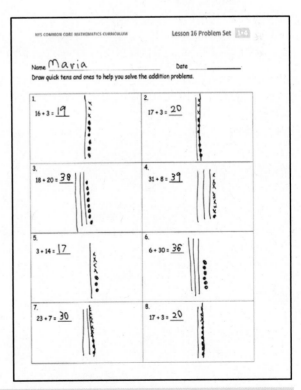

You may choose to use any combination of the questions below to lead the discussion.

- Share your quick ten drawing for Problem 6 with your partner. How did you make your math drawing? Why?
- How was solving Problem 7 helpful in solving Problem 8?
- How are Problems 11 and 12 related?
- For Problem 5, a student says 3 + 14 = 44. How can you help him understand his mistake?
- How did you determine whether to add to the ones place or the tens place?
- How did the Application Problems connect to today's lesson?

Exit Ticket (3 minutes)

After the Student Debrief, instruct students to complete the Exit Ticket. A review of their work will help you assess the students' understanding of the concepts that were presented in the lesson today and plan more effectively for future lessons. You may read the questions aloud to the students.

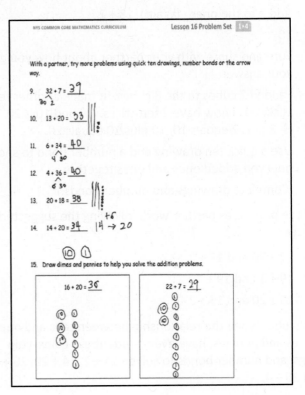

COMMON CORE™

Lesson 16:   Add ones and ones or tens and tens.
Date: 9/20/13

4.D.

© 2013 Common Core, Inc. All rights reserved. commoncore.org

Name _____   Date _____

Draw quick tens and ones to help you solve the addition problems.

1. 16 + 3 = _____	2. 17 + 3 = _____
3. 18 + 20 = _____	4. 31 + 8 = _____
5. 3 + 14 = _____	6. 6 + 30 = _____
7. 23 + 7 = _____	8. 17 + 3 = _____

COMMON CORE™   Lesson 16:   Add ones and ones or tens and tens.

Date: 9/20/13   4.D.42

With a partner, try more problems using quick ten drawings, number bonds, or the arrow way.

9.   32 + 7 = _____

10.   13 + 20 = _____

11.   6 + 34 = _____

12.   4 + 36 = _____

13.   20 + 18 = _____

14.   14 + 20 = _____

15.   Draw dimes and pennies to help you solve the addition problems.

16 + 20 = _____	22 + 7 = _____

COMMON CORE™   Lesson 16:   Add ones and ones or tens and tens.
Date: 9/20/13

4.D

Name _____ Date _____

Solve using quick ten drawings to show your work.

24 + 5	14 + 20

Draw number bonds to solve.

19 + 20	36 + 3

Draw dimes and pennies to help you solve the addition problem.

13 + 20

COMMON CORE

Lesson 16:   Add ones and ones or tens and tens.
Date: 9/20/13

4.D.44

Name _____ Date _____

Draw quick tens and ones to help you solve the addition problems.

1. 17 + 2 = _____	2. 17 + 3 = _____
3. 14 + 3 = _____	4. 24 + 10 = _____

Make a number bond or use the arrow way to solve the addition problems.

5. 6 + 24 = _____	6. 14 + 20 = _____

COMMON CORE™ Lesson 16:   Add ones and ones or tens and tens.
Date: 9/20/13

4.D.4

Solve each addition sentence and match.

22 + 1 = _____

13 + 6 = _____

3 + 26 = _____

37 + 3 = _____

22 + 10 = _____

Lesson 17

Objective: Add ones and ones or tens and tens.

Suggested Lesson Structure

■ Application Problems (5 minutes)
■ Fluency Practice (12 minutes)
▢ Concept Development (33 minutes)
■ Student Debrief (10 minutes)

Total Time **(60 minutes)**

Application Problems (5 minutes)

Use the RDW process to solve one or more of the problems.

a. Ben had 7 fish. He bought 4 fish at the store. How many fish does Ben have?

b. Maria has fish. She had 7 fish in her tank and bought some more fish until she had 9 fish. How many fish did Maria buy?

c. Anton has 8 fish. A few of the fish died and now Anton has 4 fish. How many fish died?

Note: Today, students solve similar math stories within a new context. Notice students who easily solved the problems with cubes but found today's problems more challenging. These students may need support visualizing story contexts.

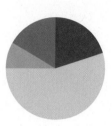

Fluency Practice (12 minutes)

- Core Addition Fluency Review: Missing Addends **1.OA.6**   (5 minutes)
- Relating Addition and Subtraction **1.OA.4**   (2 minutes)
- Analogous Addition Sentences **1.NBT.4**   (5 minutes)

Core Addition Fluency Review: Missing Addends (5 minutes)

Materials: (S) Missing Addends Core Addition Fluency Review

Note: This review sheet contains the majority of addition facts with sums of 5–10, which is part of the required core fluency for Grade 1. The focus on missing addends strengthens students' ability to count on, a

Level 2 strategy that first graders should master. Keep this activity out so students can use it in the next fluency activity.

Students complete as many problems as they can in three minutes. Choose a counting sequence for early finishers to practice on the back of their papers. When time runs out, read the answers aloud so students can correct their work. Encourage students to remember how many problems they answered correctly in the allotted time so they can work to improve their scores on future Missing Addends Core Addition Fluency Reviews.

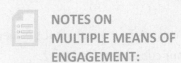

NOTES ON MULTIPLE MEANS OF ENGAGEMENT:

Encourage students to set goals for improvement on sprints and fluency reviews. Provide scaffolds, strategies, and opportunities for practice to help them reach their personal goals.

Relating Addition and Subtraction (2 minutes)

Materials: (S) Missing Addends Core Addition Fluency Review from previous activity

Note: This fluency activity targets the first grade's core fluency requirement. Reviewing the relationship between addition and subtraction is especially beneficial for students who continue to find subtraction challenging.

Students choose a column from the review sheet and rewrite each problem as a subtraction equation, seeing how many they can do in two minutes.

Analogous Addition Sentences (5 minutes)

Materials: (S) Personal white boards, dice

Note: This is the second day students are doing this partner activity. As students work, ask if it is easier the second day.

Follow instructions in G1–M4–Lesson 16.

Concept Development (33 minutes)

Materials: (T) Ten-sticks, chart paper (S) Ten-sticks from math toolkit, personal white boards, game cards for Addition and Subtraction with Cards

Students gather in the meeting area with their partners and materials.

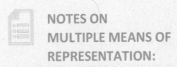

NOTES ON MULTIPLE MEANS OF REPRESENTATION:

Highlight the critical vocabulary such as *quick ten drawings, number bonds, tens, ones,* and *addends,* and use pictorial representations to support student understanding. Have students use these terms as they share their thinking. This will support vocabulary development.

T: (Write 19 + 2 on chart paper and show 19 red cubes on the floor.) What are we adding to 19?

S: 2.

T: 2 what?

S: 2 ones.

Lesson 17:   Add ones and ones or tens and tens.
Date: 9/20/13

4.D.48

T: Where should we add the 2 ones, to the tens or the ones? Turn and talk to your partner about why?

S: The ones! → To 9 ones! → It's easier to add ones together.

T: Use your cubes to solve 19 + 2.

T: (Circulate to observe the different strategies students are using and select students to demonstrate.)

S: We knew that 19 needs 1 more to make the next ten. So we took 1 from the 2 and made a ten. Now we have 20 and 1. That's 21. → We saw 10 ones in 9 + 1. We now have 2 tens and 1 one. That's 21. → We added the ones together. 9 + 2 = 11. One more ten is 21.

T: Excellent strategies! Just like we did yesterday, let's add the ones together. 9 and 2 is?

S: 11.

T: What more do we still have to add?

S: 1 ten.

T: 11 and 10 is?

S: 21.

T: Say the number sentence starting with 19.

S: 19 + 2 = 21.

Have students represent their work in quick ten drawings.

T: Let's represent our work using a number bond. Which number did we break apart?

S: We broke apart 19 into 10 and 9. That makes it easier to see the ones. I can add 9 and 2 first, then add 10.

T: Great. (Chart the number bond and complete the number sentence.) (Point to each number as you say it.) 9 and 2 is?

S: 11.

T: 11 and 10 is?

S: 21.

T: 19 + 2 is?

S: 21.

T: (Write 19 + 20 on the chart.) Show 19 using your cubes or quick ten drawings.

S: (Show or draw 1 ten-stick and 9 ones.)

T: Before adding the next addend with your cubes, we should ask…

S: Am I adding tens or am I adding ones?

T: Correct! So which are we adding? Tens or ones?

S: Tens.

T: Yes. Add 2 tens. (Pause.) 1 ten and 2 tens is?

$19 + 2 = 21$

$19 + 2 = 21$

$10 \quad 9$

$9 + 2 = 11$

$11 + 10 = 21$

S: 3 tens.

T: How many ones are there?

S: 9 ones.

T: 3 tens 9 ones is?

S: 39.

Guide students as they make the number bond to represent 19 + 20 and write two addition sentences.

Repeat the process following the suggested sequence:

- 16 + 2 and 16 + 20
- 2 + 13 and 20 + 13
- 10 + 28 and 28 + 1
- 8 + 27

Have students practice asking, "Do I add to the ones or add to the tens?" before representing their work with cubes or quick tens and the number bond with two sentences. When appropriate, have students choose just one method to solve and explain their choice to their partner or to the whole group. For more challenging examples, have students add dimes and pennies when using the sequence above.

For the remainder of time, have partners play Addition and Subtraction with Cards (follow instructions from G1–M4–Lesson 12) with the new cards labeled *D*.

Problem Set (10 minutes)

Students should do their personal best to complete the Problem Set within the allotted 10 minutes. For some classes, it may be appropriate to modify the assignment by specifying which problems they work on first.

Student Debrief (10 minutes)

Lesson Objective: Add ones and ones or tens and tens.

The Student Debrief is intended to invite reflection and active processing of the total lesson experience.

Invite students to review their solutions for the Problem Set. They should check work by comparing answers with a partner before going over answers as a class. Look for misconceptions or misunderstandings that can be addressed in the Debrief. Guide students in a conversation to debrief the Problem Set and process the lesson.

You may choose to use any combination of the questions below to lead the discussion.

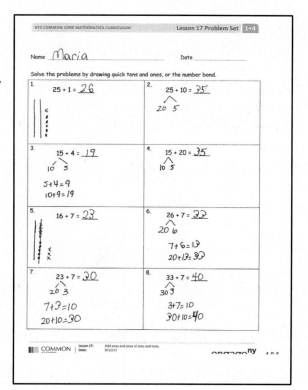

COMMON CORE™

Lesson 17:   Add ones and ones or tens and tens.
Date: 9/20/13

© 2013 Common Core, Inc. All rights reserved. commoncore.org

4.D.50

- Share the problems you solved using quick tens and a number bond in the Problem Set with your partner. Why did you choose to solve these problems using the quick ten or a number bond?
- How can solving 11(a) help you solve 11(b)?
- Look at Problems 3 and 5. In both problems, we added ones to ones. In the answer, why did the tens stay the same in Problem 3 but the tens changed in Problem 5?
- How can your fluency work with the die (Analogous Addition Sentences) help you solve addition problems in today's lesson?

Exit Ticket (3 minutes)

After the Student Debrief, instruct students to complete the Exit Ticket. A review of their work will help you assess the students' understanding of the concepts that were presented in the lesson today and plan more effectively for future lessons. You may read the questions aloud to the students.

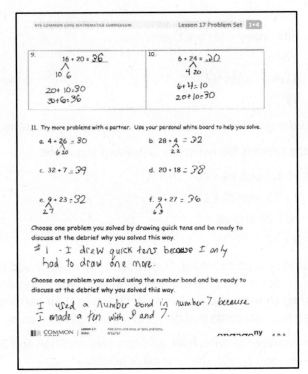

Lesson 17:   Add ones and ones or tens and tens.
Date: 9/20/13

4.D.

Name _____   Date _____

Core Addition Fluency Review: Missing Addends

1. $5 + \underline{\hphantom{xx}} = 5$ 16. $6 + \underline{\hphantom{xx}} = 7$ 31. $9 + \underline{\hphantom{xx}} = 9$

2. $4 + \underline{\hphantom{xx}} = 5$ 17. $1 + \underline{\hphantom{xx}} = 7$ 32. $0 + \underline{\hphantom{xx}} = 9$

3. $2 + \underline{\hphantom{xx}} = 5$ 18. $0 + \underline{\hphantom{xx}} = 7$ 33. $1 + \underline{\hphantom{xx}} = 9$

4. $3 + \underline{\hphantom{xx}} = 5$ 19. $7 + \underline{\hphantom{xx}} = 7$ 34. $2 + \underline{\hphantom{xx}} = 9$

5. $0 + \underline{\hphantom{xx}} = 5$ 20. $3 + \underline{\hphantom{xx}} = 7$ 35. $7 + \underline{\hphantom{xx}} = 9$

6. $1 + \underline{\hphantom{xx}} = 5$ 21. $4 + \underline{\hphantom{xx}} = 7$ 36. $6 + \underline{\hphantom{xx}} = 9$

7. $1 + \underline{\hphantom{xx}} = 6$ 22. $4 + \underline{\hphantom{xx}} = 8$ 37. $5 + \underline{\hphantom{xx}} = 9$

8. $0 + \underline{\hphantom{xx}} = 6$ 23. $5 + \underline{\hphantom{xx}} = 8$ 38. $3 + \underline{\hphantom{xx}} = 9$

9. $6 + \underline{\hphantom{xx}} = 6$ 24. $6 + \underline{\hphantom{xx}} = 8$ 39. $4 + \underline{\hphantom{xx}} = 9$

10. $5 + \underline{\hphantom{xx}} = 6$ 25. $2 + \underline{\hphantom{xx}} = 8$ 40. $4 + \underline{\hphantom{xx}} = 10$

11. $3 + \underline{\hphantom{xx}} = 6$ 26. $3 + \underline{\hphantom{xx}} = 8$ 41. $5 + \underline{\hphantom{xx}} = 10$

12. $4 + \underline{\hphantom{xx}} = 6$ 27. $0 + \underline{\hphantom{xx}} = 8$ 42. $6 + \underline{\hphantom{xx}} = 10$

13. $2 + \underline{\hphantom{xx}} = 6$ 28. $8 + \underline{\hphantom{xx}} = 8$ 43. $3 + \underline{\hphantom{xx}} = 10$

14. $2 + \underline{\hphantom{xx}} = 7$ 28. $7 + \underline{\hphantom{xx}} = 8$ 44. $1 + \underline{\hphantom{xx}} = 10$

15. $5 + \underline{\hphantom{xx}} = 7$ 30. $1 + \underline{\hphantom{xx}} = 8$ 45. $2 + \underline{\hphantom{xx}} = 10$

Name _____   Date _____

Solve the problems by drawing quick tens and ones or a number bond.

1. 25 + 1 = ____	2. 25 + 10 = ____
3. 15 + 4 = ____	4. 15 + 20 = ____
5. 16 + 7 = ____	6. 26 + 7 = ____
7. 23 + 7 = ____	8. 33 + 7 = ____

9. 16 + 20 = _____	10. 6 + 24 = _____

11. Try more problems with a partner. Use your personal white board to help you solve.

    a. 4 + 26   b. 28 + 4

    c. 32 + 7   d. 20 + 18

    e. 9 + 23   f. 9 + 27

Choose one problem you solved by drawing quick tens and be ready to discuss.

Choose one problem you solved using the number bond and be ready to discuss.

Name _____ Date _____

Find the totals using quick ten drawings or number bonds.

1. 17 + 8	2. 28 + 7
3. 24 + 10	4. 19 + 20

COMMON CORE™

Lesson 17:   Add ones and ones or tens and tens.
Date: 9/20/13

4.D.

© 2013 Common Core, Inc. All rights reserved. commoncore.org

Name _____   Date _____

Use quick ten drawings or number bonds to make true number sentences.

1. 13 + 20 = _____	2. 23 + 6 = _____
3. 10 + 23 = _____	4. 28 + 6 = _____
5. 26 + 7 = _____	6. 20 + 17 = _____

7. How did you solve Problem 5? Why did you choose to solve it that way?

Solve using quick ten drawings or number bonds.

8. 23 + 9 = _____	9. 27 + 7 = _____
10. 24 + 10 = _____	11. 20 + 18 = _____
12. 28 + 9 = _____	13. 29 9 = _____

14. How did you solve Problem 11? Why did you choose to solve it that way?

G1-M4-Topic D Flashcards (and Review Subtraction)

35 + 4 D	**24 + 3** D
24 + 6 D	**28 + 4** D
35 + 5 D	**22 + 8** D
17 + 7 D	**31 + 6** D

24 + 9	**8 + 28**
26 + 8	**3 + 33**
7 + 32	**29 + 7**
3 + 18	**18 - 3**
17 - 4	**19 - 5**

Lesson 18

Objective: Share and critique peer strategies for adding two-digit numbers.

Suggested Lesson Structure

■ Application Problems   (5 minutes)
■ Fluency Practice   (12 minutes)
■ Concept Development   (33 minutes)
■ Student Debrief   (10 minutes)
    Total Time   **(60 minutes)**

Application Problems (5 minutes)

Use the RDW process to solve one or both of the problems.

a.   Some ducks were in a pond. 4 baby ducks joined them. Now there are 6 ducks in the pond. How many ducks were in the pond at first?

b.   Some frogs were in the pond. Three jumped out and now there are 5 frogs in the pond. How many frogs were in the pond at first?

Note: Today's Application Problems use *add to* and *take from* problems with the unknown in the *starting position*. For most students, this is a difficult problem type, and it is for this reason that the numbers in the stories are small.

Notice how students attempt the problem. Those who simply add the two numbers in the first problem or subtract the two numbers in the last problem may need additional reinforcement in reading one sentence at a time as they review their drawings to find the matching story parts.

Fluency Practice (12 minutes)

- Core Addition Fluency Review: Missing Addends **1.OA.6**   (5 minutes)
- Relating Addition and Subtraction **1.OA.4**   (2 minutes)
- Analogous Addition Sentences **1.NBT.4**   (5 minutes)

Lesson 18:   Share and critique peer strategies for adding two-digit numbers.
Date: 9/20/13

4.D.60

Core Addition Fluency Review: Missing Addends (5 minutes)

Materials: (S) Missing Addends Core Addition Fluency Review
(from G1–M4–Lesson 17)

Note: This review sheet contains the majority of addition facts with sums of 5–10, which is part of the required core fluency for Grade 1. The focus on missing addends strengthens students' ability to count on, a Level 2 strategy that first graders should master.

Students complete as many problems as they can in three minutes. Choose a counting sequence for early finishers to practice on the back of their papers. When time runs out, read the answers aloud so students can correct their work. Celebrate improvement by having students compare yesterday's total correct with today's total correct. Share a class cheer for the student(s) with the most improved score.

NOTES ON MULTIPLE MEANS OF ENGAGEMENT:

Scaffold sprints and fluency reviews for students who may be having a difficult time remembering basic math facts. Privately provide a modified version of the sprint or review so students can feel successful while building fluency with math facts.

Relating Addition and Subtraction (2 minutes)

Materials: (S) Missing Addends Core Addition Fluency Review from previous activity

Note: This fluency activity targets the first grade's core fluency requirement and **1.OA.4**.

Students choose a column from the review sheet and rewrite each problem as a subtraction equation, seeing how many they can do in two minutes.

Analogous Addition Sentences (5 minutes)

Materials: (S) Personal white boards, dice or numeral cards 0–10.

Note: Today, assign partners of equal ability and give students with a strong understanding of sums and differences to 12 numeral cards instead of dice. The cards go up to 10, so they will be more of a challenge since there will be more opportunities to make ten.

Repeat the activity from G1–M2–Lesson 16.

Concept Development (33 minutes)

Materials: (T) Student work samples (template at end of lesson), projector (S) Personal white boards

Have students come to the meeting area and sit in a semi-circle.

  T: (Write 17 + 4 on the board.) Turn and talk to your partner about how you would solve this problem.
  S: (Discuss as teacher circulates and listens.)

Lesson 18:   Share and critique peer strategies for adding two-digit numbers.
Date: 9/20/13

4.D

T: (Project Student A work.) Turn and talk to your partner about how he showed his solution to 17 + 4 and think about how we can label his work.

S: Let's label it the arrow way. → He got to the next ten by adding 3. Then he added the 1 that was left and got 21. → You can see his thinking in the number sentences, too.

T: Yes! The arrow way and the number sentences clearly show what he was thinking. I am going to label this work *The Arrow Way*. (Label work A.)

T: (Project Student B work.) How did this student show how to solve 17 + 4?

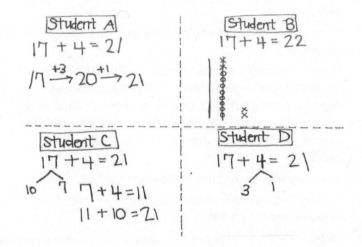

S: She drew quick tens.

T: (Label this work *Quick Ten Drawing*.)

S: (Continue.) It looks like she added the ones together. She showed how she made a ten by drawing a line through the 10 ones. → She added 2 tens and 2 ones and got 22. → I noticed a mistake! She drew 18 first instead of 17! She drew an extra circle. She added 4 correctly using X's, but because she started out by drawing the wrong number, her answer is wrong. → She should have drawn 17 and 4. She should have gotten 21 as the answer.

T: What are some ways this student can improve her work?

S: She needs to count carefully especially when she's drawing her ones. → She should check her work with her partner. Then she might have caught her mistake.

T: Even though drawing is easy for many of you, it's not always the best way to get the correct answer because sometimes you have to make so many circles and X's. Somewhere along the way, you can lose count and make a mistake.

T: Work carefully and show 17 + 4 using the quick ten drawing on your board. Then check your work with your partner.

S: (Make a quick ten drawing showing 21 as the sum and check with partner.)

T: (Project Student C and D work.) Let's compare Student C's work and Student D's work. Did they solve the problem in the same way? What similarities and differences do you notice? Turn and talk to your partner.

S: They both used number bonds.

T: (Label these works *Number Bond*.)

S: (Continue.) They used number bonds but broke apart different numbers. → Student C added the ones first. → Student D made the next ten.

T: Turn and talk to your partner about which student work best shows the tens.

S: I think Student D shows the tens the best because I can see that 17 + 3 = 20 and that is 2 tens. → I think Student C shows the tens the best because I can see that 17 is 10 and 7. I see the 10 in 17.

Lesson 18:   Share and critique peer strategies for adding two-digit numbers.
Date: 9/20/13

4.D.62

T: Can both students' work be correct even though they broke apart different numbers?

S: Yes. → You can break apart different numbers and get the correct answer, as long as you add every part.

T: What is a compliment you can give to each of these students?

S: They drew correct number bonds. → Student C added the ones together first. She clearly showed her two steps by writing both addition sentences. → Student D made the next ten from 17. He did a good job breaking apart 4 into 3 and 1 so that he could make 20 with 17 and 3.

T: What are some ways they could improve their work?

S: Student D could have written two addition sentences to show how he got 21.

MP.3

NOTES ON MULTIPLE MEANS OF REPRESENTATION:

Facilitate student discussions to provide options for comprehension. Guide students to recognize strategies that can make math easier, for example, breaking a larger number into number bonds as well as looking for patterns and structures in their work.

T: (Write 19 + 5 on the board.) It's your turn to solve a problem. You may use any method to solve but you must show your work. When you are finished, swap your work with your partner and study it. Give them a compliment and a suggestion about how to improve their work.

Have students swap boards with their partner and discuss the following:

-   How did your partner show their solution?
-   How was their work different from your work?
-   How was your work the same?
-   Give your partner a compliment on their work.
-   Give a suggestion for how they could improve their work.

T: (Project 3 work samples from the class, showing each of the methods: a quick ten drawing, a number bond, and the arrow way.) Which student work best helps you not count all?

S: The number bond because I counted on. → The arrow way because I got to the next ten and counted on.

T: Good thinking! Why does the quick ten allow you to count all?

S: The drawing shows all the numbers so I can count them all instead of counting on.

T: How is the student work shown different from your partner's work?

S: My partner drew the quick tens. → My partner drew circles and X's for the ones. → My partner bonded a different number. → My partner started with a different number to get to 20 using the arrow way.

If time allows, have students solve 18 + 6 and share another set of student work from the class.

Problem Set (10 minutes)

Students should do their personal best to complete the Problem Set within the allotted 10 minutes. For some classes, it may be appropriate to modify the assignment by specifying which problems they work on first. Some of the problems may have more than one correct student work for each problem.

Lesson 18:   Share and critique peer strategies for adding two-digit numbers.
Date: 9/20/13

4.D

Student Debrief (10 minutes)

Lesson Objective: Share and critique peer strategies for adding two-digit numbers.

The Student Debrief is intended to invite reflection and active processing of the total lesson experience.

Invite students to review their solutions for the Problem Set. They should check work by comparing answers with a partner before going over answers as a class. Look for misconceptions or misunderstandings that can be addressed in the Debrief. Guide students in a conversation to debrief the Problem Set and process the lesson.

You may choose to use any combination of the questions below to lead the discussion.

- Look at Problem 2. What did you do to fix the student work?

- Look at Problem 2(b). What suggestion do you have for this student so she can improve her work?

- Look at Problem 3(a). How can you help this student improve?

- Compare your work on Problem 4 with your partner. Did you solve the same way? Do you think their way was an easier or harder way to solve? Explain why.

- Project Student Work A–D from today's Concept Development. Which student work best helps you not count all?

- How did today's fluency help you to be successful with the lesson?

Exit Ticket (3 minutes)

After the Student Debrief, instruct students to complete the Exit Ticket. A review of their work will help you assess the students' understanding of the concepts that were presented in the lesson today and plan more effectively for future lessons. You may read the questions aloud to the students.

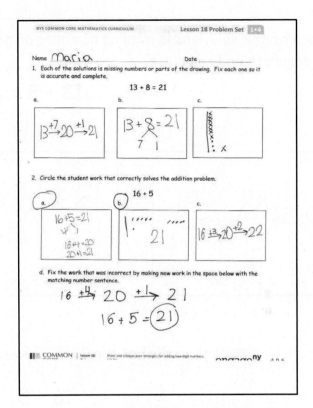

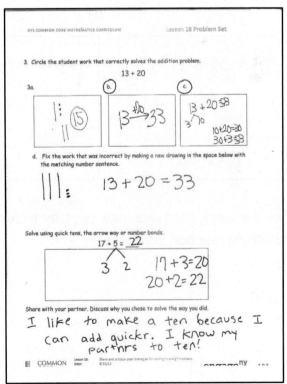

Name _____   Date _____

1. Each of the solutions is missing numbers or parts of the drawing. Fix each one so it is accurate and complete.

$$13 + 8 = 21$$

a.

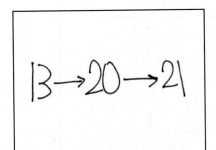

b.

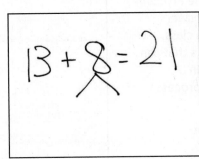

c.

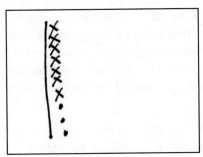

2. Circle the student work that correctly solves the addition problem.

$$16 + 5$$

a.

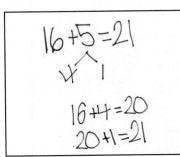

b.

c.

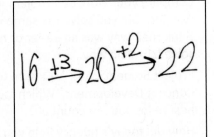

d. Fix the work that was incorrect by making new work in the space below with the matching number sentence.

COMMON CORE   Lesson 18:   Share and critique peer strategies for adding two-digit numbers.
Date: 9/20/13

4.D

© 2013 Common Core, Inc. All rights reserved. commoncore.org

3. Circle the student work that correctly solves the addition problem.

13 + 20

a.

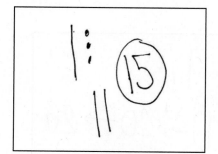

b.

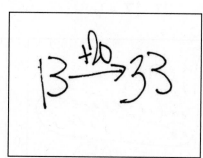

c.

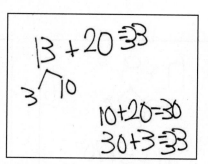

d. Fix the work that was incorrect by making a new drawing in the space below with the matching number sentence.

Solve using quick tens, the arrow way, or number bonds.

17 + 5 = ____

Share with your partner. Discuss why you chose to solve the way you did.

Name _____   Date _____

Circle the work that correctly solves the addition problem.

17 + 9

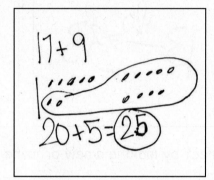

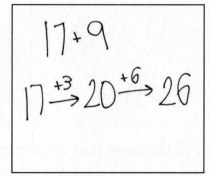

Fix the work that was incorrect by making a new drawing in the space below with the matching number sentence.

Name _____   Date _____

Two students both solved the addition problem below using different methods.

$$18 + 9$$

$$18 + 9 = 27$$

2   7

$$18 + 2 = 20$$
$$20 + 7 = 27$$

$$18 + 9 = 27$$

$$18 \xrightarrow{+2} 20 \xrightarrow{+7} 27$$

$$18 + 2 = 20$$
$$20 + 7 = 27$$

re they both correct? Why or why not?

Another two students solved the same problem using quick tens.

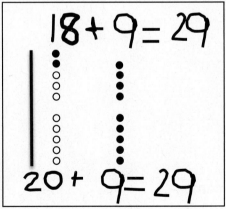

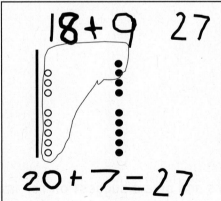

re they both correct? Why or why not?

Circle any student work that is correct.

$$19 + 6$$

Student A	Student B	Student C

Student A:

$19 + 6$

XXXXX (tally marks)

$20 + 6 = 26$

Student B:

$19 + 6$

$1 \nearrow 5$

$19 + 1 = 20$

$20 + 5 = 25$

Student C:

$19 + 6$

$19 \Rightarrow 20 \overset{5}{\Rightarrow} 25$

Fix the student work that was incorrect by making new drawings in the space below.

Choose the correct answers and give a suggestion for improvement.

Student Work Samples

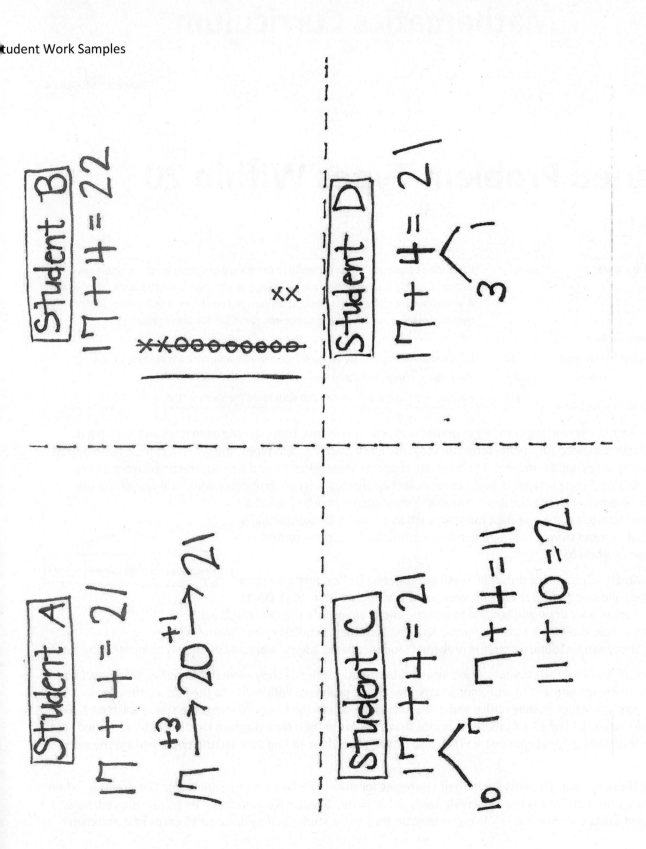

Student B

$17 + 4 = 22$

xx

x x o o o o o o o o

Student D

$17 + 4 = 21$

3 1

Student A

$17 + 4 = 21$

$17 \xrightarrow{+3} 20 \xrightarrow{+1} 21$

Student C

$17 + 4 = 21$

$17 \overset{7}{\underset{10}{\langle}}$

$7 + 4 = 11$

$11 + 10 = 21$

COMMON CORE™

Lesson 18: Share and critique peer strategies for adding two-digit numbers.
Date: 9/20/13

4.D.70

Topic E
Varied Problem Types Within 20

1.OA.1

Focus Standard:	1.OA.1	Use addition and subtraction within 20 to solve word problems involving situations of adding to, taking from, putting together, taking apart, and comparing, with unknowns in all positions, e.g., by using objects, drawings, and equations with a symbol for the unknown number to represent the problem. (See CCLS Glossary, Table 1.)
Instructional Days:	4	
Coherence -Links from:	G1–M2	Introduction to Place Value Through Addition and Subtraction Within 20
-Links to:	G1–M6	Place Value, Comparison, Addition and Subtraction to 100
	G2–M4	Addition and Subtraction Within 200 with Word Problems to 100

As students begin working with larger numbers in word problems, representing each item and drawing it individually can become cumbersome. In previous work with problem types, the two parts have been almost exclusively single-digit numbers. For example, students were adding 9 and 6 or subtracting 8 from 14 to solve. During Topic E, students begin to represent quantities in larger groupings while still visualizing the relationship between the numbers. For example, students may be adding a two-digit number and a one-digit number, such as 12 and 4, or subtracting a two-digit number from a two-digit number, such as 16 – 12, represented in the tape diagram to the right.

tape diagram

In Lesson 19, students are presented with *put together/take apart with total unknown* and *add to with result unknown* word problems within 20 (**1.OA.1**). As they solve, they draw and box the two parts, and then include the numeral label within the box, producing tape diagrams. This enables them to quickly identify where the quantity can be found within the drawing. Students begin adding a bracket as shown to identify the total.

Lessons 20 and 21 allow students to explore number relationships as they solve *put together/take apart with addend unknown* and *add to with change unknown* word problems within 20. As they do so, they explore number relationships as they notice and discuss how the size of the boxes relate to the size of each part. For example, when adding 12 + 4, students notice that the part in their tape diagram that contains 12 is much longer than the part that contains 4. They also notice that when adding 10 + 10, the two parts are the same size.

During these lessons, students share their strategies for drawing when a part is unknown. For example, when given the problem, "Maria has 15 playing cards in her hand. She has 8 black cards. If the rest are red, how many red cards does she have?" In order to solve this, some students may draw all 15 cards first and then place a box around the 8 black cards Maria already has. Other students will draw the 8 black cards and then count on as they draw to 15. Still other students will label 15 for the total, draw one part labeled 8, and then work towards identifying the missing part. Students will continue to work on recognizing what kind of unknown they are looking for: a part or a total.

During Lesson 22, students use their experiences and understanding to write their own word problems of varied types based on given tape diagrams.

While the addition and subtraction within the problems for Topic E will be within 20, fluency work will continue to support students' skill and understanding from Topics A through D using numbers to 40. This fluency work will prepare them for the increased complexity of addition in the final topic, Topic F.

A Teaching Sequence Towards Mastery of Varied Problem Types Within 20

Objective 1: Use tape diagrams as representations to solve *put together/take apart with total unknown* and *add to with result unknown* word problems.
(Lesson 19)

Objective 2: Recognize and make use of part–whole relationships within tape diagrams when solving a variety of problem types.
(Lessons 20–21)

Objective 3: Write word problems of varied types.
(Lesson 22)

Lesson 19

Objective: Use tape diagrams as representations to solve *put together/take apart with total unknown* and *add to with result unknown* word problems.

Suggested Lesson Structure

■ Fluency Practice   (10 minutes)
■ Concept Development   (40 minutes)
■ Student Debrief   (10 minutes)
   Total Time   **(60 minutes)**

Fluency Practice (10 minutes)

▪ Sprint: Analogous Addition Within 40 **1.OA.6, 1.NBT.4**   (10 minutes)

Sprint: Analogous Addition Within 40 (10 minutes)

Materials: (S) Analogous Addition Within 40 Sprint

Note: The progression of this Sprint mirrors the progression of concepts taught in Topic D thus far. It begins with addition sentences conducive to counting on, transitions into sentences in which the sums of the ones are less than ten, and ends with problems that cross ten.

Concept Development (40 minutes)

Materials: (T) Document camera (S) Problem Set

Note: During this lesson, students will complete the Problem Set as the teacher guides instruction. This method allows students to alternately practice a problem and then analyze both the process and the solution before moving on to their next practice problem. Although today's Problem Set includes both *put together* and *add to* problem types, they all have the result or total unknown. The focus of today's lesson is to support the use of the tape diagram within the RDW process:

- ▪ Read.
- ▪ Draw and label.
- ▪ Write a number sentence and a statement.

In Lesson 20, students will grapple with solving both addition and subtraction problem types. Students should keep their Problem Sets in a folder, along with the Application Problems from Lessons 13–18.

	Lesson 19:	Use tape diagrams as representations to solve *put together/take apart*
		with total unknown and *add to with result unknown* word problems.
	Date:	9/20/13

Distribute Problem Sets and have students work from their seats.

T: (Project Problem 1 on the board.) Let's read the problem together.

S/T: Lee saw 6 yellow squash and 7 pumpkins growing in his garden. How many vegetables did he see growing in his garden?

T: On your own, work on solving the problem. Remember that we always *read* the problem, *draw* and label, and *write* the number sentence and the statement that answers the question.

S/T: (Reread the problem as students begin to solve. Provide a maximum of 2 minutes for students to draw and label.)

T: How did you use drawing to make sense of the problem? Talk with a partner and explain your drawing.

S: (Provide students 30–45 seconds to share with a partner.) I drew the 6 squash in a straight line and then 7 pumpkins. I figured out that was 13. (Project students' work as they describe their drawings to the class. Choose student work that most closely resembles the tape diagram shown to the right.)

T: Look at this student's work. Where in the drawing can I find the squash?

S: (Point to the picture.)

T: (If the 6 squash are not inside a rectangle or circle to show the part, include this next sentence.) The label helps find this part of the drawing. Let's put a rectangle around it so I can keep track of this part more easily.

T: How many are there?

S: 6.

T: How can I tell quickly? (If the number is not labeled in the drawing, or is not near the picture, reword the second question to, "What can I do so I can tell quickly?")

S: He wrote 6 next to his picture.

Repeat the process asking about the pumpkins, using the same student work sample.

T: (Ask a student to read the question from the story again for the class.) How many vegetables are there?

NOTES ON MULTIPLE MEANS OF ENGAGEMENT:

Appropriate scaffolds help all students feel successful. Students may use translators, interpreters, or sentence frames to present their solutions or respond to feedback. Models shared may include concrete manipulatives.

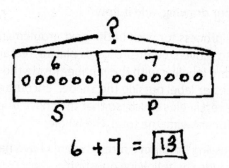

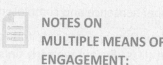

Problem 1: Lee saw 6 squash and 7 pumpkins growing in his garden. How many vegetables did he see growing in his garden?

NOTES ON MULTIPLE MEANS OF ENGAGEMENT:

If you anticipate students struggling with the problems due to the size of the numbers or the complexity of the language, follow up with a similar problem that uses either smaller quantities or less complex language as a scaffold step. Be sure to provide at least one challenging problem to all students, as we help support them in building stamina and perseverance in problem solving.

Lesson 19: Use tape diagrams as representations to solve *put together/take apart with total unknown* and *add to with result unknown* word problems.

Date: 9/20/13

4.E.4

S: 13 vegetables.

T: So from here (pointing to one end of the squash) to here (pointing to the other end of the pumpkins) we have 13 vegetables?

S: Yes!

T: Let's show that above our drawing, so we can keep track. (Draw as shown, so that the bracket, or arms, represent that everything from one end to the other has a total of 13. Label with 13 and *T* for total.) When we connect our two parts like this, and show the total, we call it a **tape diagram**. If you didn't show this in your drawing, add it now.

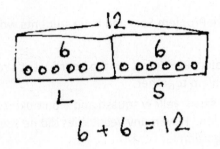

$$6 + 6 = 12$$

Repeat the process for each of the next problems. Use the questions to move students towards placing rectangles around each part and labeling with the number inside the part, as well as using a letter label outside the shape. Encourage students to make their rectangles touch, so that they have one large rectangle for showing the total, the whole.

Problem 2: Kiana caught 6 lizards. Her brother caught 6 snakes. How many reptiles do they have altogether?

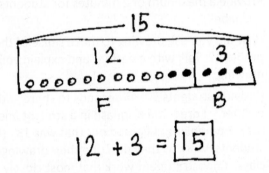

$$12 + 3 = \boxed{15}$$

When discussing Problem 3 after students have had a chance to solve it, include the following question.

• How could using a color change at 10 help you keep track of the number of soccer balls on the field?

Before moving on to the next problem, ensure that all students have added labels to each part of their drawing and have written the number sentence and completed the statement.

Problem 3: Anton's team has 12 soccer balls on the field and 3 soccer balls in the coach's bag. How many soccer balls does Anton's team have?

Choose probing questions appropriate to the successes and challenges of the class. Encourage early finishers to write their own word problems on another sheet of paper. They can write the problem on one side and then write the solution using a drawing, number sentence, and statement on the other side.

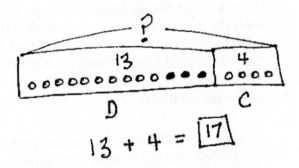

$$13 + 4 = \boxed{17}$$

Problem 4: Emi had 13 friends over for dinner. Four more friends came over for cake. How many friends came over to Emi's house?

COMMON CORE | Lesson 19:   Use tape diagrams as representations to solve *put together/take apart with total unknown* and *add to with result unknown* word problems.   4

    Date: 9/20/13

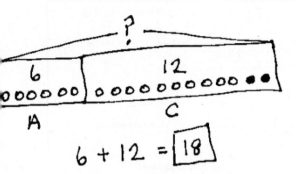

$$6 + 12 = \boxed{18}$$

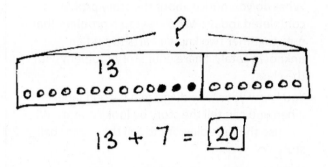

$$13 + 7 = \boxed{20}$$

Problem 5: Six adults and 12 children were swimming in the lake. How many people were swimming in the lake?

Problem 6: Rose has a vase with 13 flowers. She puts 7 more flowers in the vase. How many flowers are in the vase?

Student Debrief (10 minutes)

Lesson Objective: Use tape diagrams as representations to solve *put together/take apart with total unknown* and *add to with result unknown* word problems.

The Student Debrief is intended to invite reflection and active processing of the total lesson experience.

Guide students in a conversation to debrief the Problem Set and process the lesson. Look for misconceptions or misunderstandings that can be addressed in the Debrief.

You may choose to use any combination of the questions below to lead the discussion.

- We called our drawings today **tape diagrams.** Think about the diagrams we draw in science class. Why might we use the word *diagram* here? What are the important parts of our tape diagram?

- Look at Problem 2. What do you notice about the size of each rectangle around the parts? Why is that?

- Look at Problem 5. How is the tape diagram similar to the one you made for Problem 2? How is it different? Compare the size of the two rectangles around each part of Problem 5. What do you notice?

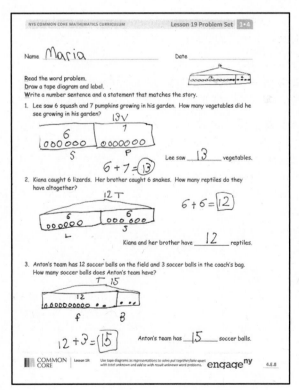

COMMON CORE   Lesson 19:   Use tape diagrams as representations to solve *put together/take apart with total unknown* and *add to with result unknown* word problems.   4.E.6

Date: 9/20/13

2013 Common Core, Inc. All rights reserved. commoncore.org

- What do you notice about the story problems we completed today? Who created a problem that puts together two known parts to find an unknown total? Share your story problem with the class.
- You know your tape diagram has good labels when you can tell the story by looking at it. Who can use the tape diagram to tell the soccer ball story?
- How can a tape diagram help us share our thinking?

Exit Ticket (3 minutes)

After the Student Debrief, instruct students to complete the Exit Ticket. A review of their work will help you assess the students' understanding of the concepts that were presented in the lesson today and plan more effectively for future lessons. You may read the questions aloud to the students.

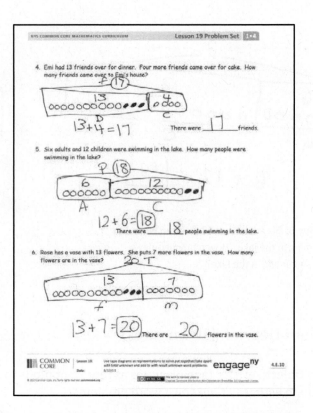

A

Number correct: _____

Name _____ Date _____

*Write the missing number.

1	6 + 1 = ☐		16	6 + 3 = ☐	
2	16 + 1 = ☐		17	16 + 3 = ☐	
3	26 + 1 = ☐		18	26 + 3 = ☐	
4	5 + 2 = ☐		19	4 + 5 = ☐	
5	15 + 2 = ☐		20	15 + 4 = ☐	
6	25 + 2 = ☐		21	8 + 2 = ☐	
7	5 + 3 = ☐		22	18 + 2 = ☐	
8	15 + 3 = ☐		23	28 + 2 = ☐	
9	25 + 3 = ☐		24	8 + 3 = ☐	
10	4 + 4 = ☐		25	8 + 13 = ☐	
11	14 + 4 = ☐		26	8 + 23 = ☐	
12	24 + 4 = ☐		27	8 + 5 = ☐	
13	5 + 4 = ☐		28	8 + 15 = ☐	
14	15 + 4 = ☐		29	28 + ☐ = 33	
15	25 + 4 = ☐		30	25 + ☐ = 33	

COMMON CORE — Lesson 19: Use tape diagrams as representations to solve *put together/take apart with total unknown* and *add to with result unknown* word problems. — 4.E.8

Date: 9/20/13

B

Number correct: ⬡

Name _____   Date _____

*Write the missing number.

1	$5 + 1 = \square$		16	$6 + 3 = \square$	
2	$15 + 1 = \square$		17	$16 + 3 = \square$	
3	$25 + 1 = \square$		18	$26 + 3 = \square$	
4	$4 + 2 = \square$		19	$3 + 5 = \square$	
5	$14 + 2 = \square$		20	$15 + 3 = \square$	
6	$24 + 2 = \square$		21	$9 + 1 = \square$	
7	$5 + 3 = \square$		22	$19 + 1 = \square$	
8	$15 + 3 = \square$		23	$29 + 1 = \square$	
9	$25 + 3 = \square$		24	$9 + 2 = \square$	
10	$6 + 2 = \square$		25	$9 + 12 = \square$	
11	$16 + 2 = \square$		26	$9 + 22 = \square$	
12	$26 + 2 = \square$		27	$9 + 5 = \square$	
13	$4 + 3 = \square$		28	$9 + 15 = \square$	
14	$14 + 3 = \square$		29	$29 + \square = 34$	
15	$24 + 3 = \square$		30	$25 + \square = 34$	

COMMON CORE   **Lesson 19:**   Use tape diagrams as representations to solve *put together/take apart with total unknown* and *add to with result unknown* word problems.
Date: 9/20/13

4

Name _____   Date _____

Read the word problem.
Draw a tape diagram and label.
Write a number sentence and a statement that matches the story.

1. Lee saw 6 squash and 7 pumpkins growing in his garden. How many vegetables did he see growing in his garden?

Lee saw _____ vegetables.

2. Kiana caught 6 lizards. Her brother caught 6 snakes. How many reptiles do they have altogether?

Kiana and her brother have _____ reptiles.

3. Anton's team has 12 soccer balls on the field and 3 soccer balls in the coach's bag. How many soccer balls does Anton's team have?

Anton's team has _____ soccer balls.

4. Emi had 13 friends over for dinner. Four more friends came over for cake. How many friends came over to Emi's house?

There were _____ friends.

5. Six adults and 12 children were swimming in the lake. How many people were swimming in the lake?

There were _____ people swimming in the lake.

6. Rose has a vase with 13 flowers. She puts 7 more flowers in the vase. How many flowers are in the vase?

There are _____ flowers in the vase.

Name _____   Date _____

Read the word problem.
Draw a tape diagram and label.
Write a number sentence and a statement that matches
the story.

1. Peter counts the number of lightning bolts during a storm, and Lee counts the
    rumbles of thunder. Peter counts 14 lightning bolts, and Lee counts 6 rumbles of
    thunder. How many lightning bolts and thunder rumbles did they count in all?

They count _____ lightning bolts and thunder rumbles.

**COMMON
CORE**™

Lesson 19:   Use tape diagrams as representations to solve *put together/take apart*
             with total unknown and *add to with result unknown* word problems.
Date: 9/20/13

4.E.12

Name _____ Date _____

<u>R</u>ead the word problem.
<u>D</u>raw a tape diagram and label.
<u>W</u>rite a number sentence and a statement that matches
the story.

1. Darnel is playing with his 4 red robots. Ben joins him with 13 blue robots. How
   many robots do they have altogether?

                                        They have _____ robots.

2. Rose and Emi have a jump rope contest. Rose jumps 14 times and Emi jumps 6
   times. How many times did Rose and Emi jump?

                                        They jumped _____ times.

COMMON CORE Lesson 19: Use tape diagrams as representations to solve *put together/take apart*
with total unknown and *add to with result unknown* word problems.

Date: 9/20/13

4.

3. Pedro counts the airplanes taking off and landing at the airport. He sees 17 airplanes take off and 6 airplanes land. How many airplanes did he count altogether?

Pedro counts _____ airplanes.

4. Tamra and Willie score all the points for their team in their basketball game. Tamra scores 13 points, and Willie scores 8 points. What was their team's score for the game?

The team's score was _____ points.

COMMON CORE™

Lesson 19: Use tape diagrams as representations to solve *put together/take apart with total unknown* and *add to with result unknown* word problems.

Date: 9/20/13

4.E.14

Lesson 20

Objective: Recognize and make use of part–whole relationships within tape diagrams when solving a variety of problem types.

Suggested Lesson Structure

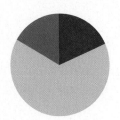

- ■ Fluency Practice   (11 minutes)
- ▪ Concept Development   (39 minutes)
- ■ Student Debrief   (10 minutes)
  - **Total Time**   **(60 minutes)**

Fluency Practice (11 minutes)

- Beep Counting by Ones and Tens **1.OA.5, 1.NBT.3**   (2 minutes)
- Number Bond Addition and Subtraction **1.OA.6**   (4 minutes)
- Addition and Subtraction with Cards **1.NBT.4**   (5 minutes)

Beep Counting by Ones and Tens (2 minutes)

Note: This fluency activity allows students to practice their counting sequences as well as practicing mentally adding 10 and subtracting 10 from a given number.

Say a series of four numbers but replace one of the numbers with the word "beep" (e.g., "1, 2, 3, beep"). When signaled, students say the number that was replaced by the word "beep" in the sequence. Scaffold number sequences, beginning with easy sequences and moving to more complex ones. Choose sequences that count forward and backward by ones and tens within 40.

Suggested sequence type: 10, 11, 12, beep; 20, 21, 22, beep; 20, 19, 18, beep; 30, 29, 28 beep; 0, 10, 20, beep; 1, 11, 21, beep; 40, 30, 20, beep; 39, 29, 19, beep. Continue with similar sequences, changing the sequential placement of the beep.

Number Bond Addition and Subtraction (4 minutes)

Materials: (S) Personal white boards

Note: This fluency activity builds students' ability to add and subtract within 10 or 20, while reinforcing the relationship between addition and subtraction. The first two to three minutes should be spent reviewing the core fluency within 10. In the last one to two minutes, allow students who are very strong with sums and differences to 10 to work with a partner and choose totals between 10 and 20.

Lesson 20:   Recognize and make use of part–whole relationships within tape
             diagrams when solving a variety of problem types.
Date: 9/20/13

4.

Write a number bond for a number between 0 and 10, with a missing part or whole. Students write an addition and subtraction sentence with a box for the missing number in each equation. They then solve for the missing number.

Addition and Subtraction with Cards (5 minutes)

Materials: (S) Topics A and C Addition and Subtraction with Cards game cards (from G1–M4–Lesson 12) and additional Topic D cards (from G1–M4–Lesson 17)

Note: This fluency game reviews the problem types presented in Topics A–D, as well as reviews subtraction from Module 2.

Follow the directions in G1–M4–Lesson 12's Concept Development.

Concept Development (38 minutes)

Materials: (S) Problem Set, highlighter

Note: During Lesson 20, the suggested delivery of instruction is an integration of student work on the Problem Set with guided instruction interspersed between each problem. Today, the unknown in each problem will vary between a part and the total. The sequence of problems has been designed to support students in using the RDW process, particularly to keep track of information as they determine if they are looking for a part or the total, and to use the visual representation of the information to support calculations.

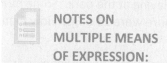

NOTES ON MULTIPLE MEANS OF EXPRESSION:

Partnering students and asking them to explain their work to each other can support students' language development. Students can ask each other the same questions that the teacher asks. Be sure to have students switch roles so that all students have the opportunity to practice verbalizing their thinking and listening.

Suggested Delivery of Instruction for Solving Word Problems

1. Model the problem, calculate, and write a statement.

Choose two pairs of students who have been accurately solving the Application Problems from Topic D and who have been using simple shapes in a straight line when drawing. Invite these two pairs of students to work on chart paper while the others work independently or in pairs at their seats. Vary the selected students as the problems become more complex. Review the following questions before beginning the first problem:

NOTES ON MULTIPLE MEANS OF ENGAGEMENT:

Appropriate scaffolds help all students feel successful. Students may use translators, interpreters, or sentence frames to present their solutions or respond to feedback. Models shared may include concrete manipulatives.

- Can you draw something?
- What can you draw?
- What can you tell from looking at your drawing?

As students work, circulate. Reread Problem 1 and reiterate the questions above. After a maximum of two minutes, have the pairs of students share their labeled diagrams. Give everyone two to three minutes to

Lesson 20: Recognize and make use of part–whole relationships within tape diagrams when solving a variety of problem types.

Date: 9/20/13

4.E.16

finish work on that question, sharing their work and thinking with a peer. All should write their equations and statements of the answer.

2. Assess the solution for reasonableness.

Give students one to two minutes to assess and explain the reasonableness of their solution. For about one minute, have the demonstrating students receive and respond to feedback and questions from their peers.

3. As a class, notice the ways the drawing depicts the story and the solution.

Ask questions to help students recognize how each part of their drawing matches the story and solution. This will help students begin to see how the same process can help them solve varying word problems. Keep at least one chart paper sample of each solution for reference later in the lesson.

Problem 1

Nine dogs were playing at the park. Some more dogs came to the park. Then there were 11 dogs. How many more dogs came to the park?

To support students' methods for keeping track of their information, ask some of the following questions:

- What labels did the student use to show the part consisting of the dogs that were playing at first?
- How did she separate them from the part consisting of the dogs that came later?
- What label did she use for the total number of dogs?
- Where did she put the label for the total number of dogs? How did that help?

Be sure to discuss the solution and the number sentence, noting which number from the number sentence is the solution number. This number should have a rectangle around it, as shown.

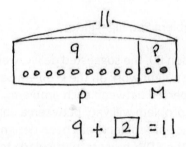

Problem 1: Nine dogs were playing at the park. Some more dogs came to the park. Then there were 11 dogs. How many more dogs came to the park?

Problem 2

Sixteen strawberries are in a basket for Peter and Julio. Peter ate 8 of them. How many are there for Julio to eat?

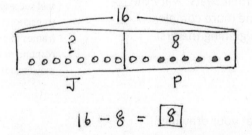

Problem 2: Sixteen strawberries are in a basket for Peter and Julio. Peter ate 8 of them. How many are there for Julio to eat?

Lesson 20: Recognize and make use of part–whole relationships within tape diagrams when solving a variety of problem types.

Date: 9/20/13

Problem 3

Thirteen children are on the roller coaster. Three adults are on the roller coaster. How many people are on the roller coaster?

Have the class read one sentence of the problem at a time, while the students at the board show where the information is within their drawing, pointing out the number and letter labels. Discuss where the solution can be found within the number sentence, and ensure that everyone has placed a rectangle around this number.

Some students will initially assume this problem requires subtraction. Walking through each sentence to ask, "Is this a new part, or does this include the part I already drew?" can support students internalizing a process for making sense of word problems.

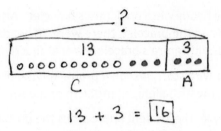

Problem 3: Thirteen children are on the roller coaster. Three adults are on the roller coaster. How many people are on the roller coaster?

Problem 4

Thirteen people are on the roller coaster now. Three adults are on the roller coaster, and the rest are children. How many children are on the roller coaster?

While this problem uses the same context as Problem 3, the problem type is different. As students consider the question, "Is this a new part, or is this a part of what I already drew?" they will recognize that in this problem, the unknown number is a part of the total 13.

During the Debrief, Problems 3 and 4 will be compared.

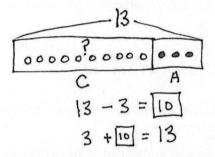

Problem 4: Thirteen people are on the roller coaster now. Three adults are on the roller coaster, and the rest are children. How many children are on the roller coaster?

Problem 5

Ben has 6 baseball practices in the morning this month. If Ben also has 6 practices in the afternoon, how many baseball practices does Ben have?

Choose probing questions appropriate to the successes and challenges of the class. Notice students who are improving, and ask them to share their increasing understanding.

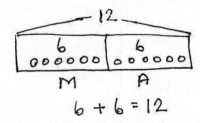

Problem 5: Ben has 6 baseball practices in the morning this month. If Ben also has 6 practices in the afternoon, how many baseball practices does Ben have?

	Lesson 20:	Recognize and make use of part–whole relationships within tape diagrams when solving a variety of problem types.	4.E.18
	Date:	9/20/13	

© 2013 Common Core, Inc. All rights reserved. **commoncore.org**

Problem 6

Some yellow beads were on Tamra's bracelet. After she put 14 purple beads on the bracelet, there were 18 beads. How many yellow beads did Tamra's bracelet have at first?

As an *add to with start unknown* problem type, this will most likely be the most challenging problem of the set.

In this example, the student approaches the problem by first drawing an empty box for the yellow beads and putting the question mark in it. Next, the 14 are drawn and the total of 18 is labeled. Finally, the student counts up from 14 to 18 while drawing in the additional 4 beads to find the missing part.

The number sentences are written. The most probable solution equation would be the center one, 14 + ___ = 18. Not many first graders will opt to start with a part unknown or subtract 14 from 18.

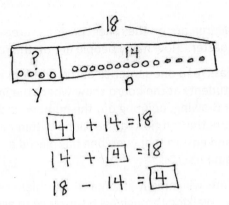

Problem 5: Some yellow beads were on Tamra's bracelet. After she put 14 purple beads on the bracelet, there were 18 beads. How many yellow beads did Tamra's bracelet have at first?

Student Debrief (10 minutes)

Lesson Objective: Recognize and make use of part–whole relationships within tape diagrams when solving a variety of problem types.

The Student Debrief is intended to invite reflection and active processing of the total lesson experience.

Guide students in a conversation to debrief the Problem Set and process the lesson. Look for misconceptions or misunderstandings that can be addressed in the Debrief.

You may choose to use any combination of the questions below to lead the discussion.

- How are Problems 3 and 4 alike? How are they different? How did your drawings help you to solve each problem?

- In which problems could making ten help you? Explain your thinking.

- Look at Problem 2 and Problem 3. What is similar and what is different between the two problems? What do you notice about the size of the rectangles around each part in Problem 2? What do you notice in Problem 3?

- Look at Problem 6. How did you solve this problem? What did you draw first? Next? Did anyone do it a different way?

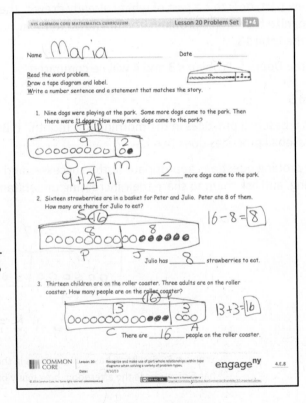

Lesson 20:

Recognize and make use of part–whole relationships within tape diagrams when solving a variety of problem types.

Date: 9/20/13

4.

- Using a highlighter, underline the question in each problem. Highlight the part of the tape diagram that shows the answer to the question. What do you notice?
- Some people only write numbers and not circles inside the parts of a tape diagram. Why do we draw the circles sometimes? Why do we just use numbers at times?

Exit Ticket (3 minutes)

After the Student Debrief, instruct students to complete the Exit Ticket. A review of their work will help you assess the students' understanding of the concepts that were presented in the lesson today and plan more effectively for future lessons. You may read the questions aloud to the students.

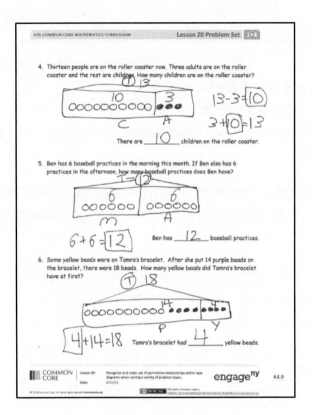

COMMON CORE

Lesson 20:   Recognize and make use of part–whole relationships within tape diagrams when solving a variety of problem types.

Date: 9/20/13

4.E.20

Name _____   Date _____

R̲ead the word problem.
D̲raw a tape diagram and label.
W̲rite a number sentence and a statement that matches the story.

1. Nine dogs were playing at the park. Some more dogs came to the park. Then there were 11 dogs. How many more dogs came to the park?

_____ more dogs came to the park.

2. Sixteen strawberries are in a basket for Peter and Julio. Peter ate 8 of them. How many are there for Julio to eat?

Julio has _____ strawberries to eat.

3. Thirteen children are on the roller coaster. Three adults are on the roller coaster. How many people are on the roller coaster?

There are _____ people on the roller coaster.

Lesson 20:   Recognize and make use of part–whole relationships within tape
diagrams when solving a variety of problem types.
Date: 9/20/13

4. Thirteen people are on the roller coaster now. Three adults are on the roller coaster, and the rest are children. How many children are on the roller coaster?

There are _____ children on the roller coaster.

5. Ben has 6 baseball practices in the morning this month. If Ben also has 6 practices in the afternoon, how many baseball practices does Ben have?

Ben has _____ baseball practices.

6. Some yellow beads were on Tamra's bracelet. After she put 14 purple beads on the bracelet, there were 18 beads. How many yellow beads did Tamra's bracelet have at first?

Tamra's bracelet had _____ yellow beads.

COMMON CORE™   Lesson 20:   Recognize and make use of part–whole relationships within tape diagrams when solving a variety of problem types.   **4.E.22**

Date: 9/20/13

Name _____   Date _____

<u>R</u>ead the word problem.

<u>D</u>raw a tape diagram and label.

<u>W</u>rite a number sentence and a statement that matches the story.

There were 6 turtles in the tank. Dad bought some more turtles. Now there are 12 turtles. How many turtles did Dad buy?

Dad bought _____ turtles.

COMMON CORE™

Lesson 20:   Recognize and make use of part–whole relationships within tape diagrams when solving a variety of problem types.

Date: 9/20/13

4.

Name _____   Date _____

Read the word problem.
Draw a tape diagram and label.
Write a number sentence and a statement that matches
the story.

1. Rose has 12 soccer practices this month. Six practices are in the afternoon, but
    the rest are in the morning. How many practices will be in the morning?

Rose has _____ practices in the morning.

2. Ben catches 16 fish. He puts some back in the lake. He brings home 7 fish. How
    many fish did he put back in the lake?

Ben put _____ fish back in the lake.

COMMON CORE   Lesson 20:   Recognize and make use of part–whole relationships within tape
                                 diagrams when solving a variety of problem types.   4.E.24
                   Date: 9/20/13

3. Nikil solved 9 problems on the first sprint. He solved 12 problems on the second sprint. How many problems did he solve on the two sprints?

Nikil solved _____ problems on the sprints.

4. Shanika returned some books to the library. She had 16 books at first, and she still has 13 books left. How many books did she return to the library?

Shanika returned _____ books to the library.

COMMON CORE   Lesson 20:   Recognize and make use of part–whole relationships within tape
diagrams when solving a variety of problem types.

Date: 9/20/13

4.

Lesson 21

Objective: Recognize and make use of part–whole relationships within tape diagrams when solving a variety of problem types.

Suggested Lesson Structure

■ Fluency Practice   (12 minutes)
■ Concept Development   (38 minutes)
■ Student Debrief   (10 minutes)
    Total Time   **(60 minutes)**

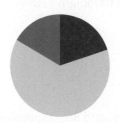

Fluency Practice (12 minutes)

- Race and Roll Addition **1.OA.6**   (4 minutes)
- Number Bond Addition and Subtraction **1.OA.6**   (4 minutes)
- Take Out 1 or 10 **1.OA.6**   (2 minutes)
- Longer/Shorter **K.CC.7**   (2 minutes)

Race and Roll Addition (4 minutes)

Materials: 1 die per set of partners

Note: In this fluency activity, students practice adding and subtracting within 20. The competitive nature of Race and Roll Addition and Subtraction promotes students' engagement while increasing their brains' ability to retain information (since the partners are trying to stand quickly).

All students start at 0. Partners take turns rolling a die, saying a number sentence, and adding the number rolled to the total. For example, Partner A rolls 6 and says, "0 + 6 = 6," then Partner B rolls 3 and says, "6 + 3 = 9." They continue rapidly rolling and saying number sentences until they get to 20 without going over. Partners stand when they reach 20. For example, if they are at 18 and roll 5, they would take turns rolling until one of them rolls a 2. Then they would both stand.

Number Bond Addition and Subtraction (4 minutes)

Materials: (S) Personal white boards

Note: This fluency activity builds a student's ability to add and subtract within 10. Reviewing the relationship between addition and subtraction is especially beneficial for students who continue to find subtraction challenging.

$$5 + \boxed{3} = 8 \qquad 8 - 5 = \boxed{3}$$
$$\boxed{3} + 5 = 8 \qquad 8 - \boxed{3} = 5$$

	Lesson 21:	Recognize and make use of part–whole relationships within tape diagrams when solving a variety of problem types.	
	Date:	9/20/13	4.E.26

Write a number bond for a number between 0 and 10, with a missing part or whole. Today, students write *two* addition and *two* subtraction sentences with a box for the missing number in each equation. They then solve for the missing number.

Take Out 1 or 10 (2 minutes)

Note: This activity reviews place value in order to prepare students for Topic F.

Choose numbers between 10 and 20 and follow the paradigm below.

> T: Say 15 the Say Ten way.
>
> S: Ten 5.
>
> T: Take out 1.
>
> S: Ten 4.

Repeat for 25 and 35. Then, take out 10 from 15, 25, and 35, respectively.

Longer/Shorter (2 minutes)

Materials: (T) Board or document camera

Note: Working with visualizing proportional relationships between numbers can support students' number sense development. By using tape diagram models, students can recognize methods for representing numbers in relation to other numbers.

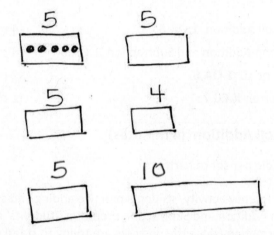

Write one pair of numbers on the board at a time (e.g., 5 and 5). Draw a rectangle under the first number.

> T: This rectangle is long enough to hold this row of 5 dots. (Draw 5 dots so that they fill the space.)
>
> T: (Point to the second number, which in this first example is also 5.) I'm going to start drawing a rectangle that is long enough to hold a row of 5 dots of the same size. Tell me when to stop.
>
> T/S: (Begin drawing a rectangle, and give students the chance to say "Stop!" when it is approximately the same size as the first rectangle.)
>
> T: Why did you say stop there?
>
> S: It is about the same size as the first rectangle.

Repeat this process for the following sequence of numbers: 5 and 4, 5 and 10, 1 and 3, 4 and 6, 10 and 20. Only draw the dots for the first example. Have students talk about how the first number relates to the second number using language such as *a little longer, a little shorter, much longer, double,* etc. Have students who find this challenging use a number line with their left pointer finger on zero and their right on the number (endpoint).

Lesson 21:   Recognize and make use of part–whole relationships within tape
diagrams when solving a variety of problem types.
Date: 9/20/13

4.E

Concept Development (38 minutes)

Materials: (S) Problem Set

Note: Like Lessons 19 and 20, the suggested delivery of instruction for Lesson 21 is an integration of student work on Problem Sets with guided instruction interspersed between each problem. If students have been highly successful with the past days' lessons, today, have them try representing the quantities in each part using the number and label, without including the shapes inside each part. The goal is to support students in identifying a process for making sense of a problem.

By working with the tape diagrams as drawings related to the varying problem types, students can internalize an entry point into any problem. *Can you draw something? What can you draw? What can you tell from looking at your drawing?* Tape diagrams, even without shapes inside each part, can be considered a type of drawing. Remember to have students hold on to the Problem Sets so they can be used as a reference later in the topic.

Suggested Delivery of Instruction for Solving Word Problems

1. Model the problem, calculate, and write a statement.

Choose two pairs of students who have been accurately solving the Application Problems from Topic D and who have been using simple shapes in a straight line when drawing. Invite these two pairs of students to work on chart paper while the others work independently or in pairs at their seats. Vary the selected students as the problems become more complex. Review the following questions before beginning the first problem:

- Can you draw something?
- What can you draw?
- What can you tell from looking at your drawing?

As students work, circulate and support. After two minutes, have the two pairs of students share only their labeled diagrams. Give everyone two to three minutes to finish work on that question, sharing their work and thinking with a peer. All should write their equations and statements of the answer.

2. Assess the solution for reasonableness.

Give students one to two minutes to assess and explain the reasonableness of their solution. For about one minute, have the demonstrating students receive and respond to feedback and questions from their peers.

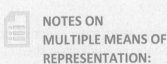

**NOTES ON
MULTIPLE MEANS OF
REPRESENTATION:**

Encourage students who have difficulty moving to the tape diagram representation as the position of the unknown changes to draw a number bond as part of their work. Some students more easily relate to the tape diagram through its similarities with number bonds.

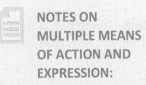

**NOTES ON
MULTIPLE MEANS
OF ACTION AND
EXPRESSION:**

If students do not have experience with a context such as the one used in Problem 2, act out the problem with a few student volunteers before having the class begin to draw and solve the problem.

Lesson 21:   Recognize and make use of part–whole relationships within tape
diagrams when solving a variety of problem types.
Date: 9/20/13

4.E.28

3. As a class, notice the ways the drawing depicts the story and the solution.

Ask questions to help students recognize how each part of their drawing matches the story and solution. This will help students begin to see how the same process can help them solve varying word problems. Keep at least one chart paper sample of each solution for reference later in the lesson.

Problem 1

Rose drew 7 pictures, and Will drew 11 pictures. How many pictures did they draw altogether?

This problem, a *put together with total unknown*, is one of the easiest problem types. After the students have explained their drawing and solution accurately, point to sections of the tape diagram and ask the class questions such as, "What does this part represent? How do you know? What did the student draw or write to help us remember?"

For the next five problems, move quickly from one to the next, having only the students at the board share their work, so that students have time to work through and discuss all six problems. Choose one or two probing questions similar to Problems 1 and 2 to support student development as needed.

Problem 2

Darnel walked 7 minutes to Lee's house. Then he walked to the park. Darnel walked for a total of 18 minutes. How many minutes did he walk to get to the park?

Problem 3

Emi has some goldfish. Tamra has 14 Beta fish. Tamra and Emi have 19 fish in all. How many goldfish does Emi have?

Problem 4

Shanika built a block tower using 14 blocks. Then she added 4 more blocks to the tower. How many blocks are there in the tower now?

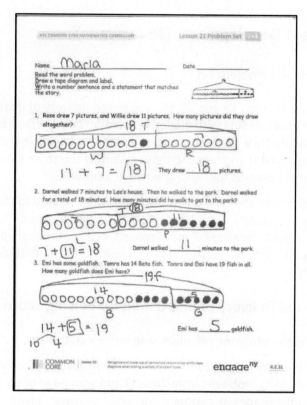

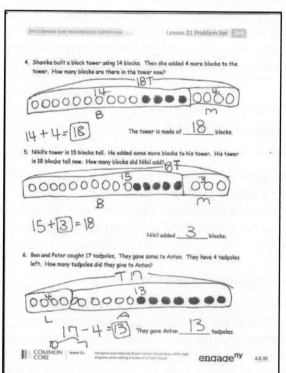

Lesson 21: Recognize and make use of part–whole relationships within tape diagrams when solving a variety of problem types.

Date: 9/20/13

Problem 5

Nikil's tower has 15 blocks. He added some more blocks to his tower. His tower is 18 blocks tall now. How many blocks did Nikil add?

Problem 6

Ben and Peter caught 17 tadpoles. They gave some to Anton. They have 4 tadpoles left. How many tadpoles did they give to Anton?

Student Debrief (10 minutes)

Lesson Objective: Recognize and make use of part–whole relationships within tape diagrams when solving a variety of problem types.

The Student Debrief is intended to invite reflection and active processing of the total lesson experience.

Guide students in a conversation to debrief the Problem Set and process the lesson. Look for misconceptions or misunderstandings that can be addressed in the Debrief.

You may choose to use any combination of the questions below to lead the discussion.

- Look at Problem 1. What did you draw? How did your drawing help you solve the problem?
- Look at Problem 2. What did you draw first? How is your drawing similar or different from the drawing you made for Problem 1?
- Look at Problem 3. How did you draw this problem? How is your drawing similar to or different from your partner's drawing?
- Look at Problem 5. Did you solve this the same way you solved Problem 3, or did you solve it in a different way? Share your drawing and explain your thinking.
- Last week, we were looking at smaller, single-digit addition facts inside two-digit addition problems. Can you find any simpler addition facts inside your number sentences? Share your examples. How can you draw your tape diagrams in ways that help you see simple problems inside the larger ones?
- Using a highlighter, underline the question in each problem. Highlight the part of the tape diagram that shows the answer to the question. What do you notice?
- Some people only write numbers and not circles inside the parts of a tape diagram. Why might we want to include the circles in each part? Why might we choose to use only the number and leave out the circles in each part sometimes?

Exit Ticket (3 minutes)

After the Student Debrief, instruct students to complete the Exit Ticket. A review of their work will help you assess the students' understanding of the concepts that were presented in the lesson today and plan more effectively for future lessons. You may read the questions aloud to the students.

COMMON CORE

Lesson 21:   Recognize and make use of part–whole relationships within tape diagrams when solving a variety of problem types.

Date: 9/20/13

4.E.30

Name _____ Date _____

<u>R</u>ead the word problem.
<u>D</u>raw a tape diagram and label.
<u>W</u>rite a number sentence and a statement that matches
the story.

1. Rose drew 7 pictures, and Willie drew 11 pictures. How many pictures did they draw altogether?

They drew _____ pictures.

2. Darnel walked 7 minutes to Lee's house. Then he walked to the park. Darnel walked for a total of 18 minutes. How many minutes did he walk to get to the park?

Darnel walked _____ minutes to the park.

3. Emi has some goldfish. Tamra has 14 Beta fish. Tamra and Emi have 19 fish in all. How many goldfish does Emi have?

Emi has _____ goldfish.

COMMON CORE | **Lesson 21:** Recognize and make use of part–whole relationships within tape diagrams when solving a variety of problem types.

Date: 9/20/13

4.E

4. Shanika built a block tower using 14 blocks. Then she added 4 more blocks to the tower. How many blocks are there in the tower now?

The tower is made of _____ blocks.

5. Nikil's tower is 15 blocks tall. He added some more blocks to his tower. His tower is 18 blocks tall now. How many blocks did Nikil add?

Nikil added _____ blocks.

6. Ben and Peter caught 17 tadpoles. They gave some to Anton. They have 4 tadpoles left. How many tadpoles did they give to Anton?

They gave Anton _____ tadpoles.

 Lesson 21:   Recognize and make use of part–whole relationships within tape diagrams when solving a variety of problem types.

Date: 9/20/13

4.E.32

Name _____   Date _____

<u>R</u>ead the word problem.
<u>D</u>raw a tape diagram and label.
<u>W</u>rite a number sentence and a statement that matches
the story.

1. Shanika read some pages on Monday. On Tuesday, she read 6 pages. She read 13
   pages in the 2 days. How many pages did she read on Monday?

        Shanika read _____ pages on Monday.

COMMON CORE™

Lesson 21:   Recognize and make use of part–whole relationships within tape
             diagrams when solving a variety of problem types.
Date: 9/20/13

4.E

Name _____   Date _____

Read the word problem.
Draw a tape diagram and label.
Write a number sentence and a statement that matches
the story.

1. Fatima has 12 colored pencils in her bag. She has 6 regular pencils, too. How many
pencils does Fatima have?

Fatima has _____ pencils.

2. Julio swam 7 laps in the morning. In the afternoon he swam some more laps. He
swam a total of 14 laps. How many laps did he swim in the afternoon?

Julio swam _____ laps in the afternoon.

COMMON CORE™   Lesson 21:   Recognize and make use of part–whole relationships within tape
diagrams when solving a variety of problem types.

Date: 9/20/13

3. Peter built 18 models. He built 13 airplanes and some cars. How many car models did he build?

Peter built _____ car models.

4. Kiana found some shells at the beach. She gave 8 shells to her brother. Now she has 9 shells left. How many shells did Kiana find at the beach?

Kiana found _____ shells.

Lesson 22

Objective: Write word problems of varied types.

Suggested Lesson Structure

■ Fluency Practice   (15 minutes)
  Concept Development   (33 minutes)
■ Student Debrief   (12 minutes)

  Total Time   **(60 minutes)**

Fluency Practice (15 minutes)

- Race and Roll Addition **1.OA.6**   (3 minutes)
- Sprint: Related Addition and Subtraction Within 10 and 20 **1.OA.6**   (10 minutes)
- Longer/Shorter **K.CC.7**   (2 minutes)

Race and Roll Addition (3 minutes)

Materials: 1 die per set of partners

Note: In previous Race and Roll Addition games, students raced to 20. Today, change the target number to 10 and practice both addition and subtraction. As students play, pay attention to their automaticity. When students demonstrate strong fluency to 10, increase the target number to 12.

Repeat Race and Roll Addition from G1–M4–Lesson 21. Instead of racing to 20 and stopping, students start at 0 and roll and add until they hit 10. Once they do, they roll to get back to 0 by subtracting.

Sprint: Related Addition and Subtraction Within 10 and 20 (10 minutes)

Materials: (S) Related Addition and Subtraction Within 10 and 20 Sprint

Note: During the last few days of fluency, students have been reviewing the relationship between addition and subtraction using the context of a number bond. In this Sprint, students apply this knowledge to solve equations, first within 10, and then within 20. Students who reach the final two questions of the fourth quadrants will be challenged to apply their understanding of analogous addition equations to analogous subtraction equations (**2.NBT.5**).

Lesson 22:   Write word problems of varied types.
Date: 9/20/13

4.E.36

Longer/Shorter (2 minutes)

Materials: (T) Board or document camera

Write one pair of numbers on the board at a time (e.g., 10 and 20). Draw a rectangle under the first number.

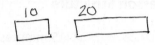

- T: This rectangle can fit a row of 10 dots.
- T: (Point to the second number, which in this example is 20.) I'm going to start to draw a rectangle that can fit a row of 20 dots of the same size. Tell me when to stop.
- T/S: (Begin drawing a rectangle, and give students the chance to say "Stop!" when it is approximately twice the size of the first rectangle.)
- T: Why did you say stop there?
- S: It is about double the length of the first rectangle. A rectangle for 20 has to fit 10 + 10.

Repeat this process for the following sequence of numbers: 10 and 5, 4 and 4, 4 and 8, 4 and 2, 8 and 10, 10 and 9. Only draw the actual dots for the first example. With each example, help students talk about how the first number compares, or relates, to the second number using language such as *a little longer, a little shorter, much longer, double*, etc.

Concept Development (33 minutes)

Materials: (T) Chart paper (S) Folder with Application Problems from Lessons 13–18 and Problem Sets from Lessons 19–21, personal white board

Have students place the tape diagram template inside their personal white boards, and bring all materials to the meeting area.

- T: (Display the tape diagram shown in the image to the right.) I found this drawing on a piece of paper on the floor. It went with someone's word problem from this week. Does anyone know which one it went to? Look through your Problem Sets with a partner and see if you can figure it out. Talk about how you know.

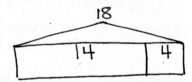

- S: (Look back at Problem Sets with their partners and discuss what is the same about the problem and the tape diagram.)
- T: Which problem does this tape diagram go with?

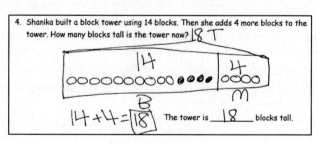

Lesson 21 Problem 4

S: This tape diagram goes with the problem about Shanika's tower (Problem 4 in Lesson 21). (Explains how the referents align with the problem story.) → I think it goes with the one about Tamra's yellow and purple beaded bracelet. (Problem 6 in Lesson 20). (Explains how the referents align with the problem story.)

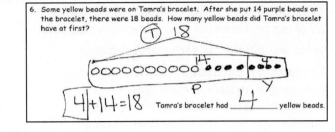

Lesson 20 Problem 6

T: Hmm. They both sound like they could match this tape diagram.

T: (Draw tape diagram shown in the image on the right.) This is a tape diagram for a problem from yesterday's lesson. Which problem does this match?

S: (Look back at Problem Set for Lesson 21 with partner and discuss what is the same about the problem and the tape diagram.)

T: Which problem does the tape diagram go with?

S: It's the one where Nikil builds a tower with 15 blocks and then adds some more. It's Problem 5. (Explains how the referents align with the problem story.)

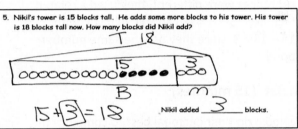

Lesson 21 Problem 5

T: With your partner, try to come up with a *different* story that could go with this tape diagram. You can use your tape diagram template as you discuss your idea.

T: (While students are discussing, circulate and listen.)

Listen to the students as they generate their story ideas, and choose three student math stories to be used as samples for the class. Present the stories in the following order:

- A story that parallels the examples using a different topic. (An *add to with a change unknown* problem type, where the 3 is the unknown number, e.g., 15 + ? = 18.)

- An *add to with a result unknown* problem type, e.g., 15 + 3 = ?.

- A different *add to or take from with a change unknown* problem or an *add to with the start unknown* problem, e.g., 3 + ? = 18, 18 - ? = 15, or ? + 15 = 18.

As the students share the problem with the class, redraw the tape diagram, label appropriately for the given story, and write the accompanying number sentences and statement.

NOTES ON
MULTIPLE MEANS OF
ACTION AND
EXPRESSION:

Giving students an opportunity to share their thinking allows them to evaluate their process and practice. English language learners also benefit from hearing others explain their thinking.

NOTES ON
MULTIPLE MEANS OF
REPRESENTATION:

Highlight the vocabulary used in the Problem Set to ensure understanding of all words. This supports vocabulary development, especially with English language learners.

COMMON CORE

Lesson 22: Write word problems of varied types.
Date: 9/20/13

4.E.38

T: What was similar in all of these problems?

S: All of our problems used the same tape diagram.

T: What was *different* in each story problem?

S: The topic was different. → Sometimes the unknown or mystery number was different. → Sometimes my number sentence was an addition sentence and sometimes it was a subtraction sentence. → The statement answered the question, and the question was different for each story problem.

T: How could knowing the answer to one story problem help you with a different story problem?

S: Sometimes they *do* use the same number sentence. → Even when the number sentences were different, they used a related fact, like $15 + 3 = 18$ can still help you with $18 - 15 = 3$, since they use the same number bond.

Problem Set (15 minutes)

Students should do their personal best to complete the Problem Set within the allotted 15 minutes. For some classes, it may be appropriate to modify the assignment by specifying which problems they work on first. Some problems do not specify a method for solving. Students solve these problems using the RDW approach used for Application Problems.

Student Debrief (12 minutes)

Lesson Objective: Write word problems of varied types.

The Student Debrief is intended to invite reflection and active processing of the total lesson experience.

Invite students to review their solutions for the Problem Set. They should check work by comparing answers with a partner before going over answers as a class. Look for misconceptions or misunderstandings that can be addressed in the Debrief. Guide students in a conversation to debrief the Problem Set and process the lesson.

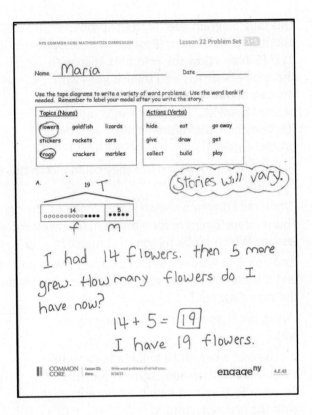

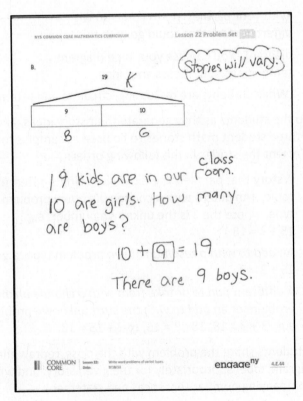

COMMON CORE™
Lesson 22:   Write word problems of varied types.
Date: 9/20/13

4.

ou may choose to use any combination of the questions below to lead the discussion.

- Look at Problem A. What story problem did you write? Share with the class. Posed to the rest of the class: What is the unknown number in their question? What number sentence would help you solve the question? Invite one or two more students to share. How did you decide on your labels for your tape diagrams?

- Which problems were the easiest for you to think of ideas for? Which were harder? Why?

- Look at your application problems from last week and your Problem Sets from this week. What do you notice about your work? What part of your word problem work has been improving?

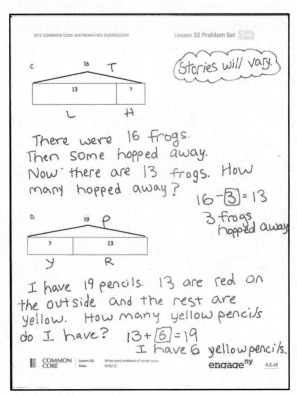

xit Ticket (3 minutes)

fter the Student Debrief, instruct students to complete he Exit Ticket. A review of their work will help you ssess the students' understanding of the concepts that ere presented in the lesson today and plan more ffectively for future lessons. You may read the uestions aloud to the students.

COMMON CORE

Lesson 22:   Write word problems of varied types.
Date: 9/20/13

4.E.40

A

Number correct: _____

Name _____ Date _____

*Write the missing number. Pay attention to the + and – signs.

1	$2 + 2 = \square$		16	$2 + \square = 8$	
2	$2 + \square = 4$		17	$6 + \square = 8$	
3	$4 - 2 = \square$		18	$8 - 6 = \square$	
4	$3 + 3 = \square$		19	$8 - 2 = \square$	
5	$3 + \square = 6$		20	$9 + 2 = \square$	
6	$6 - 3 = \square$		21	$9 + \square = 11$	
7	$4 + \square = 7$		22	$11 - 9 = \square$	
8	$3 + \square = 7$		23	$9 + \square = 15$	
9	$7 - 3 = \square$		24	$15 - 9 = \square$	
10	$7 - 4 = \square$		25	$8 + \square = 15$	
11	$5 + 4 = \square$		26	$15 - \square = 8$	
12	$4 + \square = 9$		27	$8 + \square = 17$	
13	$9 - 4 = \square$		28	$17 - \square = 8$	
14	$9 - 5 = \square$		29	$27 - \square = 8$	
15	$9 - \square = 4$		30	$37 - \square = 8$	

COMMON CORE™

Lesson 22: Write word problems of varied types.
Date: 9/20/13

4.

B

Number correct:

Name _____   Date _____

Write the missing number. Pay attention to the + and − signs.

1	$3 + 3 = \square$		16	$2 + \square = 9$	
2	$3 + \square = 6$		17	$7 + \square = 9$	
3	$6 - 3 = \square$		18	$9 - 7 = \square$	
4	$4 + 4 = \square$		19	$9 - 2 = \square$	
5	$4 + \square = 8$		20	$9 + 5 = \square$	
6	$8 - 4 = \square$		21	$9 + \square = 14$	
7	$4 + \square = 9$		22	$14 - 9 = \square$	
8	$5 + \square = 9$		23	$9 + \square = 16$	
9	$9 - 5 = \square$		24	$16 - 9 = \square$	
10	$9 - 4 = \square$		25	$8 + \square = 16$	
11	$3 + 4 = \square$		26	$16 - \square = 8$	
12	$4 + \square = 7$		27	$8 + \square = 16$	
13	$7 - 4 = \square$		28	$16 - \square = 8$	
14	$7 - 3 = \square$		29	$26 - \square = 8$	
15	$7 - \square = 3$		30	$36 - \square = 8$	

COMMON CORE | Lesson 22: | Write word problems of varied types.
Date: | 9/20/13

4.E.42

Name _____   Date _____

Use the tape diagrams to write a variety of word problems. Use the word bank if needed. Remember to label your model after you write the story.

Topics (Nouns)		
flowers	goldfish	lizards
stickers	rockets	cars
frogs	crackers	marbles

Actions (Verbs)		
hide	eat	go away
give	draw	get
collect	build	play

A.

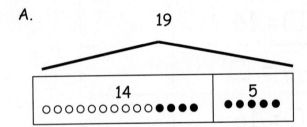

19

14   5

COMMON CORE

Lesson 22:   Write word problems of varied types.
Date: 9/20/13

4.

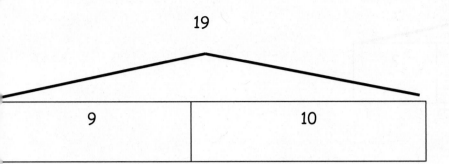

COMMON CORE™

Lesson 22: Write word problems of varied types.
Date: 9/20/13

4.E.44

C.

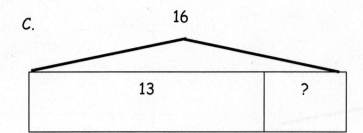

D.

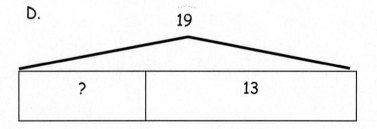

Name _____   Date _____

Circle the 2 story problems that match the tape diagram.

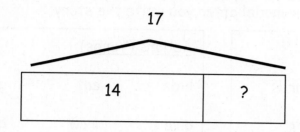

A. There are 14 ants on the picnic blanket. Then some more ants came over. Now there are 17 ants on the picnic blanket. How many ants came over?

B. Fourteen children are on the playground from one class. Then 17 children from another class came to the playground. How many children are on the playground now?

C. Seventeen grapes were on the plate. Willie ate 14 grapes. How many grapes are on the plate now?

Name _____   Date _____

Use the tape diagrams to write a variety of word problems. Use the word bank if needed. Remember to label your model after you write the story.

Topics (Nouns)		
flowers	goldfish	lizards
stickers	rockets	cars
frogs	crackers	marbles

Actions (Verbs)		
hide	eat	go away
give	draw	get
collect	build	play

A.

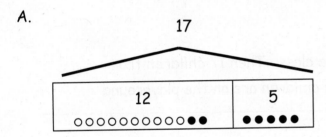

COMMON CORE™

Lesson 22: Write word problems of varied types.
Date: 9/20/13

4.

B.

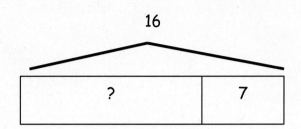

Mathematics Curriculum

1
GRADE

Topic F

Addition of Tens and Ones to a Two-Digit Number

1.NBT.4

Focus Standard:	1.NBT.4	Add within 100, including adding a two-digit number and a one-digit number, and adding a two-digit number and a multiple of 10, using concrete models or drawings and strategies based on place value, properties of operations, and/or the relationship between addition and subtraction; relate the strategy to a written method and explain the reasoning used. Understand that in adding two-digit numbers, one adds tens and tens, ones and ones; and sometimes it is necessary to compose a ten.
Instructional Days:	7	
Coherence -Links from:	G1–M2	Introduction to Place Value Through Addition and Subtraction Within 20
-Links to:	G1–M6	Place Value, Comparison, Addition and Subtraction to 100
	G2–M4	Addition and Subtraction Within 200 with Word Problems to 100

In Topic F, students begin adding like units within pairs of two-digit numbers. Lesson 23 focuses on taking interpretations of two-digit numbers a step further, having students interpret numbers such as 25 as 1 ten and 15 ones as well as 2 tens and 5 ones and as 25 ones. Working with this concept supports student understanding in the next lessons, when students add pairs such as 14 + 16 and initially make 2 tens and 10 ones.

During Lessons 24 and 25, students interchangeably add sets of two-digit numbers where the ones digits produce a sum less than or equal to 10. For example, when adding 17 + 13, students decompose the second addend into 10 and 3. They then add 10 to 17, making 27, and then add the remaining ones. In Lesson 25, students also practice adding ones to the first addend and then adding the remaining ten.

$$17 + 13 = 30$$
10   3

$$17 + 10 = 27$$
$$27 + 3 = 30$$

Lesson 24

$$17 + 13 = 30$$
3   10

$$17 + 3 = 20$$
$$20 + 10 = 30$$

Lesson 25

Topic F:	Addition of Tens and Ones to a Two-Digit Number
Date:	9/20/13

4

Lesson 26 and 27, students add tens and ones when the ones digits have a sum greater than 10, such as 19 + 15. Students continue to decompose the second addend, alternating between adding on the ten first and making the next ten, as shown to the right. In Lesson 27, students solve the same problem using the varying strategies taught throughout the topic. Students continue to strengthen their use of Level 3 strategies for adding numbers to 40.

The module closes with Lessons 28 and 29, wherein students solve problem sets of varied types to support flexibility in thinking as they add any pair of two-digits whose sum is within 40. In Lesson 29, students again share methods and representations for finding the sums.

$$19 + 15$$
$$\diagup\quad\diagdown$$
$$10\quad 5$$

$$19 + 10 = 29$$
$$29 + 5 = 34$$
$$\diagup\ \diagdown$$
$$1\quad 4$$

Adding on ten first

$$19 + 15$$
$$\diagup\quad\diagup\ \diagdown$$
$$1\quad 14$$

$$19 + 1 = 20$$
$$20 + 14 = 34$$
$$\diagup\ \diagdown$$
$$10\quad 4$$

Adding to make the next ten first

A Teaching Sequence Towards Mastery of Addition of Tens and Ones to a Two-Digit Number

Objective 1: Interpret two-digit numbers as tens and ones including cases with more than 9 ones.
(Lesson 23)

Objective 2: Add a pair of two-digit numbers when the ones digits have a sum less than or equal to 10.
(Lessons 24–25)

Objective 3: Add a pair of two-digit numbers when the ones digits have a sum greater than 10.
(Lessons 26–27)

Objective 4: Add a pair of two-digit numbers with varied sums in the ones.
(Lessons 28–29)

Lesson 23

Objective: Interpret two-digit numbers as tens and ones, including cases with more than 9 ones.

Suggested Lesson Structure

■ Application Problem   (5 minutes)
■ Fluency Practice   (10 minutes)
■ Concept Development   (35 minutes)
■ Student Debrief   (10 minutes)
   Total Time   **(60 minutes)**

Application Problem (5 minutes)

Kim picks up 10 loose pencils and puts them in a cup. Ben has 1 package of 10 pencils that he adds to the cup. How many pencils are now in the cup? Use the RDW process to solve the problem.

Note: This problem bridges the objectives from Lessons 19 through to today's lesson. During the Debrief, students complete a place value chart to match the story and reinterpret the number 20 in several ways. As in Topic D, throughout Topic F the Application Problem starts the lesson so that fluency activities flow into the Concept Development.

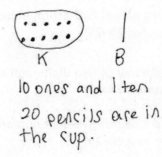

Fluency Practice (10 minutes)

- Grade 1 Core Fluency Differentiated Practice Sets **1.OA.6**   (5 minutes)
- Count by 10 with Dimes **1.NBT.5, 1.MD.3**   (2 minutes)
- Tens and Ones **1.NBT.4**   (3 minutes)

Grade 1 Core Fluency Differentiated Practice Sets (5 minutes)

Materials: (S) Core Fluency Practice Sets

Note: Throughout Topic F and for the remainder of the year, each day's fluency includes an opportunity for review and mastery of the sums and differences with totals through 10 by means of the Core Fluency Practice Sets or Sprints. Five options are provided in this lesson for the Core Fluency Practice Set, with Sheet A being

Lesson 23:   Interpret two-digit numbers as tens and ones, including cases with more than 9 ones.
Date: 9/20/13

the simplest addition fluency of the grade and Sheet E being the most complex. Start all students on Sheet A. Keep a record of student progress so that you can move students to more complex sheets as they are ready.

Students complete as many problems as they can in 90 seconds. We recommend 100% accuracy and completion before moving to the next level. Collect any Practice Sheets that have been completed within the 90 seconds and check the answers. The next time Core Fluency Practice Sets are used, students who have successfully completed their set today can be provided with the next level.

For early finishers, you might assign a counting pattern and start number. Celebrate improvement as well as advancement. Students should be encouraged to compete with themselves rather than their peers. Interview students on practice strategies. Notify caring adults of each child's progress.

Count by 10 with Dimes (2 minutes)

Materials: (T) 10 dimes

Note: This fluency activity strengthens students' ability to recognize a dime and identify its value, while providing practice with counting forward and back by 10.

Lay out and take away dimes in 5-group formation as students count by 10 both the regular way and the Say Ten way.

Tens and Ones (3 minutes)

Materials: (T) 100-bead Rekenrek

Note: This fluency activity reviews how to decompose two-digit numbers into tens and ones with the Rekenrek so that students can see alternate decompositions in today's lesson.

    T: (Show a 16 on the Rekenrek). How many tens do you see?
    S: 1 ten.
    T: How many ones?
    S: 6 ones.
    T: Say the number the Say Ten way.
    S: Ten 6.
    T: Good. 1 ten plus 6 ones is?
    S: 16.
    T: 16 + 10 is?
    S: 26.

Slide over the next row and repeat for 26 and then 36. Continue with the following suggested sequence: 15, 25, 35, 45, 55, 65, 75; 17, 27, 37, 57, 97. Then, follow the same script, but ask students to subtract 10 instead of add 10, using the following suggested sequence: 39, 29, 19, 9; 51, 41, 31, etc.

COMMON CORE™

| Lesson 23: | Interpret two-digit numbers as tens and ones, including cases with more than 9 ones. |
| Date: | 9/20/13 |

4.F.4

Concept Development (35 minutes)

Materials: (T) Chart paper, place value chart template from G1–M4–Lesson 2 (optional) (S) Personal white boards, ten-sticks from math toolkit

Have students gather in the meeting area in a semi-circle formation.

T: (Ask three student volunteers to come to the front.) Show us 3 tens using your magic counting sticks.

S: (Each student shows clasped hands.)

T: How many tens do you see?

S: 3 tens.

T: How many loose ones do you see?

S: 0 ones.

T: What is the value of 3 tens?

S: 30.

T: (Write 30 = 3 tens and fill in the place value chart. Continue to chart student responses as they make other combinations of 30 using tens and ones.)

T: (Ask one student to unclasp her hands.) How many tens do you see?

S: 2 tens.

T: How many loose ones do you see?

S: 10 ones.

T: Do we still have 30? Explain how you know.

S: Yes! → We didn't add anything or take anything away. → 1 ten became 10 ones, but they are the same amount. → They have the same value.

T: How is 30 made here? (Chart the students' answer.)

S: With 2 tens and 10 ones.

Repeat the process and ask the remaining students to unbundle their tens one at a time to show 1 ten 20 ones and, finally, 30 ones.

T: Let's look at the chart. The number 30 can be represented in many different ways. 30 can be made of?

S: 3 tens, 2 tens 10 ones. 1 ten 20 ones, 30 ones!

T: Get together with your partner and another pair of students. Show as many tens as you can using your magic counting sticks. (Wait.)

Combinations of **30** in tens and ones

tens	ones
3	0

30 = 3 tens 0 ones

tens	ones
2	10

30 = 2 tens 10 ones

tens	ones
1	20

30 = 1 ten 20 ones

tens	ones
0	30

30 = 30 ones

NOTES ON MULTIPLE MEANS OF REPRESENTATION:

Careful selection of pairs for collaborative work is essential to achieving expected outcomes. This lesson will work well with hetero-geneous groupings of students. Pair one student with a clear understanding of the concept with another student who might need more practice with tens and ones. Pair an English language learner with another student who expresses their reasoning especially well.

Lesson 23: Interpret two-digit numbers as tens and ones, including cases with more than 9 ones.

Date: 9/20/13

4

T: What is the largest amount of tens you can make?

S: 4 tens.

T: What is 4 tens?

S: 40.

T: Show more ways to make 40 and record them on your boards.

S: We made 3 tens 10 ones. → 2 tens 20 ones. → 1 ten 30 ones. → 40 ones.

T: (Ask four volunteers to come to the front.) Show 37 using your magic counting sticks with as many tens as possible.

S: (Show 3 tens 7 ones.)

T: (Tap the third student on the shoulder.) If Student 3 unbundles his ten, how many tens and ones will we have?

S: 2 tens 17 ones.

T: Let's check. Student 3, unbundle your magic counting sticks! Were we correct? Are there 2 tens and 17 ones?

S: Yes!

T: Explain to your partner how 2 tens 17 ones is the same as 37.

S: 17 ones is the same as 1 ten and 7 ones. 2 tens and 1 ten is 3 tens. 7 more ones is 37.

T: Show 37 as 3 tens 7 ones again. If only 1 student shows 1 ten, how many ones will there be to make 37? 37 is the same as 1 ten and how many ones?

S: 1 ten 27 ones.

T: How did you know?

S: (Point to each student with unclasped hands.) 10, 20, 7 is 27. → Two students will have to unbundle their sticks, so that's 20. 20 ones and 7 ones is 27 ones.

T: Let's check. Student 1, keep your hands clasped. The other students with tens, unbundle and show 10 ones. (Wait.) 37 is the same as how many tens and how many ones?

S: 1 ten 27 ones.

Repeat the process, showing 0 tens 37 ones.

Have students work in pairs using linking cubes or working in groups of four using magic counting sticks to make all combinations of tens and ones to make 13, 23, 27, 34, and 38.

Next, write a number in the tens and ones place using the place value chart template (see image below) and ask students to determine the total value:

T: (Write 1 ten 15 ones on a place value chart.) What is the value of 1 ten 15 ones? You may use your cubes or work with your classmates and their magic counting sticks to show your thinking.

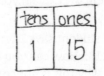

S: 10 plus 15 is 25. → 1 ten is 10 ones. 10 ones and 15 ones is 25 ones. → 15 ones is the same as 1 ten 5 ones. Add another 1 ten and I have 2 tens 5 ones, that's 25.

T: So the value of 1 ten 15 ones is?

COMMON CORE | **Lesson 23:** Interpret two-digit numbers as tens and ones, including cases with more than 9 ones.
| **Date:** 9/20/13

4.F.6

S: 25!

Repeat the process with the following sequence:

- 1 ten 5 ones, 25 ones

- 3 tens 5 ones, 2 tens 15 ones, 1 ten 25 ones

- 31 ones, 2 ten 11 ones, 1 ten 21 ones, 3 tens 1 one

- 2 ten 16 ones, 3 tens 6 ones

- 1 ten 29 ones, 3 tens 9 ones

Students may work in pairs and use their linking cubes or in groups of 4 using fingers to solve while others visualize every 10 ones as 1 ten.

Problem Set (10 minutes)

Students should do their personal best to complete the Problem Set within the allotted 10 minutes. For some classes, it may be appropriate to modify the assignment by specifying which problems they work on first.

Student Debrief (10 minutes)

Lesson Objective: Interpret two-digit numbers as tens and ones, including cases with more than 9 ones.

The Student Debrief is intended to invite reflection and active processing of the total lesson experience.

Invite students to review their solutions for the Problem Set. They should check work by comparing answers with a partner before going over answers as a class. Look for misconceptions or misunderstandings that can be addressed in the Debrief. Guide students in a conversation to debrief the Problem Set and process the lesson.

You may choose to use any combination of the questions below to lead the discussion.

- How did you solve Problem 4? Explain your thinking.

- Look at Problem 1(d). A student says 2 tens 13 ones can be written as 213. How can you help this student understand why this is not correct?

**NOTES ON
MULTIPLE MEANS OF
REPRESENTATION:**

As students complete the Problem Set, allow those who need more concrete practice to use their ten-sticks and ones cubes. Some students may not be able to visualize ones as tens especially when completing Problem 4. Support these students by having them lay out the numbers as they are matching. Their path to abstract thinking may be a little longer than those of other students.

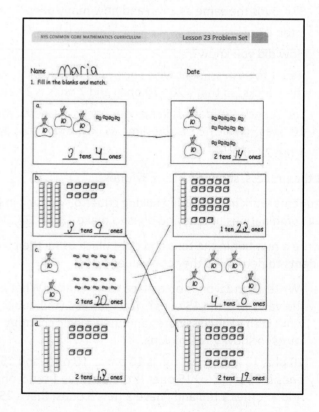

Lesson 23:   Interpret two-digit numbers as tens and ones, including cases with more than 9 ones.
Date: 9/20/13

- Look at Problem 2. Circle the place value charts that have two digits in the ones place. What do you notice?
- Look at Problem 3. Circle the statement that is not true. Write down as many combinations of tens and ones to make the statement true.
- How can using Say Ten counting help you find your combinations of tens and ones?
- How did the Application Problem connect to today's lesson? How could we write the total number of pencils in the place value chart? What other combinations of tens and ones can we use to make this number?

xit Ticket (3 minutes)

fter the Student Debrief, instruct students to complete ne Exit Ticket. A review of their work will help you ssess the students' understanding of the concepts that ere presented in the lesson today and plan more ffectively for future lessons. You may read the uestions aloud to the students.

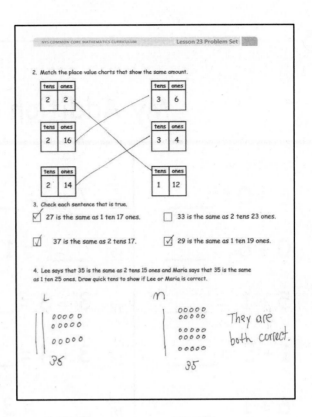

COMMON CORE™

Lesson 23: Interpret two-digit numbers as tens and ones, including cases with more than 9 ones.
Date: 9/20/13

4.F.8

2013 Common Core, Inc. All rights reserved. commoncore.org

Name _____ Date _____

My Addition Practice

1. $6 + 0 =$ ___	11. $7 + 1 =$ ___	21. $5 + 3 =$ ___
2. $0 + 6 =$ ___	12. ___ $= 1 + 7$	22. ___ $= 5 + 4$
3. $5 + 1 =$ ___	13. $3 + 3 =$ ___	23. $6 + 4 =$ ___
4. $1 + 5 =$ ___	14. $3 + 4 =$ ___	24. $4 + 6 =$ ___
5. $6 + 1 =$ ___	15. ___ $= 3 + 5$	25. ___ $= 4 + 4$
6. $1 + 6 =$ ___	16. $6 + 3 =$ ___	26. $3 + 4 =$ ___
7. $6 + 2 =$ ___	17. $7 + 3 =$ ___	27. $5 + 5 =$ ___
8. $5 + 2 =$ ___	18. ___ $= 7 + 2$	28. ___ $= 4 + 5$
9. $2 + 5 =$ ___	19. $2 + 7 =$ ___	29. $3 + 7 =$ ___
10. $2 + 4 =$ ___	20. $2 + 8 =$ ___	30. ___ $= 3 + 6$

Today I finished _____ problems.

I solved _____ problems correctly.

COMMON CORE | Lesson 23: | Interpret two-digit numbers as tens and ones, including cases with more than 9 ones.

Date: 9/20/13

4

Name _____   Date _____

My Missing Addend Practice

1. $6 + \_\_\_ = 6$	11. $3 + \_\_\_ = 6$	21. $4 + \_\_\_ = 7$
2. $0 + \_\_\_ = 6$	12. $4 + \_\_\_ = 8$	22. $7 = 3 + \_\_\_$
3. $5 + \_\_\_ = 6$	13. $10 = 5 + \_\_\_$	23. $2 + \_\_\_ = 7$
4. $4 + \_\_\_ = 6$	14. $5 + \_\_\_ = 9$	24. $2 + \_\_\_ = 8$
5. $0 + \_\_\_ = 7$	15. $5 + \_\_\_ = 7$	25. $9 = 2 + \_\_\_$
6. $6 + \_\_\_ = 7$	16. $8 = 5 + \_\_\_$	26. $2 + \_\_\_ = 10$
7. $1 + \_\_\_ = 7$	17. $5 + \_\_\_ = 9$	27. $10 = 3 + \_\_\_$
8. $7 + \_\_\_ = 8$	18. $8 + \_\_\_ = 10$	28. $3 + \_\_\_ = 9$
9. $1 + \_\_\_ = 8$	19. $7 + \_\_\_ = 10$	29. $4 + \_\_\_ = 9$
10. $6 + \_\_\_ = 8$	20. $10 = 6 + \_\_\_$	30. $10 = 4 + \_\_\_$

Today I finished _____ problems.

I solved _____ problems correctly.

Name _____   Date _____

My Related Addition and Subtraction Practice

1. $5 + \_\_\_ = 6$	11. $7 + \_\_\_ = 10$	21. $4 + \_\_\_ = 8$
2. $1 + \_\_\_ = 6$	12. $10 - 7 = \_\_\_$	22. $8 - 4 = \_\_\_$
3. $6 - 1 = \_\_\_$	13. $5 + \_\_\_ = 7$	23. $4 + \_\_\_ = 7$
4. $9 + \_\_\_ = 10$	14. $7 - 5 = \_\_\_$	24. $7 - 4 = \_\_\_$
5. $1 + \_\_\_ = 10$	15. $5 + \_\_\_ = 8$	25. $5 + \_\_\_ = 9$
6. $10 - 9 = \_\_\_$	16. $8 - 5 = \_\_\_$	26. $9 - 5 = \_\_\_$
7. $5 + \_\_\_ = 10$	17. $4 + \_\_\_ = 6$	27. $6 + \_\_\_ = 9$
8. $10 - 5 = \_\_\_$	18. $6 - 4 = \_\_\_$	28. $9 - 6 = \_\_\_$
9. $8 + \_\_\_ = 10$	19. $3 + \_\_\_ = 6$	29. $4 + \_\_\_ = 7$
10. $10 - 8 = \_\_\_$	20. $6 - 3 = \_\_\_$	30. $7 - 4 = \_\_\_$

Today I finished _____ problems.

I solved _____ problems correctly.

COMMON CORE   **Lesson 23:**   Interpret two-digit numbers as tens and ones, including cases with more than 9 ones.

Date: 9/20/13

4.

Name _____ Date _____

My Subtraction Practice

1. 6 - 0 = ____	11. 6 - 3 = ____	21. 8 - 4 = ____
2. 6 - 1 = ____	12. 7 - 3 = ____	22. 8 - 3 = ____
3. 7 - 1 = ____	13. 9 – 3 = ____	23. 8 - 5 = ____
4. 8 - 1 = ____	14. 10 - 8 = ____	24. 9 - 5 = ____
5. 6 - 2 = ____	15. 10 - 6 = ____	25. 9 - 4 = ____
6. 7 - 2 = ____	16. 10 – 4 = ____	26. 7 - 3 = ____
7. 9 - 2 = ____	17. 10 - 5 = ____	27. 10 - 7 = ____
8. 10 - 10 = ____	18. 7 – 6 = ____	28. 9 - 7 = ____
9. 10 - 9 = ____	19. 7 – 5 = ____	29. 9 - 6 = ____
10. 10 - 7 = ____	20. 6 - 4 = ____	30. 8 - 6 = ____

Today I finished _____ problems.

I solved _____ problems correctly.

COMMON CORE™ Lesson 23: Interpret two-digit numbers as tens and ones, including cases with more than 9 ones.
Date: 9/20/13

4.F.12

Name _____   Date _____

My Mixed Practice

1. $4 + 2 = $ ___	11. $2 + $ ___ $ = 6$	21. $8 - 5 = $ ___
2. $2 + $ ___ $ = 6$	12. $6 - 2 = $ ___	22. $3 + $ ___ $ = 8$
3. $6 = 3 + $ ___	13. $6 - 4 = $ ___	23. $8 = $ ___ $ + 5$
4. $2 + 5 = $ ___	14. $5 + $ ___ $ = 7$	24. ___ $ + 2 = 9$
5. $7 = 5 + $ ___	15. $7 - 5 = $ ___	25. $9 = $ ___ $ + 7$
6. $4 + 3 = $ ___	16. $7 - 4 = $ ___	26. $9 - 2 = $ ___
7. $7 = $ ___ $ + 4$	17. $7 - 3 = $ ___	27. $9 - 7 = $ ___
8. $8 = $ ___ $ + 4$	18. $8 = 6 + $ ___	28. $9 - 6 = $ ___
9. $4 + 5 = $ ___	19. $8 - 2 = $ ___	29. $9 = $ ___ $ + 4$
10. $9 = $ ___ $ + 4$	20. $8 - 6 = $ ___	30. $9 - 6 = $ ___

Today I finished _____ problems.

I solved _____ problems correctly.

COMMON CORE **Lesson 23:** Interpret two-digit numbers as tens and ones, including cases with more than 9 ones.

Date: 9/20/13

4.

Name _____ Date _____

Fill in the blanks and match the pairs that show the same amount.

a.

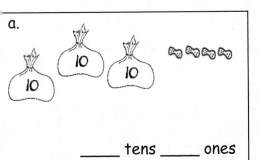

_____ tens _____ ones

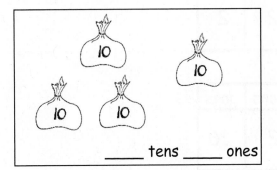

_____ tens _____ ones

b.

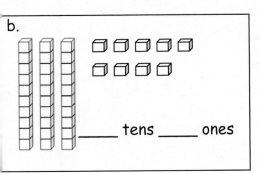

_____ tens _____ ones

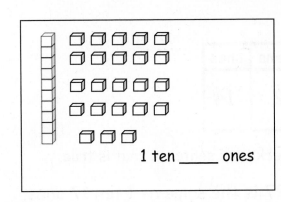

1 ten _____ ones

c.

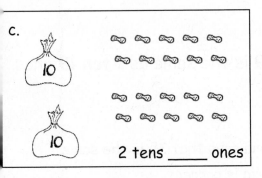

2 tens _____ ones

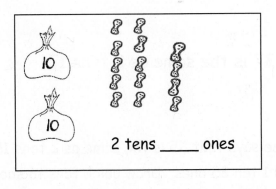

2 tens _____ ones

d.

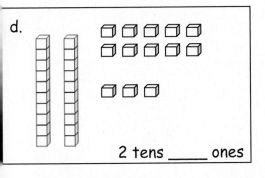

2 tens _____ ones

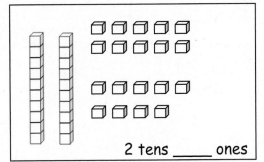

2 tens _____ ones

COMMON CORE™

Lesson 23:   Interpret two-digit numbers as tens and ones, including cases with more than 9 ones.

Date: 9/20/13

4.F.14

2. Match the place value charts that show the same amount.

tens	ones
2	2

tens	ones
3	6

tens	ones
2	16

tens	ones
3	4

tens	ones
2	14

tens	ones
1	2

3. Check each sentence that is true.

☐ 27 is the same as 1 ten 17 ones.

☐ 33 is the same as 2 tens 23 ones

☐ 37 is the same as 2 tens 17.

☐ 29 is the same as 1 ten 19 ones.

4. Lee says that 35 is the same as 2 tens 15 ones, and Maria says that 35 is the same as 1 ten 25 ones. Draw quick tens to show if Lee or Maria is correct.

COMMON CORE | **Lesson 23:** Interpret two-digit numbers as tens and ones, including cases with more than 9 ones.
Date: 9/20/13

4.

Name _____   Date _____

Match the place value charts that show the same amount.

tens	ones
2	12

tens	ones
2	16

tens	ones
2	8

tens	ones
1	18

tens	ones
3	6

tens	ones
3	2

Tamra says that 24 is the same as 1 ten 14 ones, and Willie says that 24 is the same as 2 tens 14 ones. Draw quick tens to show if Tamra or Willie is correct.

COMMON CORE™

Lesson 23:   Interpret two-digit numbers as tens and ones, including cases with more than 9 ones.

Date: 9/20/13

4.F.16

Name _____   Date _____

1.   Fill in the blanks and match the pairs that show the same amount.

a.

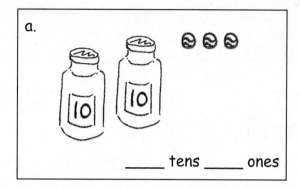

_____ tens _____ ones

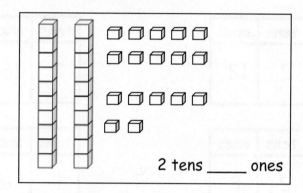

2 tens _____ ones

b.

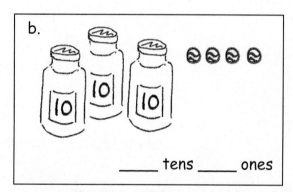

_____ tens _____ ones

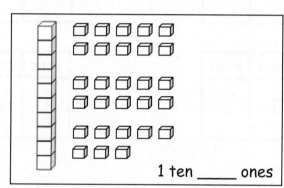

1 ten _____ ones

c.

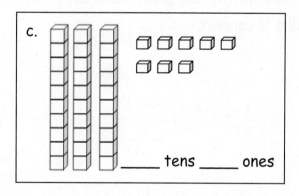

_____ tens _____ ones

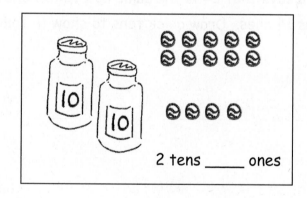

2 tens _____ ones

d.

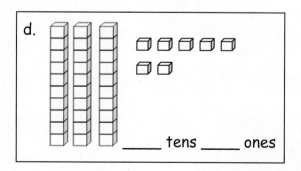

_____ tens _____ ones

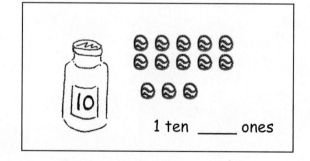

1 ten _____ ones

Lesson 23:   Interpret two-digit numbers as tens and ones, including cases with
               more than 9 ones.
Date: 9/20/13

4.

. Match the place value charts that show the same amount.

tens	ones
2	18

tens	ones
3	8

tens	ones
1	16

tens	ones
2	1

tens	ones
0	21

tens	ones
2	6

3. Check each sentence that is true.

☐ 35 is the same as 1 ten 25 ones.   ☐ 28 is the same as 1 ten 18 ones.

☐ 36 is the same as 2 tens 16 ones.   ☐ 39 is the same as 2 tens 29 ones.

4. Emi says that 37 is the same as 1 ten 27 ones, and Ben says that 37 is the same as 2 tens 7 ones. Draw quick tens to show if Emi or Ben is correct.

COMMON CORE

Lesson 23:   Interpret two-digit numbers as tens and ones, including cases with more than 9 ones.

Date: 9/20/13

4.F.18

Lesson 24

Objective: Add a pair of two-digit numbers when the ones digits have a sum less than or equal to 10.

Suggested Lesson Structure

- Application Problem   (5 minutes)
- Fluency Practice   (14 minutes)
- Concept Development   (31 minutes)
- Student Debrief   (10 minutes)

Total Time   **(60 minutes)**

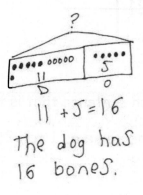

Application Problem (5 minutes)

A dog hides 11 bones behind his doghouse. Later, his owner gives him 5 bones. How many bones does the dog have? Use the RDW process to share your thinking as you solve the problem.

Extension: All the bones are brown or white. The same number of bones are brown as white. How many brown bones does the dog have?

Note: This problem reviews the *add to with result unknown* problem type so that they can focus on the drawing and labeling of the tape diagram. In the extension, students are challenged to consider the relationship between the two parts. Keep at least one student work sample to use as a comparison during the following day's Debrief.

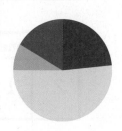

Fluency Practice (14 minutes)

- Grade 1 Core Fluency Differentiated Practice Sets **1.OA.6**   (5 minutes)
- Number Bond Addition and Subtraction **1.OA.6**   (4 minutes)
- Count by 10 or 1 with Dimes and Pennies **1.NBT.5, 1.MD.3**   (3 minutes)
- Add Tens **1.NBT.4**   (2 minutes)

Grade 1 Core Fluency Differentiated Practice Sets (5 minutes)

Materials: (S) Core Fluency Practice Sets from G1–M4–Lesson 23

Note: This activity assesses students' progress toward mastery of the required addition fluency for first graders. Give Practice Set B to students who correctly answered all questions on Practice Set A in the previous lesson. All other students should try to improve their scores on Practice Set A.

Students complete as many problems as they can in 90 seconds. Assign a counting pattern and start number for early finishers, or tell them to practice make ten addition or subtraction on the backs of their papers. Collect and correct any Practice Sets completed within the allotted time.

Number Bond Addition and Subtraction (4 minutes)

Materials: (S) Personal white boards, die per pair

Note: This fluency activity addresses Grade 1's core fluency requirement and strengthens understanding of the relationship between addition and subtraction.

Repeat the activity from G1–M4–Lesson 21. Today, assign partners of equal ability and an appropriate range of numbers for each pair. Allow partners to choose a number for their whole and roll the die to determine the one of the parts. Both students write two addition and two subtraction sentences with a box for the missing number in each equation and solve for the missing number. They then exchange boards and check each other's work.

$$5 + \boxed{3} = 8 \qquad 8 - 5 = \boxed{3}$$
$$\boxed{3} + 5 = 8 \qquad 8 - \boxed{3} = 5$$

Count by 10 or 1 with Dimes and Pennies (3 minutes)

Materials: (T) 10 dimes and 10 pennies

Note: This activity uses dimes and pennies as abstract representations of tens and ones to help students become familiar with coins, while simultaneously providing practice with counting forward and back by 10 or 1.

- Minute 1: Place and take away dimes in a 5-group formation as students count along by 10.
- Minute 2: Begin with 2 pennies. Ask how many ones there are. Instruct students to start at 2 and add and subtract 10 as you place and take away dimes.
- Minute 3: Begin with 2 dimes. Ask how many tens there are. Instruct students to begin at 20 and add and subtract 1 as you place and take away pennies.

Add Tens (2 minutes)

Materials: (T) 100-bead Rekenrek

Note: Reviewing how to add multiples of 10 enables students to utilize their understanding of place value to add 2 two-digit numbers in today's lesson.

T: (Show 14 on the Rekenrek.) Add 10.
S: 14 + 10 = 24.

| **COMMON CORE** | Lesson 24: | Add a pair of two-digit numbers when the ones digits have a sum less than or equal to 10. | **4.F.20** |
| | Date: | 9/20/13 | |

T: Add 20.

S   14 + 20 = 34.

Repeat, displaying other teen numbers and instructing students to add 10 and 20. If students find it challenging to mentally add 20, scaffold by asking them to add 2 tens and modeling with the Rekenrek before asking them to add 20.

Concept Development (31 minutes)

Materials: (T) 5 ten-sticks (3 red and 2 yellow), chart paper (S) 4 ten-sticks from math toolkit, personal white board

Students gather in the meeting area with their partners and materials.

T: (Write 24 + 13.) Partner A, show 24 with your cubes. Partner B, show 13 with your cubes.

S: (Show 24 or 13 with cubes.)

T: Combine your cubes to show the easiest way to find the total.

S: (Add cubes.)

T: How did you add 24 and 13?

S: We put the tens together and the ones together.
→ We put 2 tens and 1 ten together. We put 4 ones and 3 ones together. → We have 3 ten-sticks and 7 ones. We made 37.

T: I love the way you combined the tens with tens and ones with ones together. 2 tens and 1 ten is?

S: 3 tens.

T: 4 ones and 3 ones is?

S: 7 ones.

T: 3 tens 7 ones is?

S: 37.

T: 24 + 13 is?

S: 37.

T: (Complete the number sentence. Then show 24 using red cubes.) You are experts at working with tens. You know how to add tens to any number just like we practiced during fluency today. Let's use that skill to add 24 and 13.   Let's add 10 from 13 to 24 first.

T: (Place the ten-stick next to 2 ten-sticks.) 1 ten more than 2 tens 4 is?

S: 3 tens 4.

T: What do I need to still add?

S: 3 ones.

NOTES ON MULTIPLE MEANS OF EXPRESSION:

At this stage of development, students will typically start in the highest place, in this case, the tens place. This is an acceptable strategy for addition at any level. Starting with the ones place only makes the standard algorithm easier and is not necessary until students are adding larger numbers with regrouping in multiple places.

Lesson 24:   Add a pair of two-digit numbers when the ones digits have a sum less than or equal to 10.

Date: 9/20/13

4.F

T: (Place 3 yellow cubes on top of 4 red cubes.) 34 and 3 is?

S: 37.

T: We just used our expertise on tens by adding 1 ten to 24 first.

T: Let's use a number bond to do the same thing. How did we break apart 13?

S: 10 and 3.

T: (Draw the number bond.) What did we do first? (Point to the number bond.)

S: Add 10. (Write 24 + 10.)

T: 24 + 10 is?

S: 34.

T: Next? (Point to the number bond.)

S: Add 3.

T: 34 + 3 is?

S: 37.

T: Now you write the two addition sentences to show how we added 1 ten first.

S: (Write 24 + 10 = 34 and 34 + 3 = 37.)

T: Let's try a new problem. (Write 24 + 16.) Partner A, make 24 with your linking cubes. Partner B, make 16. (Wait.) What part of 16 did we add first before?

S: 10!

T: Add 10 to 24. What do you get?

S: (Lay down a ten-stick next to 2 ten-sticks.) 34.

T: What more do we have to add?

S: 6.

T: How much do you have altogether?

S: 40.

T: Show us what you did.

S: We made another ten-stick with 4 and 6. Now we have 4 ten-sticks. That's 40. → 4 ones and 6 ones is 10 ones. 3 tens and 10 ones is the same as 40. That's what we did yesterday!

T: Make a number bond and write two number sentences to record how you solved 24 + 16. We started with 24. Let's break apart 16 into?

S: 10 and 6. (Break apart 16 into 10 and 6.)

NOTES ON MULTIPLE MEANS OF ENGAGEMENT:

Appropriate scaffolds help all students feel successful. Some students may get the tens and ones confused when adding. Students may use place value charts to write the numbers in that they are adding to help them move towards visualizing. Using their ten-sticks and ones cubes will also help these students eventually move from concrete to abstract.

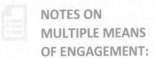

24 + 13
  /   \
 10   3

24 + 10 = 34
34 + 3 = 37

24 + 16
  /   \
 10   6

24 + 10 = 34
34 + 6 = 40

COMMON CORE   Lesson 24:   Add a pair of two-digit numbers when the ones digits have a sum less than or equal to 10.

Date: 9/20/13

4.F.22

If needed, have students represent their process of adding 24 and 16 in quick ten drawings, talking through the steps with their partners. Ask students to also write two addition sentences to record their steps.

Repeat the process following the suggested sequence: 22 + 14, 23 + 16, 23 + 17, 19 + 21, 22 + 18, and 12 + 28 (start with 28, the bigger addend, then add 10 and 2).

Problem Set (10 minutes)

Students should do their personal best to complete the Problem Set within the allotted 10 minutes. For some classes, it may be appropriate to modify the assignment by specifying which problems they work on first. Some problems do not specify a method for solving. Students solve these problems using the RDW approach used for Application Problems.

Student Debrief (10 minutes)

Lesson Objective: Add a pair of two-digit numbers when the ones digits have a sum less than or equal to 10.

The Student Debrief is intended to invite reflection and active processing of the total lesson experience.

Invite students to review their solutions for the Problem Set. They should check work by comparing answers with a partner before going over answers as a class. Look for misconceptions or misunderstandings that can be addressed in the Debrief. Guide students in a conversation to debrief the Problem Set and process the lesson.

NOTES ON
MULTIPLE MEANS OF
ENGAGEMENT:

Remember to provide challenging extensions for your advanced students. Give them one two-digit number and the sum. Have students find the mystery two-digit addend.

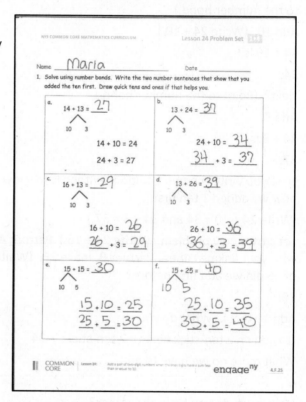

You may choose to use any combination of the questions below to lead the discussion.

- How did you solve Problem 1(d)? Which addend did you start with and why?
- How can setting up for Problem 1(e) help you solve Problem 1(f)?
- How can setting up for Problem 2(e) help you solve Problem 2(f)?
- What new strategy did we use to add 2 two-digit addends?
- How did the Application Problem connect to today's lesson?

Lesson 24:   Add a pair of two-digit numbers when the ones digits have a sum less than or equal to 10.

Date: 9/20/13

4.

Exit Ticket (3 minutes)

After the Student Debrief, instruct students to complete the Exit Ticket. A review of their work will help you assess the students' understanding of the concepts that were presented in the lesson today and plan more effectively for future lessons. You may read the questions aloud to the student

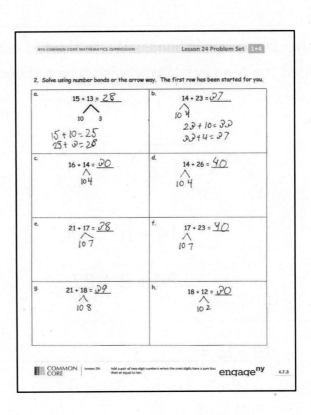

COMMON CORE™ | **Lesson 24:** Add a pair of two-digit numbers when the ones digits have a sum less than or equal to 10.

Date: 9/20/13

4.F.24

Name _____ Date _____

1. Solve using number bonds. Write the two number sentences that show that you added the ten first. Draw quick tens and ones if that helps you.

a.

14 + 13 = _____

/\
10   3

14 + 10 = 24

24 + 3 = 27

b.

13 + 24 = _____

/\
10   3

24 + 10 = _____

_____ + 3 = _____

c.

16 + 13 = _____

/\
10   3

16 + 10 = _____

_____ + 3 = _____

d.

13 + 26 = _____

/\
10   3

26 + 10 = _____

_____ + _____ = _____

e.

15 + 15 = _____

/\
10   5

_____ + _____ = _____

_____ + _____ = _____

f.

15 + 25 = _____

/\

_____ + _____ = _____

_____ + _____ = _____

. Solve using number bonds or the arrow way. The first row has been started for you.

a. $15 + 13 =$ _____ 10 3	b. $14 + 23 =$ _____
c. $16 + 14 =$ _____	d. $14 + 26 =$ _____
e. $21 + 17 =$ _____	f. $17 + 23 =$ _____
g. $21 + 18 =$ _____	h. $18 + 12 =$ _____

Lesson 24:   Add a pair of two-digit numbers when the ones digits have a sum less
than or equal to 10.
Date: 9/20/13

4.F.26

Name _____   Date _____

a. 13 + 26 = _____	b. 19 + 21 = _____

a.   13 + 26 = _____

     ⋀

_____ + _____ = _____

_____ + _____ = _____

b.   19 + 21 = _____

     ⋀

_____ + _____ = _____

_____ + _____ = _____

COMMON CORE™ | **Lesson 24:** Add a pair of two-digit numbers when the ones digits have a sum less than or equal to 10.

Date: 9/20/13

4.F

ame _____ Date _____

Solve using number bonds. Write the two number sentences that show that you added the ten first. Draw quick tens and ones if that helps you.

a. 13 + 16 = ____

    10   3

            16 + 10 = 26

            26 + 3 = 29

b.

    16 + 23 = ____

    10   6

            23 + 10 = _____

            _____ + 6 = _____

c.

    16 + 14 = ____

    10   4

            16 + 10 = ____

            ____ + 4 = ____

d.   14 + 26 = ____

    10   4

            26 + 10 = ____

            ____ + ____ = ____

e.   17 + 13 = ____

    10   3

            ____ + ____ = ____

            ____ + ____ = ____

f.   27 + 13 = ____

            ____ + ____ = ____

            ____ + ____ = ____

Lesson 24:	Add a pair of two-digit numbers when the ones digits have a sum less than or equal to 10.
Date:	9/20/13

4.F.28

2. Solve using number bonds. The first row has been started for you.

a. 14 + 13 = _____ 10 3 14 + 10 = _____ _____ + 3 = _____	**b.** 24 + 14 = _____ ___ + ___ = _____ ___ + ___ = _____
c. 15 + 14 = ____	**d.** 24 + 15 = ____
e. 22 + 17 = ____	**f.** 27 + 12 = ____
g. 18 + 12 = ____	**h.** 28 + 12 = ____

Lesson 25

Objective: Add a pair of two-digit numbers when the ones digits have a sum less than or equal to 10.

Suggested Lesson Structure

Application Problem	(5 minutes)
Fluency Practice	(16 minutes)
Concept Development	(29 minutes)
Student Debrief	(10 minutes)
Total Time	**(60 minutes)**

Application Problem (5 minutes)

A chipmunk hides 11 acorns under a tree. Later, he gives 5 acorns to his friend. How many acorns does the chipmunk have? Use the RDW process to solve the problem.

Extension: A squirrel has double the number of acorns the chipmunk had to begin with. How many acorns does the squirrel have?

Note: Today's problem challenges students to pay attention to the differences in a story problem. During the Debrief, students compare yesterday's Application Problem with today's, analyzing the parts and the whole or total in each problem.

Fluency Practice (16 minutes)

- Get to 10 or 20 **1.OA.6**   (4 minutes)
- Sprint Targeting Core Fluency: Missing Addends for Sums of Ten(s) **1.OA.6**   (10 minutes)
- Take Out 1 or 2 **1.OA.5**   (2 minutes)

Get to 10 or 20 (4 minutes)

Materials: (S) 1 dime and 10 pennies

Note: This activity uses dimes and pennies as abstract representations of tens and ones to help students become familiar with coins, while simultaneously providing practice with missing addends to ten(s).

Lesson 25:	Add a pair of two-digit numbers when the ones digits have a sum less than or equal to 10.	4.F.30
Date:	9/20/13	

For the first two minutes:

- Step 1: Lay out 0–10 pennies in 5-group formation and ask students to identify the amount shown (e.g., 9 ones).
- Step 2: Ask for the addition sentence to get to 10 (e.g., 9 ones + 1 one = 10 ones).

For the next two minutes:

- Repeat Steps 1 and 2, then add a dime and ask students to identify the amount shown (e.g., 1 ten 9 ones = 19 or 9 cents + 10 cents = 19 cents) and a new addition sentence (e.g., 19 cents + 1 cent = 20 cents).

Vary the unit terminology throughout the activity (ones, pennies, cents, tens, dimes).

Sprint Targeting Core Fluency: Missing Addends for Sums of Ten(s) (10 minutes)

Materials: (S) Missing Addends for Sums of Ten(s) Sprint

Note: The first two quadrants of this Sprint focuses on partners to 10, which reviews the core fluency standard and prepares students for today's lesson. The third and fourth quadrants relate partners to 10 to corresponding partners to 20. This adds excitement to the grade level fluency goals as students see how these equations relate to larger numbers.

Take Out 1 or 2 (2 minutes)

Note: This anticipatory fluency practices taking out 1 or 2 from two-digit numbers in order to prepare students to use this skill when adding 2 two-digit numbers in upcoming lessons.

Choose numbers between 0 and 10 and follow the paradigm below.

- T: Take out 1 from each number. 6. (Snap.)
- S: 1 and 5.

Continue with other numbers within 10. Then start again at 6.

- T: 6.
- S: 1 and 5.
- T: 16.
- S: 1 and 15.
- T: 26.
- S: 1 and 25.
- T: 36.
- S: 1 and 35.

After students take out 1 for a minute, start again and take out 2.

Lesson 25: Add a pair of two-digit numbers when the ones digits have a sum less than or equal to 10.

Date: 9/20/13

4.F

Concept Development (29 minutes)

Materials: (T) 5 ten-sticks (4 red and 1 yellow) (S) 4 ten-sticks from math toolkit, personal white board

Students gather in the meeting area with their materials in a semi-circle formation.

The first 10 minutes of Lesson 25's Concept Development can be used to solidify the learning that has occurred in Lesson 24. Three sets of problems have been provided for students who are ready to extend their double-digit addition skills. The teaching sequence from Lesson 24 may be used to guide instruction. Students should be encouraged to use their cubes, quick ten drawing, or the number bond to solve their problems. Note that Problems 10–12 involve numbers greater than 40. Encourage students to use place value language to describe and compare strategies for solving. Ask questions such as, "What is another way this can be solved? Why did you choose your method?"

NOTES ON MULTIPLE MEANS FOR ACTION AND EXPRESSION:

More advanced students may choose to show how they solved some problems using the arrow way. This shows you that these students are thinking more abstractly while adding two-digit numbers.

Problems 1–4	Problems 5–8	Problems 9–12
15 + 12	24 + 13	37 + 22
15 + 13	26 + 13	46 + 23
15 + 15	27 + 13	46 + 24
16 + 14	12 + 28	53 + 17

After 10 minutes of practice, proceed with the following:

T: (Write 17 + 13.) How could we solve this?

S: 17 + 10 = 27. 27 + 3 = 30. (As students describe, show the number bond and write two number sentences.)

T: Great job! So far, we have been practicing to add the tens first as an easy way to add two-digit numbers. What if I wanted to add my tens at the end? How else might we start?

S: We can add the ones first. 17 + 3 is 20, and then 20 + 10 is 30. (As students describe, use the number bond and number sentences as shown.)

T: Great strategies! Earlier today, we were adding on tens first. This time, we can add the ones first. Let's try some more!

$17 + 13 = 30$

$17 + 10 = 27$
$27 + 3 = 30$

$17 + 13 = 30$

$17 + 3 = 20$
$20 + 10 = 30$

COMMON CORE | **Lesson 25:** | Add a pair of two-digit numbers when the ones digits have a sum less than or equal to 10. | 4.F.32
Date: 9/20/13

Repeat the process following the suggested sequence: 18 + 12, 28 + 12, 18 + 22, 16 + 23, 16 + 24, and 21 + 19. Students may choose to continue practicing adding on the tens first or try adding the ones first using the number bond or the arrow way and explain their choice.

Problem Set (10 minutes)

Students should do their personal best to complete the Problem Set within the allotted 10 minutes. For some classes, it may be appropriate to modify the assignment by specifying which problems they work on first.

NOTES ON MULTIPLE MEANS FOR ACTION AND EXPRESSION:

Encourage students to explain their thinking about adding or subtracting tens. Students may learn as much from each other's reasoning as from the lesson. As the teacher, you will learn more about their level of thinking and ability to express that thinking.

Student Debrief (10 minutes)

Lesson Objective: Add a pair of two-digit numbers when the ones digits have a sum less than or equal to 10.

The Student Debrief is intended to invite reflection and active processing of the total lesson experience.

Invite students to review their solutions for the Problem Set. They should check work by comparing answers with a partner before going over answers as a class. Look for misconceptions or misunderstandings that can be addressed in the Debrief. Guide students in a conversation to debrief the Problem Set and process the lesson.

You may choose to use any combination of the questions below to lead the discussion.

- Look at Problem 1(c) and 1(d). Why can't we use the strategy to get to the next ten in 1(c) while we can in 1(d)?

- In Problem 2(g), which addend did you start with? Why?

- Share your strategy for solving 2(h) with your partner. How are your strategies similar or different?

- Look at Problem 2(h). How might a number bond look different for using the adding the ten strategy compared to the adding the ones strategy?

- Look at Problem 2(c). How can you use the arrow way to show the different ways to solve this problem?

- How is the adding the ten strategy similar and different compared to the adding the ones strategy? How does that show in your number bonds and the two number sentences that follow the number bond?

- How did the Application Problem connect to today's lesson?

Exit Ticket (3 minutes)

After the Student Debrief, instruct students to complete the Exit Ticket. A review of their work will help you assess the students' understanding of the concepts that were presented in the lesson today and plan more effectively for future lessons. You may read the questions aloud to the students.

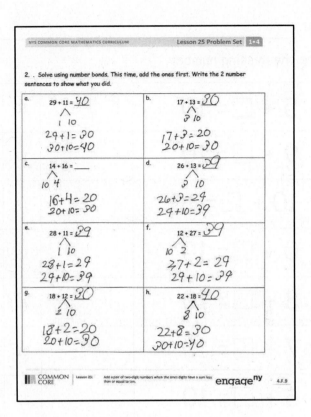

NYS COMMON CORE MATHEMATICS CURRICULUM   Lesson 25 Problem Set 1•4

2. . Solve using number bonds. This time, add the ones first. Write the 2 number sentences to show what you did.

a. $29 + 11 = 40$
   1   10
   $29 + 1 = 30$
   $30 + 10 = 40$

b. $17 + 13 = 30$
   3   10
   $17 + 3 = 20$
   $20 + 10 = 30$

c. $14 + 16 = \_\_\_$
   10 4
   $16 + 4 = 20$
   $20 + 10 = 30$

d. $26 + 13 = 39$
   3   10
   $26 + 3 = 24$
   $29 + 10 = 39$

e. $28 + 11 = 39$
   1   10
   $28 + 1 = 29$
   $29 + 10 = 39$

f. $12 + 27 = 39$
   10 2
   $27 + 2 = 29$
   $29 + 10 = 39$

g. $18 + 12 = 30$
   2   10
   $18 + 2 = 20$
   $20 + 10 = 30$

h. $22 + 18 = 40$
   8   10
   $22 + 8 = 30$
   $30 + 10 = 40$

COMMON CORE   Lesson 25:   Add a pair of two-digit numbers when the ones digits have a sum less than or equal to ten.   engageny   4.F.9

Lesson 25:   Add a pair of two-digit numbers when the ones digits have a sum less than or equal to 10.
Date: 9/20/13

A

Name _____   Date _____

*Write the missing number.

1	$5 + \square = 10$	16	$9 + \square = 10$
2	$9 + \square = 10$	17	$19 + \square = 20$
3	$10 + \square = 10$	18	$5 + \square = 10$
4	$0 + \square = 10$	19	$15 + \square = 20$
5	$8 + \square = 10$	20	$1 + \square = 10$
6	$7 + \square = 10$	21	$11 + \square = 20$
7	$6 + \square = 10$	22	$3 + \square = 10$
8	$4 + \square = 10$	23	$13 + \square = 20$
9	$3 + \square = 10$	24	$4 + \square = 10$
10	$\square + 7 = 10$	25	$14 + \square = 20$
11	$2 + \square = 10$	26	$16 + \square = 20$
12	$\square + 8 = 10$	27	$2 + \square = 10$
13	$1 + \square = 10$	28	$12 + \square = 20$
14	$\square + 2 = 10$	29	$18 + \square = 20$
15	$\square + 3 = 10$	30	$11 + \square = 20$

Number correct:

COMMON CORE   **Lesson 25:**   Add a pair of two-digit numbers when the ones digits have a sum less than or equal to 10.

Date: 9/20/13

4.

B

Number correct:

Name _____ Date _____

Write the missing number.

1	$10 + \square = 10$		16	$5 + \square = 10$	
2	$0 + \square = 10$		17	$15 + \square = 20$	
3	$9 + \square = 10$		18	$9 + \square = 10$	
4	$5 + \square = 10$		19	$19 + \square = 20$	
5	$6 + \square = 10$		20	$8 + \square = 10$	
6	$7 + \square = 10$		21	$18 + \square = 20$	
7	$8 + \square = 10$		22	$2 + \square = 10$	
8	$2 + \square = 10$		23	$12 + \square = 20$	
9	$3 + \square = 10$		24	$3 + \square = 10$	
10	$\square + 7 = 10$		25	$13 + \square = 20$	
11	$2 + \square = 10$		26	$17 + \square = 20$	
12	$\square + 8 = 10$		27	$4 + \square = 10$	
13	$1 + \square = 10$		28	$16 + \square = 20$	
14	$\square + 9 = 10$		29	$18 + \square = 20$	
15	$\square + 2 = 10$		30	$12 + \square = 40$	

COMMON CORE™ | Lesson 25: | Add a pair of two-digit numbers when the ones digits have a sum less than or equal to 10. | **4.F.36**
| | Date: | 9/20/13 | |

Name _____   Date _____

1. Solve using number bonds. This time, add the tens first. Write the 2 number sentences to show what you did.

a.
 	
    11 + 14 = _____
	b.
	
	    21 + 14 = _____

c.
 	
    14 + 15 = _____
	d.
	
	    26 + 14 = _____

e.
 	
    26 + 13 = _____
	f.
	
	    13 + 24 = _____

COMMON CORE   **Lesson 25:**   Add a pair of two-digit numbers when the ones digits have a sum less than or equal to 10.

Date: 9/20/13

4.

© 2013 Common Core, Inc. All rights reserved. commoncore.org

Solve using number bonds. This time, add the ones first. Write the 2 number sentences to show what you did.

a. $29 + 11 =$ _____	b. $17 + 13 =$ _____
c. $14 + 16 =$ _____	d. $26 + 13 =$ _____
e. $28 + 11 =$ _____	f. $12 + 27 =$ _____
g. $18 + 12 =$ _____	h. $22 + 18 =$ _____

Lesson 25:   Add a pair of two-digit numbers when the ones digits have a sum less than or equal to 10.

Date: 9/20/13

4.F.38

Name _____   Date _____

Solve using number bonds. Write the 2 number sentences to record what you did.

a.	b.
12 + 27 = _____	21 + 19 = _____

Lesson 25: Add a pair of two-digit numbers when the ones digits have a sum less
than or equal to 10.

Date: 9/20/13

4.

Name _____   Date _____

1. Solve using number bonds. This time, add the tens first. Write the 2 number sentences to show what you did.

a. 12 + 14 = _____	b. 14 + 21 = _____
c. 15 + 14 = _____	d. 25 + 14 = _____
e. 23 + 16 = _____	f. 16 + 24 = _____

COMMON CORE™

Lesson 25:   Add a pair of two-digit numbers when the ones digits have a sum less than or equal to 10.

Date: 9/20/13

4.F.40

2. Solve using number bonds. This time, add the ones first. Write the 2 number sentences to show what you did.

a. 27 + 10 = _____	b. 27 + 13 = _____
c. 13 + 26 = _____	d. 26 + 14 = _____
e. 12 + 18 = _____	f. 18 + 21 = _____
g. 19 + 11 = _____	h. 21 + 19 = _____

Lesson 25:   Add a pair of two-digit numbers when the ones digits have a sum less than or equal to 10.

Date: 9/20/13

4.

Lesson 26

Objective: Add a pair of two-digit numbers when the ones digits have a sum greater than 10.

Suggested Lesson Structure

- Application Problem   (5 minutes)
- Fluency Practice   (10 minutes)
- Concept Development   (35 minutes)
- Student Debrief   (10 minutes)

   Total Time   **(60 minutes)**

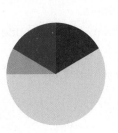

Application Problem (5 minutes)

snowed 7 days in February and the same number of days in March. How many days did it snow in those two months? Use the RDW process to solve the problem.

Extension: It snowed 3 days in January. How many days did it snow in all 3 months? How many more days did it snow in February than in January?

Note: Today's problem gives students the chance to work with equal parts. Some students may struggle when only one number is given. Circulate and notice which students are reading and making sense of the problem. Students who are struggling may need more support as they read through the problem to draw as they go.

Fluency Practice (10 minutes)

Sprint Targeting Core Fluency: Missing Addends for Sums of Ten(s) **1.OA.6**   (10 minutes)

Sprint Targeting Core Fluency: Missing Addends for Sums of Ten(s) (10 minutes)

Materials: (S) Missing Addends for Sums of Ten(s) Sprint from G1–M4–Lesson 25

Note: Students complete the same Sprint from the prior day's lesson as an opportunity to build confidence as they work to master the core fluency of the grade level and to extend this thinking to larger numbers. Between Sprints, engage the students in jumping jacks or running in place as they count from 40 to 80. This keeps their math minds going and builds confidence for the second Sprint.

	Lesson 26:	Add a pair of two-digit numbers when the ones digits have a sum greater than 10.	
	Date:	9/20/13	4.F.42

Concept Development (35 minutes)

Materials: (T) 5 ten-sticks (3 red and 2 yellow) (S) 4 ten-sticks from math toolkit, personal white board

Students gather at the meeting area with their partner and materials in a semi-circle formation.

T: (Write 19 + 15 on the chart and show with 19 red and 15 yellow linking cubes.) Partner A, make 19 with your cubes. Partner B, make 15 with yours.

S: (Show cubes in a ten-stick and some ones to match their addend.)

T: Let's add on the tens first to solve.

T/S: (Move the yellow ten-stick next to the red ten-stick.)

T: 19 and 10 is?

S: 29.

T: What do we still have to add?

S: 5.

T: Add 5 to 29. (Wait as students use their cubes to solve.)

T: How did you add 5 to 29?

S: I can count on. Twenty niiiine 30, 31, 32, 33, 34. → 29 needs 1 more to make 30, so I got 1 from 5. That gave us 30 and 4. That's 34. → 9 needs 1 more to make 10. 2 tens and 1 ten is 3 tens. Now we have 3 tens plus 4 ones. That's 34.

T: Let's draw a number bond that shows exactly how we solved 19 + 15. We are starting with 19. Why did we break apart 15 into 10 and 5?

S: We added on the ten first, so we took out 10 from 15. 5 is the other part of 15.

T: So our first number sentence is?

S: 19 + 10 = 29.

T: (Record.) Next? (Write 29 + 5 = ___.) How can we record what we did to add 5?

S: Break apart 5 into 1 and 4. We needed the 1 to make the next ten.

T: (Write the number bond.) 29 + 1 is?

S: 30.

T: 30 + 4 is?

S: 34.

T: (Complete the number sentence.)

NOTES ON MULTIPLE MEANS OF ENGAGEMENT:

Some students may need extra time to solidify their understanding of the adding on the ten strategy. Give them another sequence of problems for further practice rather than introducing a new strategy.

epeat the process following the suggested sequence, releasing students to work independently, in pairs, or
mall groups, as possible: 19 + 16, 19 + 18, 18 + 17, 17 + 15, 16 + 16, and 15 + 18.

hart the problems with their number bonds and two number sentences, listing them vertically. During the
ext component of the lesson, these solutions will be juxtaposed to solutions completing the ten first.

T: Let's look at 19 + 15 again. Partner A, make 19 with
    your cubes. Partner B, make 15. (Show 19 and 15 with
    cubes.) Before, we broke 15 into 10 and 5 because
    adding on the tens is easy. What's another strategy we
    know that uses ten?

S: Make the next ten!

T: Yes! Use your cubes to make the next ten and solve
    19 + 15.

S: 19 needs 1 more to make 20, so we took 1 from 15 to
    make 20. That gave us 3 tens and 4 ones. That's 34.
    → 19 plus 1 is 20. 20 plus 14 is 30 and 4. That's 34.
    (As students describe, make a number bond below the
    number sentence showing 15 broken apart into 1 and
    14.)

T: 19 needs how many more to make the next ten?
    (Point to 19 cubes.)

S: 1 more.

T: (Take away 1 cube from the 5 in 15 and place with 19 cubes.) How many tens did we make from 19?

S: 2 tens.

T: We still need to add 14. 20 + 14 is?

S: 34.

T: How did we break apart 15 this time? Why? (Point to how the yellow cubes are decomposed.)

S: We broke it into 1 and 14. → We took 1 from 15 because 19 needs 1 more to make the next ten.
    When we took away 1, there was still 14 left from the 15.

T: Work with your partner and write the two number sentences that show how we made the next ten
    first to solve.

S: (Write 19 + 1 = 20 and 20 + 14 = 34.)

epeat the process, modeling with cubes and number bonds using the same sequence from above and chart
he number bonds and two number sentences.

T: (Point to the chart.) Look at the two ways we solved the same addition problem. What do you
    notice about the difference in how we broke apart one of the addends?

S: When we want to add on the tens first, we always break apart the number to 10 and some ones.
    But when we want to make the next ten, we break apart the addend to get out the number we need
    and then add the rest. → If we start with 19, we take out a 1 from the other addend because 19 and
    1 makes 20. If we start with 18, we take out a 2 from the other addend because 18 + 2 = 20.

$$19 + 15$$
$$1 \quad 14$$

$$19 + 1 = 20$$
$$20 + 14 = 34$$
$$10 \quad 4$$

COMMON | Lesson 26: Add a pair of two-digit numbers when the ones digits have a sum
CORE™ | greater than 10.   **4.F.44**
         | **Date:**   9/20/13

Problem Set (10 minutes)

Students should do their personal best to complete the Problem Set within the allotted 10 minutes. For some classes, it may be appropriate to modify the assignment by specifying which problems they work on first. Some problems do not specify a method for solving.

Student Debrief (10 minutes)

Lesson Objective: Add a pair of two-digit numbers when the ones digits have a sum greater than ten.

The Student Debrief is intended to invite reflection and active processing of the total lesson experience.

Invite students to review their solutions for the Problem Set. They should check work by comparing answers with a partner before going over answers as a class. Look for misconceptions or misunderstandings that can be addressed in the Debrief. Guide students in a conversation to debrief the Problem Set and process the lesson.

You may choose to use any combination of the questions below to lead the discussion.

- How are Problems 1(a) and 1(b) related? How can solving 1(a) help you solve 1(b)?

- Which strategy is easier for you to use when you add? Adding on the ten first or making the next ten first? Explain why it's easier for you.

- Using what we learned today, try solving 49 + 11. Which strategy did you use?

- Look at the Application Problem from today and yesterday. How are they similar? How are they different?

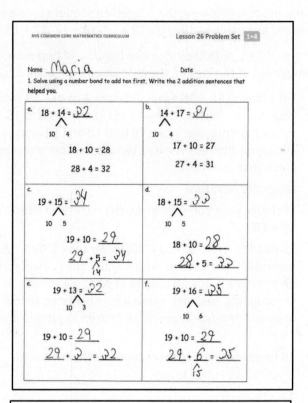

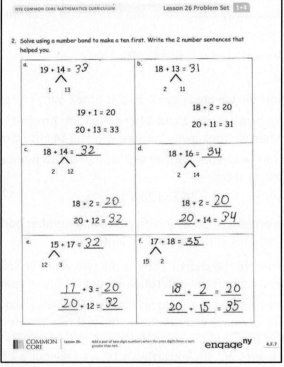

COMMON CORE™   **Lesson 26:**   Add a pair of two-digit numbers when the ones digits have a sum greater than 10.

Date: 9/20/13

4

xit Ticket (3 minutes)

fter the Student Debrief, instruct students to complete the Exit Ticket. A review of their work will help you
ssess the students' understanding of the concepts that were presented in the lesson today and plan more
ffectively for future lessons. You may read the questions aloud to the students.

Lesson 26:	Add a pair of two-digit numbers when the ones digits have a sum greater than 10.
Date:	9/20/13

4.F.46

Name _____   Date _____

1. Solve using a number bond to add ten first. Write the 2 addition sentences that helped you.

a.
$$18 + 14 = \underline{\quad}$$

10   4

$$18 + 10 = 28$$

$$28 + 4 = 32$$

b.
$$14 + 17 = \underline{\quad}$$

10   4

$$17 + 10 = 27$$

$$27 + 4 = 31$$

c.
$$19 + 15 = \underline{\quad}$$

10   5

$$19 + 10 = \underline{\quad}$$

$$\underline{\quad} + 5 = \underline{\quad}$$

d.
$$18 + 15 = \underline{\quad}$$

10   5

$$18 + 10 = \underline{\quad}$$

$$\underline{\quad} + 5 = \underline{\quad}$$

e.
$$19 + 13 = \underline{\quad}$$

10   3

$$19 + 10 = \underline{\quad}$$

$$\underline{\quad} + \underline{\quad} = \underline{\quad}$$

f.
$$19 + 16 = \underline{\quad}$$

10   6

$$19 + 10 = \underline{\quad}$$

$$\underline{\quad} + \underline{\quad} = \underline{\quad}$$

COMMON CORE

Lesson 26:   Add a pair of two-digit numbers when the ones digits have a sum greater than 10.

Date: 9/20/13

4.

. Solve using a number bond to make a ten first. Write the 2 number sentences that helped you.

a.
19 + 14 =

1   13

19 + 1 = 20

20 + 13 = 33

b.
18 + 13 =

2   11

18 + 2 = 20

20 + 11 = 31

c.   18 + 14 = _____

2   12

18 + 2 = _____

20 + 12 = _____

d.
18 + 16 = _____

2   14

18 + 2 = _____

_____ + 14 = _____

e.   15 + 17 = _____

12   3

_____ + 3 = _____

_____ + 12 = _____

f.   17 + 18 = _____

15   2

_____ + _____ = _____

_____ + _____ = _____

 COMMON CORE™ | **Lesson 26:**   Add a pair of two-digit numbers when the ones digits have a sum greater than 10.   **Date:**   9/20/13   4.F.48

Name _____   Date _____

1. Solve using number bonds to add ten first. Write the 2 number sentences that helped you.

a. 15 + 19 = _____ 　　∧ _____ + _____ = _____ _____ + _____ = _____	b. 19 + 17 = _____ 　　∧ _____ + _____ = _____ _____ + _____ = _____

2. Solve using number bonds to make a ten. Write the 2 number sentences that helped you.

c. 15 + 19 = _____ 　　∧ _____ + _____ = _____ _____ + _____ = _____	d. 19 + 17 = _____ 　　∧ _____ + _____ = _____ _____ + _____ = _____

Lesson 26:   Add a pair of two-digit numbers when the ones digits have a sum greater than 10.

Date: 9/20/13

4.

Name _____   Date _____

Solve using a number bond to add ten first. Write the 2 addition sentences that helped you.

a.
18 + 13 = ____

10   3

18 + 10 = 28

28 + 3 = 31

b.
13 + 19 = ____

10   3

19 + 10 = 29

29 + 3 = 32

c.
17 + 15 = ____

10   5

17 + 10 = _____

____ + 5 = _____

d.
17 + 16 = ____

10   6

17 + 10 = _____

____ + 6 = _____

e.
17 + 14 = ____

10   4

17 + 10 = _____

____ + ____ = _____

f.
19 + 17 = ____

10   7

19 + 10 = _____

____ + ____ = _____

Lesson 26:	Add a pair of two-digit numbers when the ones digits have a sum greater than 10.
Date:	9/20/13

4.F.50

2. Solve using a number bond to make a ten first. Write the 2 number sentences that helped you.

a.	b.
19 + 13 = ∧ 1 12 19 + 1 = 20 20 + 12 = 32	19 + 14 = ∧ 1 13 19 + 1 = 20 20 + 13 = 33
c. 18 + 15 = _____ ∧ 2 13 18 + 2 = ____ 20 + 13 = ____	d. 18 + 17 = ____ ∧ 2 15 18 + 2 = ____ ____ + 15 = ____
e. 18 + 19 = ____ ∧ 17 1 ____ + 1 = ____ ____ + 17 = ____	f. 19 + 19 = ____ ∧ 18 1 ____ + ____ = ____ ____ + ____ = ____

Lesson 27

Objective: Add a pair of two-digit numbers when the ones digits have a sum greater than ten.

Suggested Lesson Structure

■ Application Problem	(5 minutes)	
■ Fluency Practice	(12 minutes)	
■ Concept Development	(33 minutes)	
■ Student Debrief	(10 minutes)	
Total Time	**(60 minutes)**	

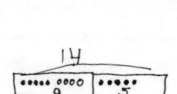

Application Problem (5 minutes)

snowed 14 days. Some snowy days, we stayed
ome. Nine snowy days we were in school. How
any snowy days did we stay home? Use the RDW
rocess to solve the problem.

xtension: How many more days did it snow when
e were in school compared to when we were
ome?

ote: Today's problem poses a *take apart with
ddend unknown* problem type. Continue to remind
tudents of the simple questions they can ask
hemselves as they attempt the problem: *Can I draw
omething? What can I draw? What does my
rawing show me that can help me with the
uestion?* The goal is that over time these questions
e internalized by the students.

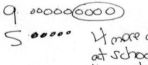

Fluency Practice (12 minutes)

Grade 1 Core Fluency Differentiated Practice Sets **1.OA.6**	(5 minutes)
Race to the Top **1.OA.6**	(5 minutes)
Take Out 1 or 2 **1.OA.5**	(2 minutes)

Grade 1 Core Fluency Differentiated Practice Sets (5 minutes)

Materials: (S) Core Fluency Practice Sets from G1–M4–Lesson 23

Note: This activity assesses students' progress toward mastery of the required addition fluency for first graders. Give the appropriate Practice Set to each student. Students who completed all questions correctly on their most recent Practice Set should be given the next level of difficulty. All other students should try to improve their scores on their current levels.

Students complete as many problems as they can in 90 seconds. Assign a counting pattern and start number for early finishers, or tell them to practice make ten addition or subtraction on the backs of their papers. Collect and correct any Practice Sets completed within the allotted time.

Race to the Top (5 minutes)

Materials: (S) Personal white boards with Race to the Top insert

Note: This fluency primarily targets the core fluency for Grade 1.

Students take turns rolling the dice, saying an addition sentence and recording the sums on the graph. The game ends when time runs out or one of the columns reaches the top of the graph.

Take Out 1 or 2 (2 minutes)

Note: This anticipatory fluency practices taking out 1 or 2 from two-digit numbers in order to prepare students to use this skill when adding two two-digit numbers in upcoming lessons.

Choose numbers between 0 and 10 and follow the script below.

    T: Take out 1 from each number. 6. (Snap.)
    S: 1 and 5.

Continue with other numbers within 10. Then start again at 6.

    T: 6.
    S: 1 and 5.
    T: 16.
    S: 1 and 15.
    T: 26.
    S: 1 and 25.
    T: 36.
    S: 1 and 35.

After students take out 1 for a minute. Then start again and take out 2.

Lesson 27:   Add a pair of two-digit numbers when the ones digits have a sum greater than ten.

Date: 9/20/13

4.

Concept Development (33 minutes)

Materials: (S) Personal white boards, 4 ten-sticks from the
math tool kit (optional)

The time allotted for Lesson 27's Concept Development can be
used to solidify the learning that has occurred in Lesson 26.
Three sets of problems have been provided for students to
practice and gain accuracy and efficiency when adding a pair of
double digit numbers. The teaching sequence from Lesson 26
may be used to guide instruction. Students should be
encouraged to use their cubes, quick ten drawings, number
bonds with pairs of number sentences to solve (MP.5). Note
that Problems 9–12 involve numbers greater than 40. This is
intended to serve as a challenge set for advanced learners.

Encourage students to use place value language as they
describe how their strategy works. Challenge them to compare
strategies with their partners and look for related problems
within the set.

NOTES ON
MULTIPLE MEANS
FOR ACTION AND
EXPRESSION:

Students may choose how they want to
solve problems—with drawings,
number bonds, or the arrow way.
Students should begin to move away
from drawing to the more abstract
method of problem solving. However,
not all students will be ready to
abstractly solve problems, so support
students wherever they are in their
learning and guide them as they
progress.

Problems 1–4	Problems 5–8	Problems 9–12
9 + 11	18 + 12	17 + 23
9 + 13	17 + 17	27 + 25
8 + 15	17 + 16	24 + 29
7 + 16	16 + 15	34 + 27

Problem Set (10 minutes)

Students should do their personal best to complete the
Problem Set within the allotted 10 minutes. For some
classes, it may be appropriate to modify the assignment
by specifying which problems they work on first.

NOTES ON
MULTIPLE MEANS
FOR ACTION AND
EXPRESSION:

Continue to challenge your advanced
students. After they have completed
Problems 9–12, give students some
word problems to solve with similar
numbers.

Student Debrief (10 minutes)

Lesson Objective: Add a pair of two-digit numbers when the ones digits have a sum greater than ten.

The Student Debrief is intended to invite reflection and active processing of the total lesson experience.

Invite students to review their solutions for the Problem Set. They should check work by comparing answers
with a partner before going over answers as a class. Look for misconceptions or misunderstandings that can
be addressed in the Debrief. Guide students in a conversation to debrief the Problem Set and process the
lesson.

COMMON
CORE™

Lesson 27:   Add a pair of two-digit numbers when the ones digits have a sum
greater than ten.
Date: 9/20/13

4.F.54

You may choose to use any combination of the questions below to lead the discussion.

- How can solving Problem 1(a) help solve 1(b)?
- Look at Problem 1(c) and 1(d). Explain how they are related. Why do they have the same answers?
- Look at 2(f). Which addend did you start with to solve this problem? Why?
- Which ten strategy, make the next ten or add on the ten, is easier for you to use when adding? Explain your choice.
- Look at today's Application Problem. Explain your drawing and solution to your partner.

Exit Ticket (3 minutes)

After the Student Debrief, instruct students to complete the Exit Ticket. A review of their work will help you assess the students' understanding of the concepts that were presented in the lesson today and plan more effectively for future lessons. You may read the questions aloud to the students.

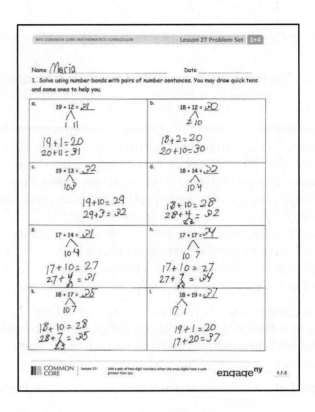

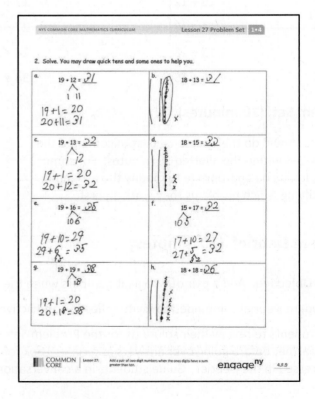

COMMON CORE   **Lesson 27:**   Add a pair of two-digit numbers when the ones digits have a sum greater than ten.
Date: 9/20/13

4

Names _____   Date _____

 Race to the Top!

2	**3**	**4**	**5**	**6**	**7**	**8**	**9**	**10**	**11**	**12**

 COMMON CORE™

Lesson 27:   Add a pair of two-digit numbers when the ones digits have a sum
greater than ten.
Date: 9/20/13

4.F.56

Name _____   Date _____

1. Solve using number bonds with pairs of number sentences. You may draw quick tens
    and some ones to help you.

a. 19 + 12 = _____	b. 18 + 12 = _____
c. 19 + 13 = _____	d. 18 + 14 = _____
e. 17 + 14 = _____	f. 17 + 17 = _____
g. 18 + 17 = _____	h. 18 + 19 = _____

Lesson 27: Add a pair of two-digit numbers when the ones digits have a sum
greater than ten.

Date: 9/20/13

4

2. Solve. You may draw quick tens and some ones to help you.

a. $19 + 12 =$ _____	b. $18 + 13 =$ _____
c. $19 + 13 =$ _____	d. $18 + 15 =$ _____
e. $19 + 16 =$ _____	f. $15 + 17 =$ _____
g. $19 + 19 =$ _____	h. $18 + 18 =$ _____

Lesson 27:   Add a pair of two-digit numbers when the ones digits have a sum greater than ten.

Date: 9/20/13

4.F.58

Name _____ Date _____

1. Solve using number bonds with pairs of number sentences. You may draw quick tens and some ones to help you.

a. 16 + 15 = _____	b. 17 + 13 = _____
c. 16 + 16 = _____	d. 17 + 15 = _____

COMMON CORE™ **Lesson 27:** Add a pair of two-digit numbers when the ones digits have a sum greater than ten.
Date: 9/20/13

4

Name _____   Date _____

1. Solve using number bonds with pairs of number sentences. You may draw quick tens and some ones to help you.

a. 17 + 14 = _____	b. 16 + 14 = _____
c. 17 + 15 = _____	d. 18 + 13 = _____
e. 18 + 15 = _____	f. 18 + 16 = _____
g. 19 + 15 = _____	h. 19 + 16 = _____

COMMON CORE™

Lesson 27:   Add a pair of two-digit numbers when the ones digits have a sum
              greater than ten.
Date: 9/20/13

4.F.60

2. Solve. You may draw quick tens and some ones to help you.

a. 17 + 14 = _____	b. 16 + 15 = _____
c. 17 + 15 = _____	d. 16 + 16 = _____
e. 19 + 16 = _____	f. 14 + 19 = _____
g. 19 + 19 = _____	h. 18 + 18 = _____

Lesson 27:   Add a pair of two-digit numbers when the ones digits have a sum greater than ten.

Date: 9/20/13

4

Lesson 28

Objective: Add a pair of two-digit numbers with varied sums in the ones.

Suggested Lesson Structure

Application Problem	(7 minutes)
Fluency Practice	(16 minutes)
Concept Development	(27 minutes)
Student Debrief	(10 minutes)
Total Time	**(60 minutes)**

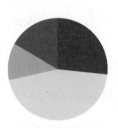

Application Problem (7 minutes)

Anton collected some crayons in his pockets. His teacher gave him 2 more. When he counted all of his crayons, he had 16 crayons. How many crayons did Anton have in his pockets originally? Use the RDW process to solve the problem.

Note: Today's problem is the challenging *add to with start unknown* problem type. Although crayons were added within the story because the start is the unknown number, the problem requires subtraction.

Several images are shown below representing students' varied approaches.

In Model A, the student draws all 16 crayons to begin with, partitioning the last two in order to find the initial 14.

In Model B, the student may have drawn the part they know, 2, with the total, 16 drawn below. The student then counts up to add more circles until the quantity matches 16, recounting to find the amount drawn.

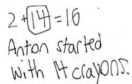

In Model C, the student represents the unknown with an empty box and builds the chunk of two on the end. This student could use a missing addend number sentence or subtraction number sentence to solve the problem.

Model A	Model B	Model C
	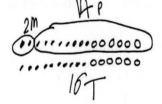	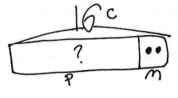

Fluency Practice (16 minutes)

- Grade 1 Core Fluency Differentiated Practice Sets **1.OA.6**   (5 minutes)
- Coin Drop **1.OA.6, 1.NBT.6**   (3 minutes)
- Make Ten: 9 Up **1.OA.6**   (3 minutes)
- Addition Strategies Review **1.OA.6**   (5 minutes)

Grade 1 Core Fluency Differentiated Practice Sets (5 minutes)

Materials: (S) Core Fluency Practice Sets from G1–M4–Lesson 23

Note: This activity assesses students' progress toward mastery of the required addition fluency for first graders. Students who completed all questions correctly on their most recent Practice Set should be given the next level of difficulty. All other students should try to improve their scores on their current levels.

Students complete as many problems as they can in 90 seconds. Assign a counting pattern and start number for early finishers, or tell them to practice make ten addition or subtraction on the backs of their papers. Collect and correct any Practice Sets completed within the allotted time.

Coin Drop (3 minutes)

Materials: (T) 4 dimes, 10 pennies, can

Note: In this activity, students practice adding and subtracting ones and tens.

> T: (Hold up a penny.) Name my coin.
> S: A penny.
> T: How much is it worth?
> S: 1 cent.
> T: Listen carefully as I drop coins in my can. Count along in your minds.

Drop in some pennies and ask how much money is in the can. Take out some pennies and show them. Ask how much money is still in the can. Continue adding and subtracting pennies for a minute or so. Then repeat the activity with dimes.

Make Ten: 9 Up (3 minutes)

Note: This fluency activity reviews how to calculate sums within 20 using the make ten strategy students learned in Module 2.

> T: When I say up, tell me how to get to ten from my number. 9 up.
> S   9 + 1 = 10.

Repeat with other numbers within 10.

Lesson 28:   Add a pair of two-digit numbers with varied sums in the ones.
Date: 9/20/13

4.

the next section, model the first few problems with a number bond and write the two-step addition sentences.

T: (Write 9 + 3 = ___.) 9 up.

S: 9 + 1 = 10.

T   (Draw a number bond under the 3 with 1 as a part and write 9 + 1 = 10, then point to the 3). How much is left to add?

S: 2.

T: (Write 2 as the other part, and the second addition sentence, 10 + 2.) 10 + 2 is?

S: 12.

T: So, 9 + 3 is?

epeat with the following suggested sequence: 9 + 3, 9 + 5, 9 + 6, 9 + 9, 9 + 8. When students are ready, onsider omitting the number bond and number sentences so students can mentally review the make a ten trategy.

ddition Strategies Review (5 minutes)

ote: This review fluency helps strengthen students' understanding of the make ten and add the ones ddition strategies, as well as their ability to recognize appropriate strategies based on problem types.

T: (Partner A, Show me 9 on your Magic Counting Sticks. Partner B, show me 6. If I want to solve 9 + 6, how can I *make a 10*?

S: Take one from the 6 and add 1 to 9.

T: Yes. Show me! We changed 9 + 6 into an easier problem. Say our new addition sentence with the solution.

S: 10 + 5 = 15.

T: If we want to add 3 to 15, should we make a ten to help us?

S: No. We already have a ten!

T: Should we add 3 to our 5 or our 10?

S: Our 5.

T: Yes! Show me! Say the addition sentence.

S: 15 + 3 = 18.

Concept Development (27 minutes)

NOTES ON MULTIPLE MEANS OF ENGAGEMENT:

Appropriate scaffolds help all students feel successful. As students are working, keep a close eye to see if any would benefit from some one-on-one problem solving with you.

Materials: (T) Chart paper (S) Personal white board, 4 ten-sticks from math toolkit (optional)

lave students gather in the meeting area with their materials.

he time allotted for Lesson 28's Concept Development is set side to consolidate and solidify the learning that has occurred

COMMON CORE™ | Lesson 28:   Add a pair of two-digit numbers with varied sums in the ones.
   | Date: 9/20/13

4.F.64

in Lessons 24–27. Three sets of problems have been provided for practice so that students gain accuracy and efficiency when adding a pair of double-digit numbers.

The teaching sequence from earlier lessons may be used to guide remedial instruction. Students should be encouraged to use their number bonds and the arrow way to solve their problems while having full access to drawing materials and manipulatives (MP.5). Note that Problems 11–15 involve sums greater than 40. This is intended to serve as a challenge set for advanced learners.

Encourage students to use place value language as they describe their methods and strategies for solving. Challenge them to compare strategies with their partners and explain their own method.

NOTES ON MULTIPLE MEANS FOR ACTION AND EXPRESSION:

Continue to challenge your advanced students. After they have completed Problems 11–15, encourage them to write a word problem to match one of the number sentences. Have students who write a word problem trade papers and solve each other's problem.

Problems 1–5	Problems 6–10	Problems 11–15
15 + 2	14 + 3	13 + 4
15 + 20	14 + 20	23 + 40
28 + 12	17 + 23	28 + 22
18 + 14	17 + 15	26 + 25
17 + 16	16 + 19	36 + 27

Problem Set (10 minutes)

Students should do their personal best to complete the Problem Set within the allotted 10 minutes. For some classes, it may be appropriate to modify the assignment by specifying which problems they work on first.

Student Debrief (10 minutes)

Lesson Objective: Add a pair of two-digit numbers with varied sums in the ones.

The Student Debrief is intended to invite reflection and active processing of the total lesson experience.

Invite students to review their solutions for the Problem Set. They should check work by comparing answers with a partner before going over answers as a class. Look for misconceptions or misunderstandings that can be addressed in the Debrief. Guide students in a conversation to debrief the Problem Set and process the lesson.

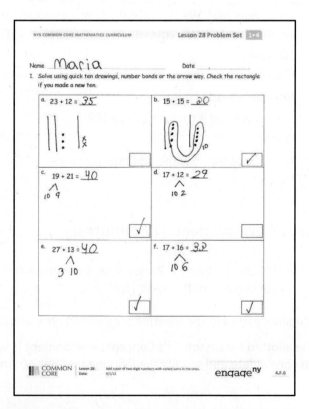

You may choose to use any combination of the questions below to lead the discussion.

- Which method did you use the most to solve today's addition problems? Explain the reason for your choice.

- Share how you solved Problem 2(f). How can solving Problem 2(f) help you solve 2(h)?

- A student says he solved Problem 1(f) by adding 2 tens and 13 ones. Is he correct? Explain his strategy for adding.

- With your partner, share how you solved your Application Problem and act out each part of the story. Explain how each part of your drawing or tape diagram represents different parts of the story.

Exit Ticket (3 minutes)

After the Student Debrief, instruct students to complete the Exit Ticket. A review of their work will help you assess the students' understanding of the concepts that were presented in the lesson today and plan more effectively for future lessons. You may read the questions aloud to the students.

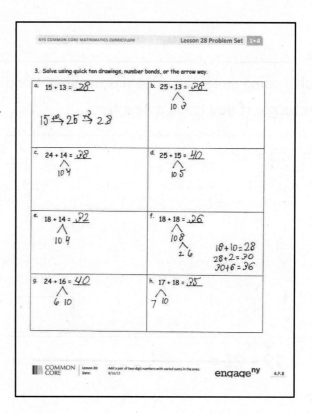

Name _____   Date _____

1. Solve using quick ten drawings, number bonds, or the arrow way. Check the
   rectangle if you made a new ten.

   a. 23 + 12 = _____

   b. 15 + 15 = _____

   c. 19 + 21 = _____

   d. 17 + 12 = _____

   e. 27 + 13 = _____

   f. 17 + 16 = _____

Solve using quick ten drawings, number bonds, or the arrow way.

a. 15 + 13 = _____	b. 25 + 13 = _____
c. 24 + 14 = _____	d. 25 + 15 = _____
e. 18 + 14 = _____	f. 18 + 18 = _____
g. 24 + 16 = _____	h. 17 + 18 = _____

COMMON CORE

Lesson 28: Add a pair of two-digit numbers with varied sums in the ones.
Date: 9/20/13

4.F.68

Name _____   Date _____

Solve using quick tens and ones, number bonds, or the arrow way.

a. 12 + 16 = _____	b. 26 + 14 = _____
c. 18 + 16 = _____	d. 19 + 17 = _____

Lesson 28:   Add a pair of two-digit numbers with varied sums in the ones.
Date: 9/20/13

4

Name _____   Date _____

Solve using quick tens and ones, number bonds, or the arrow way.

a. 13 + 16 = _____	b. 15 + 16 = _____
c. 16 + 16 = _____	d. 26 + 12 = _____
e. 22 + 17 = _____	f. 17 + 15 = _____
g. 17 + 16 = _____	h. 18 + 17 = _____

i. $24 + 13 =$ _____

j. $15 + 24 =$ _____

k. $19 + 16 =$ _____

l. $14 + 22 =$ _____

m. $27 + 12 =$ _____

n. $28 + 12 =$ _____

o. $18 + 17 =$ _____

p. $19 + 18 =$ _____

Lesson 29

Objective: Add a pair of two-digit numbers with varied sums in the ones.

Suggested Lesson Structure

▐ Application Problem   (5 minutes)
▐ Fluency Practice   (13 minutes)
▐ Concept Development   (32 minutes)
▐ Student Debrief   (10 minutes)

Total Time   **(60 minutes)**

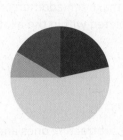

Application Problem (5 minutes)

Kiana's friend gave her 3 more stickers. Now Kiana has
16 stickers. How many stickers did Kiana already have?
Use the RDW process to solve the problem.

Note: This problem allows students to continue
practicing the challenging *add to with start unknown*
problem type. According to the Progressions Document,
students should have exposure to this problem type, but
mastery is not expected until Grade 2.

Students may employ a range of diverse strategies to
solve the problem, as depicted in the images to the right.
During the Debrief, invite students to share their
strategies as well as the drawings and notation they used
to record their thinking. If students find solving the
problem difficult, they can practice acting out their
solution with a partner as a way to check their thinking.

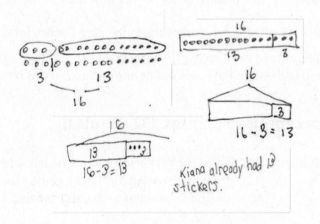

Fluency Practice (13 minutes)

Grade 1 Core Fluency Differentiated Practice Sets **1.OA.6**   (5 minutes)
Coin Drop **1.OA.6, 1.NBT.6**   (3 minutes)
Race to the Top **1.OA.6**   (5 minutes)

Grade 1 Core Fluency Differentiated Practice Sets (5 minutes)

Materials: (S) Core Fluency Practice Sets from G1–M4–Lesson 23

Note: Excitement should be building in this third consecutive day of core fluency practice. Students have had two days, and on this third day will have the chance to look back at their progress. Students who completed all questions correctly on their most recent Practice Set should be given the next level of difficulty. All other students should try to improve their scores on their current levels.

Students complete as many problems as they can in 90 seconds. Assign a counting pattern and start number for early finishers, or tell them to practice make ten addition or subtraction on the backs of their papers. Collect and correct any Practice Sets completed within the allotted time.

Coin Drop (3 minutes)

Materials: (T) 4 dimes, 10 pennies

Note: In this activity, students practice adding and subtracting ones and tens.

See yesterday's fluency for instructions.

Race to the Top (5 minutes)

Materials: (S) Personal white boards with Race to the Top insert

Note: This fluency primarily targets the core fluency for Grade 1.

Students take turns rolling the dice, saying an addition sentence and recording the sums on the graph. The game ends when time runs out or one of the columns reaches the top of the graph.

Concept Development (32 minutes)

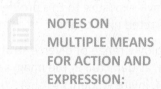

NOTES ON MULTIPLE MEANS FOR ACTION AND EXPRESSION:

Encourage students to describe and compare methods, strategies and written notation with their partners. At this point, most of your students should be as comfortable solving the problems as they are describing their thinking while solving.

Materials: (T) Chart paper (S) Personal white board, 4 ten-sticks from math toolkit (optional), game cards for Addition and Subtraction with Cards labeled *F*

Have students gather in the meeting area with their materials.

The time allotted for Lesson 29's Concept Development is also set aside to consolidate and solidify the learning that has occurred in Lessons 24–28. Just as in Lesson 28, three sets of problems have been provided for practice so that students gain accuracy and efficiency when adding a pair of double-digit numbers.

Students should be encouraged to use their number bonds and the arrow way to solve problems while having full access to drawing materials and manipulatives (MP.5). Note that Problems 11–15 involve sums greater than 40. This is intended to serve as a challenge set for advanced learners.

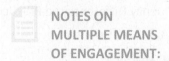

NOTES ON MULTIPLE MEANS OF ENGAGEMENT:

Appropriate scaffolds help all students feel successful. As students are working, keep a close eye to see if any would benefit from some one-on-one problem solving with you.

Lesson 29:   Add a pair of two-digit numbers with varied sums in the ones.
Date: 9/20/13

4

Challenge students to describe and compare methods, strategies, and written notation with their partners and explain why they chose to solve the way they did using terms such as tens, ones, addend, take apart, add on the tens, and make the next ten.

Problems 1–5	**Problems 6–10**	**Problems 11–15**
16 + 12	26 + 12	34 + 23
28 + 12	27 + 13	24 + 42
18 + 15	17 + 15	23 + 27
18 + 18	16 + 15	28 + 25
17 + 16	18 + 17	26 + 37

For the last five minutes, partners play Addition and Subtraction with Cards (follow instructions from G1–M4–Lesson 12) with the new cards labeled, F.

Problem Set (10 minutes)

Students should do their personal best to complete the Problem Set within the allotted 10 minutes. For some classes, it may be appropriate to modify the assignment by specifying which problems they work on first.

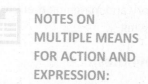

NOTES ON
MULTIPLE MEANS
FOR ACTION AND
EXPRESSION:

Continue to challenge your advanced students. After they have completed Problems 11–15 above, encourage them to write a word problem to match one of the number sentences. Have students who write a word problem trade papers and solve each other's problem.

Student Debrief (10 minutes)

Lesson Objective: Add a pair of two-digit numbers with varied sums in the ones.

The Student Debrief is intended to invite reflection and active processing of the total lesson experience.

Invite students to review their solutions for the Problem Set. They should check work by comparing answers with a partner before going over answers as a class. Look for misconceptions or misunderstandings that can be addressed in the Debrief. Guide students in a conversation to debrief the Problem Set and process the lesson.

You may choose to use any combination of the questions below to lead the discussion.

- Look at Problems 2(b) and 2(h). Did you make a new ten in both problems? Explain why this is so.

- Look at Problem 1(h). Explain which method or strategy you used to solve. Why did you choose this particular method or strategy?

- How can you solve 2(f) using doubles?

- For problems where you need to make a new ten (i.e., Problems 2(d), 2(g), 2(h), etc.), do you prefer to add on the tens first or make a new ten? Explain your choice.

- Share your drawings and solution with your partner. What was your strategy for solving this? Check your work by acting out each part of the story and matching them to the parts of your drawing.

Exit Ticket (3 minutes)

After the Student Debrief, instruct students to complete the Exit Ticket. A review of their work will help you assess the students' understanding of the concepts that were presented in the lesson today and plan more effectively for future lessons. You may read the questions aloud to the students.

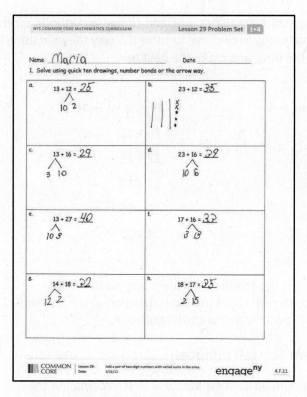

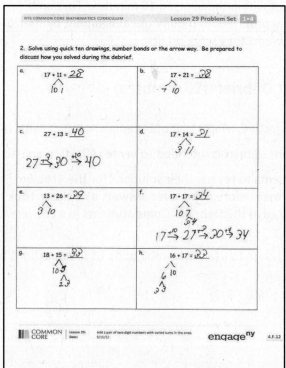

Names _____   Date _____

 Race to the Top!

2	**3**	**4**	**5**	**6**	**7**	**8**	**9**	**10**	**11**	**12**

COMMON CORE™   Lesson 29:   Add a pair of two-digit numbers with varied sums in the ones.
Date: 9/20/13

4.F.76

Name _____ Date _____

1. Solve using quick ten drawings, number bonds, or the arrow way.

a. 13 + 12 = ____	b. 23 + 12 = ____
c. 13 + 16 = ____	d. 23 + 16 = ____
e. 13 + 27 = ____	f. 17 + 16 = ____
g. 14 + 18 = ____	h. 18 + 17 = ____

Lesson 29: Add a pair of two-digit numbers with varied sums in the ones.
Date: 9/20/13

4

Solve using quick ten drawings, number bonds, or the arrow way. Be prepared to discuss how you solved during the Debrief.

a. 17 + 11 = _____	b. 17 + 21 = _____
c. 27 + 13 = _____	d. 17 + 14 = _____
e. 13 + 26 = _____	f. 17 + 17 = _____
g. 18 + 15 = _____	h. 16 + 17 = _____

Name _____   Date _____

Solve using quick ten drawings, number bonds, or the arrow way.

a. 18 + 14 = _____	b. 14 + 23 = _____
c. 28 + 12 = _____	d. 19 + 21 = _____

COMMON CORE | **Lesson 29:** | Add a pair of two-digit numbers with varied sums in the ones. | |
| | **Date:** | 9/20/13 | |

4

Name _____   Date _____

1. Solve using quick ten drawings, number bonds, or the arrow way.

a. 13 + 15 = _____	b. 26 + 12 = _____
c. 23 + 16 = _____	d. 17 + 16 = _____
e. 14 + 17 = _____	f. 27 + 12 = _____
g. 15 + 18 = _____	h. 18 + 16 = _____

 COMMON CORE™

Lesson 29:   Add a pair of two-digit numbers with varied sums in the ones.
Date: 9/20/13

4.F.80

2. Solve using quick ten drawings, number bonds or the arrow way. Be prepared to discuss how you solved during the Debrief.

a. $17 + 12 = $ ____	b. $21 + 17 = $ ____
c. $17 + 15 = $ ____	d. $27 + 12 = $ ____
e. $23 + 14 = $ ____	f. $18 + 17 = $ ____
g. $18 + 11 = $ ____	h. $18 + 18 = $ ____

Lesson 29:   Add a pair of two-digit numbers with varied sums in the ones.
Date: 9/20/13

4.

G1-M4-Topic F Flashcards (and Review Subtraction)

13 + 14 F	26 + 13 F
17 + 22 F	29 + 11 F
15 + 15 F	16 + 24 F
28 + 12 F	29 + 11 F

Lesson 29: Add a pair of two-digit numbers with varied sums in the ones.
Date: 9/20/13

4.F.82

$19 + 14$ F	$18 + 17$ F
$17 + 15$ F	$16 + 15$ F
$19 + 17$ F	$18 + 13$ F
$17 + 16$ F	$18 - 6$ F
$17 - 3$ F	$19 - 4$ F

Name _____   Date _____

. Fill in the missing numbers in the sequence.

16, ____, 18, ____, ____

39, 38, ____, 36, ____, ____

36, ____, ____, 39, ____

23, 22, ____, ____, ____

. Write the number as tens and ones in the place value chart, or use the place value chart to write the number.

a.   31

tens	ones

b.   19

tens	ones

c.   _____

tens	ones
2	6

d.   _____

tens	ones
1	5

3. Some numbers have been placed below in order from 0 to 40.

   a. Place the numbers from the rectangle in order between the tens.

3	22	19	29	35

   0   10   20   30   40

   b. Shade in the tens or the ones on the place value charts below to show which digit you looked at to help you put the pair of numbers in order from smallest to greatest.

tens	ones
2	2

tens	ones
2	9

tens	ones
2	9

tens	ones
3	5

4. Complete each sentence.

   a. 39 is _____ tens and _____ ones.

   b. 40 = _____ tens _____ ones.

   c. 2 tens and 3 ones is the same as _____ ones.

5. Match the equal amounts.

a. 21   40 ones

b. 4 tens   3 tens 6 ones

c. 36 ones   1 ten 2 ones

d. 12 ones   2 tens 1 one

6.

a. Circle the number in each pair that is **greater**.

32 40		33 28

b. Circle the number that is **less**.

36 20		21 12

7. Use <, =, or > to compare the pairs of numbers.

a.   3 tens 5 ones ◯ 2 tens 8 ones

b.   30 ◯ 3

c.   23 ◯ 32

d.   19 ◯ 21

8. Erik thinks 32 is greater than 19. Is he correct? Draw and write about tens and ones to explain your thinking.

9. Find the mystery numbers. Use the arrow way to explain how you know.

a. 10 more than 19 is _____

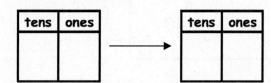

b. 10 less than 19 is _____

c. 1 more than 19 is _____

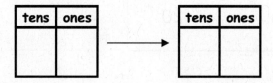

d. 1 less than 19 is _____

10. Beth said 30 – 20 is the same as 3 tens – 2 tens. Is she correct? Explain your thinking.

11. Solve for each unknown number. Use the space provided to draw quick tens, a number bond, or the arrow way to show your work.

a. 30 + 6 = _____	b. 3 tens - _____ = 1 ten
c. 11 + 10 = _____	d. 40 – 30 = _____
e. 17 + 20 = _____	f. 20 + _____ = 40
g. 15 + _____ = 35	h. 2 tens + 1 ten 2 ones = _____

Extend the counting sequence.[1]

1.NBT.1   Count to 120, starting at any number less than 120. In this range, read and write numerals and represent a number of objects with a written numeral.

Understand place value.[2]

1.NBT.2   Understand that the two digits of a two-digit number represent amounts of tens and ones. Understand the following as special cases:

     a.   10 can be thought of as a bundle of ten ones – called a "ten."

     c.   The numbers 10, 20, 30, 40, 50, 60, 70, 80, 90 refer to one, two, three, four, five, six, seven, eight, or nine tens (and 0 ones).

1.NBT.3   Compare two two-digit numbers based on meaning of the tens and ones digits, recording the results of comparisons with the symbols >, =, and <.

Use place value understanding and properties of operations to add and subtract.[3]

1.NBT.4   Add within 100, including adding a two-digit number and a one-digit number, and adding a two-digit number and a multiple of 10, using concrete models or drawings and strategies based on place value, properties of operations, and/or the relationship between addition and subtraction; relate the strategy to a written method and explain the reasoning used. Understand that in adding two-digit numbers, one adds tens and tens, ones and ones; and sometimes it is necessary to compose a ten.

1.NBT.5   Given a two-digit number, mentally find 10 more or 10 less than the number, without having to count; explain the reasoning used.

1.NBT.6   Subtract multiples of 10 in the range 10–90 from multiples of 10 in the range 10–90 (positive or zero differences), using concrete models or drawings and strategies based on place value, properties of operations, and/or the relationship between addition and subtraction; relate the strategy to a written method and explain the reasoning used.

---

[1] Focus on numbers to 40.
[2] Focus on numbers to 40
[3] Focus on numbers to 40.

Evaluating Student Learning Outcomes

A Progression Toward Mastery is provided to describe steps that illuminate the gradually increasing understandings that students develop *on their way to proficiency.* In this chart, this progress is presented from left (Step 1) to right (Step 4). The learning goal for each student is to achieve Step 4 mastery. These steps are meant to help teachers and students identify and celebrate what the student CAN do now, and what they need to work on next.

A Progression Toward Mastery

Assessment Task Item and Standards Assessed	STEP 1 Little evidence of reasoning without a correct answer. (1 Point)	STEP 2 Evidence of some reasoning without a correct answer. (2 Points)	STEP 3 Evidence of some reasoning with a correct answer or evidence of solid reasoning with an incorrect answer. (3 Points)	STEP 4 Evidence of solid reasoning with a correct answer. (4 Points)
1 **1.NBT.1**	The student is unable to complete any one sequence of numbers.	The student completes at least one sequence.	The student completes at least one sequence as well as at least two numbers in each additional sequence OR the student completes two or more sequences correctly.	The student identifies all numbers in the sequences: <ul><li>16, **17**, 18, **19**, **20**</li><li>39, 38, **37**, 36, **35**, **34**</li><li>36, **37**, **38**, 39, **40**</li><li>23, 22, **21**, **20**, **19**</li></ul>
2 **1.NBT.2**	The student does not demonstrate understanding of tens and ones, and is unable to complete more than one answer correctly.	The student demonstrates inconsistent understanding of tens and ones, completing only two answers correctly.	The student demonstrates some understanding of most aspects of tens and ones, completing at least three answers correctly.	The student completes all correctly: a. 3-1 (or 2-11; 0-31) b. 1-9 (or 0-19) c. 26 d. 15
3 **1.NBT.3**	The student demonstrates little or no understanding of number sequence, and orders one number or none correctly. For Part (b), the student was unable to shade the pairs correctly.	The student demonstrates limited understanding of the sequence of numbers as greater or less than each multiple of 10, correctly ordering at least two numbers correctly. Or, for Part (b), the student shaded at least one of the two pairs correctly.	The student demonstrates some understanding of the sequence of numbers as greater or less than each multiple of 10, correctly ordering three or four numbers. For Part (b), the student shaded at least one of the two pairs correctly.	The student correctly orders numerals: <ul><li>0 **3** 10 **19** 20 **22** **29** 30 **35** 40</li><li>Accurately shaded<ul><li>2 and 9 (ones)</li><li>2 and 3 (tens)</li></ul></li></ul>

A Progression Toward Mastery

4 1.NBT.2	The student does not demonstrate understanding of tens and ones within a given number, and is unable to complete any section correctly.	The student demonstrates inconsistent understanding of tens and ones within a given number, answering one section correctly.	The student demonstrates understanding of most aspects of tens and ones within a given number, answering at least two sections correctly.	The student identifies any correct interpretation of each quantity. For example, Part (a) is accurate with answers such as 0 tens 39 ones, 2 tens 19 ones, etc. Typical answers may be: a. 3 tens 9 ones b. 4 tens 0 ones c. 23 ones
5 1.NBT.2	The student does not demonstrate understanding of the equivalent representations of tens and ones, and is unable to match any equal amounts.	The student demonstrates limited understanding of the equivalent representations of tens and ones, matching one or two equal amounts.	The student demonstrates some understanding of the equivalent representations of tens and ones, matching three equal amounts.	The students matches all four equal amounts as follows: a. 21 = **2 tens 1 one** b. 4 tens = **40 ones** c. 36 ones = **3 tens 6 ones** d. 12 ones = **1 ten 2 ones**
6 1.NBT.3	The student demonstrates limited ability to compare numbers, correctly comparing one or none of the four sets of numbers.	The student demonstrates some ability to compare numbers, (e.g., identifying greater by not less), correctly comparing two of the four sets of numbers.	The student demonstrates the ability to compare most numbers, correctly comparing three of the four comparisons.	The students correctly identifies: a. The greater numbers as 40 33 b. The lesser numbers as 20 12
7 1.NBT.2 1.NBT.3	The student is unable to use symbols to compare numbers, and is unable to correctly answer any of the four comparisons.	The student has limited ability to use symbols to compare numbers, correctly answering one of the four comparisons.	The student has some ability to use symbols to compare numbers, correctly answering two or three of the four comparisons.	The student correctly answers: a. >￼ b. >￼ c. <￼ d. <

A Progression Toward Mastery

8 **1.NBT.2** **1.NBT.3**	The student demonstrates little to no understanding of comparing numbers based on tens and ones, answering incorrectly. There is no evidence of reasoning.	The student uses drawings or words to accurately depict at least one of the two numbers, demonstrating limited understanding of the use of place value to compare numbers.	The student demonstrates some understanding of using place value to compare numbers. The student correctly identifies the greater number but does not fully explain reasoning using place value. OR The student answers incorrectly due to error such as transcription but demonstrates strong understanding of place value through drawing or words.	The student correctly: ▪ Uses drawings or words that depict place value to accurately explain that 32 is greater than 19.
9 **1.NBT.5**	The student demonstrates little or no understanding of mentally adding or subtracting 10. Answers are incorrect and there is no evidence of reasoning.	The students demonstrates limited understanding of mentally adding or subtracting 10, identifying at least two correct mystery numbers, but does not complete any charts accurately.	The students demonstrates ability to mentally add or subtract 10, correctly identifying four mystery numbers, but reasoning is unclear because no charts have been completed accurately. OR The student accurately completes charts but makes an error in mental calculation on one or two of (a), (b), (c), or (d).	The student identifies 29, 9, 20, and 18, and accurately completes the charts to depict the arrow way.

A Progression Toward Mastery

10 1.NBT.2	The student's answer is incorrect and there is no evidence of reasoning.	The student's answer includes some indication of understanding either the connection between 30 and 3 tens or 20 and 2 tens, but the student does not follow through with this thinking to correctly answer the question.	The student's answer is correct but there is no response. OR The student's explanation is mathematically correct and rooted in an understanding of place value, but there is an error in their transcription of the numerals or other calculation error that leads to an incorrect response.	The student correctly: • Draws or writes to explain that Beth is correct. • Grounds explanation in understanding of place value in some way.

11
 	
1.NBT.4
1.NBT.6
	The student demonstrates little or no ability to add or subtract two-digit numbers to 40, answering two or fewer questions correctly.	The student demonstrates some ability to add (or subtract) two-digit numbers, answering least four of eight correctly, and demonstrates misunderstandings in place value.	The student demonstrates the ability to add (and subtract) two-digit numbers, answering at least six of eight correctly, or uses sound process throughout with at most four calculation errors.	The student correctly:
				• Solves
				  a. 36
				  b. 2 tens
				  c. 21
				  d. 10
				  e. 37
				  f. 20
				  g. 20
				  h. 3 tens 2 ones (or 32)
				• Represents process to accurately solve through drawings, number bonds, or the arrow way. The notation demonstrates use of a sound strategy for adding or subtracting.

Name _Maria_____   Date _____

1. Fill in the missing numbers in the sequence.

16, 17, 18, 19, 20

39, 38, 37, 36, 35, 34

36, 37, 38, 39, 40

23, 22, 21, 20, 19

2. Write the number as tens and ones in the place value chart, or use the place value chart to write the number.

a. 31

tens	ones
3	1

b. 19

tens	ones
1	9

c. 26

tens	ones
2	6

d. 15

tens	ones
1	5

COMMON CORE MATHEMATICS CURRICULUM

Mid-Module Assessment Task 1•4

3. Some numbers have been placed below in order from 0 to 40.

a. Place the numbers from the rectangle in order between the tens.

| 3 | 22 | 19 | 29 | 35 |

0   3   10   19   20   22 29 30   35   40

b. Shade in the tens or the ones on the place value charts below to show which digit you looked at to help you put the pair of numbers in order from smallerst to greatest.

tens	ones
2	2

tens	ones
2	9

tens	ones
2	9

tens	ones
3	5

4. Complete each sentence.

a.   39 is __3__ tens and __9__ ones.

b.   40 = __4__ tens __0__ ones.

c.   2 tens and 3 ones is the same as __23__ ones.

COMMON CORE

Module 4:   Place Value, Comparison, Addition and Subtraction to 40
Date: 9/20/13

4.S.13

© 2013 Common Core, Inc. All rights reserved. commoncore.org

5. Match the equal amounts.

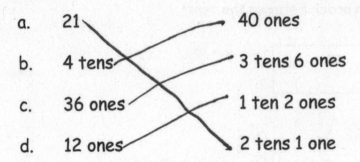

a.   21   40 ones

b.   4 tens   3 tens 6 ones

c.   36 ones   1 ten 2 ones

d.   12 ones   2 tens 1 one

6. a. Circle the number in each pair that is **greater**.

b. Circle the number that is **less**.

7. Use <, =, or > to compare the pairs of numbers.

a.   3 tens 5 ones ⑦ 2 tens 8 ones

b.   30 ⑦ 3

c.   23 Ⓒ 32

d.   19 Ⓒ 21

8. Erik thinks 32 is greater than 19. Is he correct? Draw and write about tens and ones to explain your thinking.

He is right.

3 tens 2 ones is more than 1 ten 9 ones.

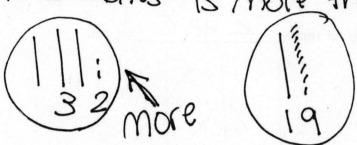

32

more

19

9. Find the mystery numbers. Use the arrow way to explain how you know.

a. 10 more than 19 is ___29___

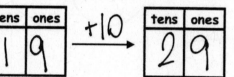

tens	ones
1	9

+10 →

tens	ones
2	9

b. 10 less than 19 is ___9___

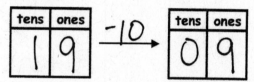

tens	ones
1	9

−10 →

tens	ones
0	9

c. 1 more than 19 is ___20___

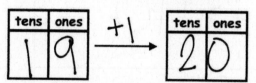

tens	ones
1	9

+1 →

tens	ones
2	0

d. 1 less than 19 is ___18___

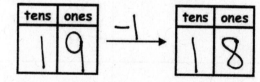

tens	ones
1	9

−1 →

tens	ones
1	8

10. Beth said 30 – 20 is the same as 3 tens – 2 tens. Is she correct? Explain your thinking. Beth is right. Its another way to write the same amount. 30 is the same as 3 tens. 20 is the same as 2 tens.

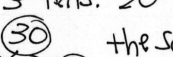

the same   the same

11. Solve for each unknown number. Use the space provided to draw quick tens, a number bond, or the arrow way to show your work.

a. $30 + 6 = 36$	b. 3 tens - $2\ tens$ = 1 ten
c. $11 + 10 = 21$	d. $40 - 30 = 10$ 4 tens 3 tens — 1 ten
e. $17 + 20 = 37$	f. $20 + 20 = 40$ $20 \xrightarrow{+10} 30 \xrightarrow{+10} 40$
g. $15 + 20 = 35$ $15 \xrightarrow{+10} 25 \xrightarrow{+10} 35$	h. 2 tens + 1 ten 2 ones = $3\ tens\ 2\ ones$

Name _____   Date _____

1. Use the RDW process to solve the following problems. Write the answer in the place value chart.

   a. Maria is having a party for 17 of her friends. She already invited some friends. She has 12 more invitations to send. How many friends has she already invited?

   Maria already invited _____ friends.

tens	ones

   b. Maria bought 11 red balloons and 8 white balloons. How many balloons did she buy?

   Maria bought _____ balloons.

tens	ones

   c. Maria had 17 friends at her party. Some of them went outside to see the piñata. There were 4 friends remaining in the room. How many friends went outside?

   _____ friends went outside.

tens	ones

2. Fill in the missing numbers in each sequence:

   a.   27, 28, _____, _____, _____, 32   b. _____, 17, _____, 19, _____

3.

   a.   Mark says that 34 is the same as 2 tens and 14 ones. Suki says that 34 is the same as 34 ones. Are they correct? Explain your thinking.

   b.   Use <, =, or > to compare the pairs of numbers.

     i.   3 tens   ◯   25 ones   ii.   1 tens 14 ones   ◯   2 tens 4 ones

     iii.   33   ◯   2 tens 12 ones   iv.   26   ◯   1 ten 25 ones

   c.   Find the mystery numbers. Explain how you know the answers.

10 more than 29 is _____   10 less than 29 is _____

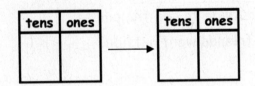   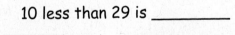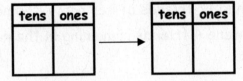

1 more than 29 is _____   1 less than 29 is _____

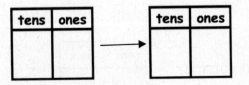   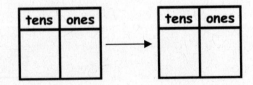

4. Solve for each unknown number. Use the space provided to draw quick tens, a number bond, or the arrow way to show your work. You may use your kit of ten-sticks if needed.

a. 18 + 3 = _____	b. 28 + 10 = _____	c. 40 - 30 = _____
d. 28 + 2 = _____	e. 28 + 6 = _____	f. 28 + 12 = _____
g. 15 + 15 = _____	h. 19 + 14 = _____	i. 16 + 18 = _____

Represent and solve problems involving addition and subtraction.

1.OA.1   Use addition and subtraction within 20 to solve word problems involving situations of adding to, taking from, putting together, taking apart, and comparing, with unknowns in all positions, e.g., by using objects, drawings, and equations with a symbol for the unknown number to represent the problem. (See CCLS Glossary, Table 1.)

Extend the counting sequence.[1]

1.NBT.1   Count to 120, starting at any number less than 120. In this range, read and write numerals and represent a number of objects with a written numeral.

Understand place value.[2]

1.NBT.2   Understand that the two digits of a two-digit number represent amounts of tens and ones. Understand the following as special cases:

   a.   10 can be thought of as a bundle of ten ones – called a "ten."

   c.   The numbers 10, 20, 30, 40, 50, 60, 70, 80, 90 refer to one, two, three, four, five, six, seven, eight, or nine tens (and 0 ones).

1.NBT.3   Compare two two-digit numbers based on meaning of the tens and ones digits, recording the results of comparisons with the symbols >, =, and <.

Use place value understanding and properties of operations to add and subtract.[3]

1.NBT.4   Add within 100, including adding a two-digit number and a one-digit number, and adding a two-digit number and a multiple of 10, using concrete models or drawings and strategies based on place value, properties of operations, and/or the relationship between addition and subtraction; relate the strategy to a written method and explain the reasoning used. Understand that in adding two-digit numbers, one adds tens and tens, ones and ones; and sometimes it is necessary to compose a ten.

1.NBT.5   Given a two-digit number, mentally find 10 more or 10 less than the number, without having to count; explain the reasoning used.

1.NBT.6   Subtract multiples of 10 in the range 10–90 from multiples of 10 in the range 10–90 (positive or zero differences), using concrete models or drawings and strategies based on place value, properties of operations, and/or relationship between addition and subtraction; relate the strategy to a written method and explain the reasoning used.

---

[1] Focus on numbers to 40.
[2] Focus on numbers to 40
[3] Focus on numbers to 40.

Module 4:   Place Value, Comparison, Addition and Subtraction to 40
Date: 9/20/13

4.

Evaluating Student Learning Outcomes

A Progression Toward Mastery is provided to describe steps that illuminate the gradually increasing understandings that students develop *on their way to proficiency*. In this chart, this progress is presented from left (Step 1) to right (Step 4). The learning goal for each student is to achieve Step 4 mastery. These steps are meant to help teachers and students identify and celebrate what the student CAN do now, and what they need to work on next.

A Progression Toward Mastery				
Assessment Task Item and Standards Assessed	**STEP 1** Little evidence of reasoning without a correct answer. **(1 Point)**	**STEP 2** Evidence of some reasoning without a correct answer. **(2 Points)**	**STEP 3** Evidence of some reasoning with a correct answer or evidence of solid reasoning with an incorrect answer. **(3 Points)**	**STEP 4** Evidence of solid reasoning with a correct answer. **(4 Points)**

1
 	
1. OA.1
1. NBT. 2
	The student's answers are incorrect and there is no evidence of reasoning.	The student's answers are incorrect but there is evidence of reasoning. For example, the student is able to write a number sentence.	The student's answers are correct, but the responses are incomplete (e.g., may be missing labels for the drawing, an addition sentence, or an explanation). The student's work is essentially strong.	The student correctly:
				▪ Solves each word problem
				  a. She needs to write 5 more cards.
				  b. She has 19 balloons.
				  c. 12 friends came late.
				▪ Circles the parts in each drawing.
				▪ Completes place value charts
				  a. 0-5
				  b. 1-9
				  c. 1-2

2 1.NBT.1	The student is unable to complete any sequence of numbers.	The student completes at least part of one sequence.	The student completes at least one sequence as well as at least one number in the additional sequence.	The student identifies all numbers in the sequences: ▪ 27, 28, **29**, **30**, **31**, 32 ▪ **16**, 17, **18**, 19, **20**

A Progression Toward Mastery

3 **1.NBT.2** **1.NBT.3** **1.NBT.5**	The student does not demonstrate understanding of comparing numbers based on tens and ones. Fewer than one section is correctly answered.	The student demonstrates inconsistent understanding of tens and ones, answering a few of the parts correctly within a section but showing errors in understanding in at least two of the three sections.	The student demonstrates understanding of tens and ones and is able to generally compare the quantities. The student correctly answers all parts of two out of the three sections.	The student correctly: a. Uses drawings or words to explain that 1 ten and 24 ones is the same as 34 ones. b. Answers (i) > (ii) = (iii) > (iv) < . c. Identifies mystery numbers as 39, 19, 30, 28 respectively and accurately completes the charts to depict the arrow way.

4
 	
1.NBT.4
1.NBT.6
	Answers two or fewer questions correctly.	Answers at least three of nine correctly, and demonstrates misunderstandngs of place value.	Answers at least six of nine correctly, or uses sound process throughout with calculation errors.	The student correctly:
				
				▪ Solves
				  a. 21
				  b. 38
				  c. 10
				  d. 30
				  e. 34
				  f. 40
				  g. 30
				  h. 33
				  i. 34
				
				▪ Represents process to accurately solve through drawings, number bonds, or the arrow way. The notation demonstrates use of a sound strategy for adding or subtracting .

Name ___Maria___   Date _____

1. Use the RDW process to solve the following problems. Write the answer in the place value chart.

a) Maria is having a party for 17 of her friends. She already invited some friends. She has 12 more invitations to send. How many friends has she already invited?

$17 = \boxed{5} + 12$ Maria already invited __5__ friends.

tens	ones
0	5

b) Maria bought 11 red balloons and 8 white balloons. How many balloons did she buy?

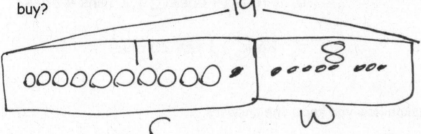

$11 + 8 = \boxed{19}$ Maria bought __19__ balloons.

tens	ones
1	9

c) Maria had 17 friends at her party. Some of them went outside to see the piñata. There were 4 friends remaining in the room. How many friends went outside?

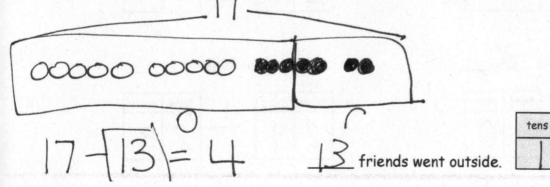

$17 - \boxed{13} = 4$ __13__ friends went outside.

tens	ones
1	3

2. Fill in the missing numbers in each sequence:

    a. 27, 28, _29_, _30_, _31_, 32   b. _16_, 17, _18_, 19, _20_

3. a. Mark says that 34 is the same as 2 tens and 14 ones. Suki says that 34 is the same as 34 ones. Are they correct? Explain your thinking.

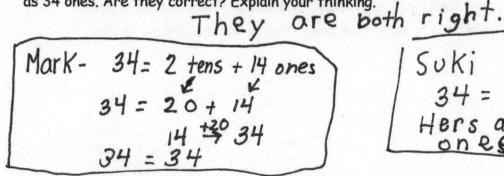

They are both right.

Mark- 34 = 2 tens + 14 ones
          34 = 20 + 14
             14 +20→ 34
         34 = 34

Suki
   34 = 34 ones
   Hers are all ones.

    b. Use <, =, or > to compare the pairs of numbers.

     a.   3 tens ⟩ 25 ones   b.   1 tens 14 ones = 2 tens 4 ones

     c.   33 ⟩ 2 tens 12 ones   d.   26 ⟨ 1 ten 25 ones

c. Find the mystery numbers. Explain how you know the answers.

    10 more than 29 is _39_   10 less than 29 is _19_

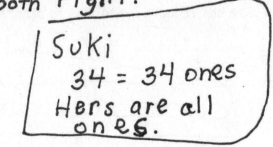

    1 more than 29 is _30_   1 less than 29 is _____

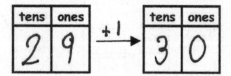

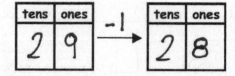

4. Solve for each unknown number. Use the space provided to draw quick tens, a number bond, or the arrow way to show your work. You may use your kit of ten sticks if needed.

a. $18 + 3 = $ 21 2 ⌃ 1	b. $28 + 10 = $ 38 20 ⌃ 8	c. $40 - 30 = $ 10 $40 - 30 = 10$ like $4 - 3 = 1$ tens
d. $28 + 2 = $ 30 20 ⌃ 8	e. $28 + 6 = $ 34 $28 \xrightarrow{+2} 30 \xrightarrow{+4} 34$	f. $28 + 12 = $ 40 20 ⌃ 8 10 ⌃ 2
g. $15 + 15 = $ 30 10 ⌃ 5 10 ⌃ 5	h. $19 + 14 = $ 33 1 ⌃ 13	i. $16 + 18 = $ 34 $16 \xrightarrow{+10} 26 \xrightarrow{+4} 30 \xrightarrow{+4} 34$